ABRAHAM LINCOLN'S WORLD

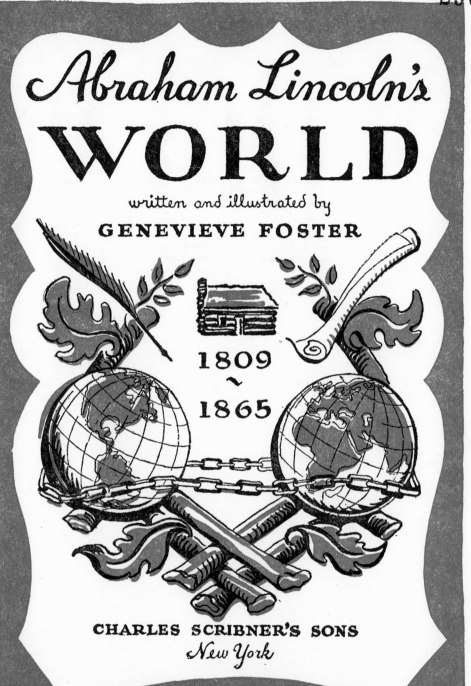

Abraham Lincoln's
WORLD

written and illustrated by
GENEVIEVE FOSTER

1809
~
1865

CHARLES SCRIBNER'S SONS
New York

ACKNOWLEDGMENT

This book is but a rearrangement of well-known historical facts. It is based for the most part on material from encyclopedias, standard textbooks on history and literature, autobiographies, letters, diaries, and the numerous biographies of the principal characters to be found on the shelves of almost any large library. In a few instances, however, I have used the account as given by a single author, and I wish here to acknowledge my indebtedness. The "Story of Brazil" is adapted from *Amazon Throne* by Bertita Harding, published by Bobbs Merrill. "A Boy of China" was inspired by the *Memoirs of Li Hung Chang* by William F. Mannix, a book which, though later found to be fictitious, was highly praised by scholars as being a true reflection of Chinese life and of the spirit of the Chinese statesman. Quotations are used by permission of Constable and Company, Ltd., London. Queen Victoria's story I believed was best told in her own words; the excerpts from her journal are used by permission from *The Letters of Queen Victoria*, published by John Murray.

Admiral Perry has described in detail his expedition to Japan, but the amusing term "Lord of the Forbidden Interior" I have borrowed from Edward M. Barrows, who uses it in his biography, *The Great Commodore*. I am sorry that out of the several hundred books I consulted, there is not space to list even the ones I most enjoyed. They contain so many fascinating incidents which had to be omitted, in order that all of the many characters might be fitted together to form a picture of their world. However, it is my hope that many readers may wish to fill in this pattern or framework with further details, and so discover for themselves some of the original stories and colorful old records.

G. F.

Evanston, Illinois.

ṽ

CONTENTS

PART I

PART II

PART III

1 8 0 9

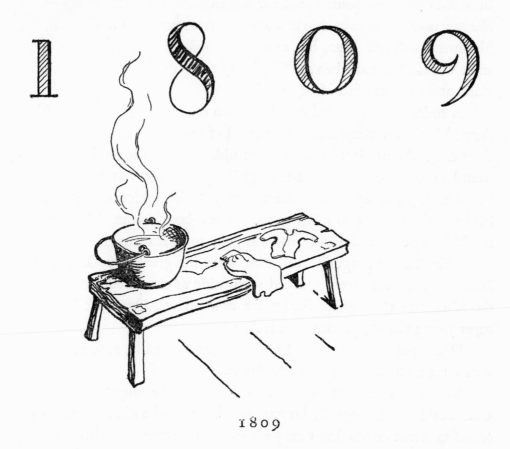

1809

FEBRUARY, 1809, just nine years after George Washington's life was over, Abraham Lincoln's life began. He was born on a Sunday morning, the twelfth day of the month. A lonely day it was. The cloud-swept sky was cold, and the forest trees spoke with strange voices in the wind. A one-room cabin was his birthplace, made of mud-plastered logs, standing stark and solitary on a clearing cut, not so long before, into the wilderness of western Kentucky.

Only a film of daylight filtered through the oiled paper of its single windowpane. Cold shadows filled the corners and stretched long wavering fingers toward the hearth. A log snapped in the fire and dropped. Nancy Lincoln on her bed of saplings wakened, turned and drew the little son only a few hours old closer within the warm circle of her arm. She saw now that he was thin and angular, not round and comforting as his sister Sarah had been, but as she watched his even breathing, her smile was tender, and when she lifted her eyes to the shadows, they were warm and dark and full of dreams for him.

A sudden gust of wind spiraled down the chimney. The bear skin flapped in the doorway, and with a whirl of snow in upon the hard dirt floor came Dennis Hanks, nine years old, and completely breathless. Tom had told them, he gasped. Aunt Betsy Sparrow was now on her way, fetching a linsey shirt for the boy and a yeller petticoat, while he— he'd run the whole two miles to see his new-born cousin! Where was he? Who'd he look like and what was goin' to be his name?

"Abraham, we figur to call him, after his gran'pappy Linkorn." Nancy's slow words were touched with pride as she lifted a corner of the homespun coverlet to display the new arrival. One look left the eager young visitor speechless with dismay.

"He'll not come to much, I reckon," he said finally, and, as if that settled the matter, went over to the fire and sat down.

So it was that Abraham Lincoln came into the world—much the same world that George Washington had known—the old slow-moving one of sails and horses. But nine years of a new century had then passed into history and a new age had begun.

Abraham Lincoln and people who were young when he was were to see the modern world come into being. They would see new nations formed, new lands opened up, new struggles for freedom won. And they would see the first of those marvelous inventions that were to change man's life completely. They would see first the steamboat, then the rail-road, then the telegraph and cable so shorten time and distance as to weave more closely together than ever before the lives of people and nations into a single story.

This book tells the story of that changing world. It weaves together again the dreams and deeds and adventures of people in every land during those years that measured the life of Abraham Lincoln.

PART ONE : WHEN

Abraham Lincoln

WAS **BORN** IN

Kentucky

People who were making History

NAPOLEON

EMPEROR OF FRANCE in 1804 and master of Europe, was defeated at Waterloo in 1815

(born 1763)
Empress JOSEPHINE was divorced by Napoleon 1809

Her grandson (born 1808) was to become Napoleon III

Their son "Napoleon II" born 1811 died 1832.

(born 1791)
MARIE LOUISE of Austria was forced to marry Napoleon in 1810

BEETHOVEN (born 1770) in 1808, first heard his great Fifth Symphony played.

WELLINGTON English commander
by
BLÜCHER of Prussia

(born 1771)
SIR WALTER SCOTT saw his first novel printed in 1814

Admiral NELSON fought Napoleon at sea (killed 1805)

ALEXANDRE DUMAS (b 1802) writer of exciting romances, was the son of a general in Napoleon's army.

AFRICA
banished to St. Helena, — died in 1821.

Czar ALEXANDER I made Napoleon fail in Russia in 1812

VICTOR HUGO the great French writer (born 1802) was staging plays at school.

and some Events that took place

when Abraham Lincoln was born

THOMAS JEFFERSON (born 1743) ended his eighth year as President of the United States in March 1809

1807
ROBERT FULTON introduced travel by
STEAMBOAT

(born 1755) **JOHN MARSHALL** as Chief Justice was making clear the meaning of the Constitution

LOUISIANA PURCHASE

In 1803 Jefferson bought land from Napoleon.

JAMES MADISON
(President from 1809 to 1817) was forced to declare the
WAR OF 1812

TECUMSEH
was the great Indian chief

1814
FRANCIS SCOTT KEY
wrote the words of
The Star Spangled Banner

(b. 1777) (b. 1782)
HENRY CLAY, DANIEL WEBSTER
JOHN C. CALHOUN (b. 1782) three young statesmen were beginning their careers

ANDREW JACKSON
Indian fighter and hero of New Orleans, was nicknamed "Old Hickory"

The **CONSTITUTION** won the name "Old Ironsides" in battle of 1812

GEORGE III
who was crowned in 1760 was still King of England and would live on until 1820

between the Years 1800 and 1815

EMPIRE of NAPOLEON 1809

Empire
Countries controlled by Napoleon
allies with Napoleon

NAPOLEON

THE WORLD'S most famous man, the most loved and the most hated, most extravagantly admired and most fearfully despised was Napoleon, self-made Emperor of France, master of all Europe and most powerful ruler in the world in the year 1809. Far in the backwoods of America, even people who could scarcely read or write like Tom and Nancy Lincoln must have heard his name, for it was echoed everywhere—Napoleon—Napoleon—no longer Napoleon BONAPARTE—but now in the fashion of all monarchs, simply Napoleon, Emperor of the French.

For years past, like a human volcano, he had been turning Europe upside down in a terrible upheaval that had shaken the whole world.

5

Slashing right and left with his sword, he had tramped about the continent, winning one lightning battle after another. He had wiped out borderlines, made new nations out of old, sent kings tumbling from their thrones, or scooting from their kingdoms, and then set their empty crowns upon the heads of his own brothers. Still he was not satisfied.

"I cannot stand still," he said. "A king, however stupid, who comes of royal blood, may fail and still be king—but I, whom they call a usurper, I must pile one success upon another if I am to last!"

Other nations he had thrown into panic, but in France Napoleon had turned his energy and his brilliant mind to bringing order out of chaos. He had straightened out the laws, and replaced an old incomprehensible muddle with an orderly system, known as the Code Napoleon, which secured to the people of France the equality they had fought for in the Revolution. He founded a National Bank, improved schools, encouraged trade and factories. The prestige of France, the fame and fortune of her emperor were at the peak. Still Napoleon was not satisfied. The passionate desire of his heart had so far been denied him.

Back and forth he paced in his shining black boots across the throne room of the Tuileries, on the last morning in November. Back and forth, crossing a shaft of sunlight and the square of brighter green it marked upon the emerald carpet. One hand was in the opening of his blue coat, the other held behind him, his head thrust forward and his mind intent upon the realization of his great desire.

Marie Louise of Austria was his proper choice—no doubt of that! Austria! He spoke the name aloud. Proud Austria, once so powerful, how he had defeated her! Four times had he humbled her proud emperor. And again Austria had risen—just this past spring of 1809. Again he had beaten her to her knees. Again Francis I, proud Hapsburg that he was, had had to sue for peace—and Austria was once more subdued. But for how long? How long would Austria remain subdued and France supreme? How long would anything he had accomplished last if he had no heir to follow him as Napoleon II? Therein lay his great desire.

His own future—the future of France—demanded that he have a

6

son! And that son, if he were to be secure upon the throne, must come of a royal mother, and who more royal or more promising or more wholly suitable could there be than seventeen-year-old Marie Louise, princess of the oldest and haughtiest royal house in Europe? Marie Louise, then, should be his bride. Her Papa Francis would not dare refuse.

The difficulty lay elsewhere. To marry Marie Louise meant that he, Napoleon, must divorce his Empress Josephine. That thought brought him to a stop abruptly. Then he turned sharply on his heel. This was a business of the head, he told himself, and not the heart. Josephine, however much he cared for her, in thirteen years of marriage had given him no son. What if she was still glamorous and beautiful, she was no longer young. She had been a widow with two children when he married her, and now she was old—six years older than he was. She would not have another child, and if she should, it would not be of royal blood, for Josephine was not a princess. Imperative it was, therefore, that Josephine should be divorced. Unfortunate, truly, but imperative. The decision made, Napoleon dismissed it from his mind, flung himself upon a sofa, and, as he had trained himself to do, fell instantly asleep.

Josephine wept and fainted, but two weeks later on December the sixteenth, the decree was final, and by early spring, Napoleon was looking forward eagerly to the arrival of her successor.

Marie Louise wept also when she heard her fate, the dreadful fate of a princess who had to marry an ogre, for was she not to marry Napoleon, the enemy of her country, the ogre of Corsica, the very devil himself! There was nothing for her to do, however, but dutifully accept her papa's choice. So eventually, after being married to him in a magnificent ceremony, in which his part was acted by her uncle, Marie Louise set out from Vienna bound for Paris to become Napoleon's bride.

It was spring, the same time of year that, forty years before, her great Aunt Marie Antoinette had set out upon the self-same journey. In the same woods outside of Paris she too was to meet her bridegroom.

Meanwhile an eager and excited forty-year-old bridegroom had been making most elaborate preparations for the welcome and the wedding. Growing with each hour more impatient, when the actual day arrived, he would stand no more on royal etiquette. Jumping into a plain two-wheeled carriage, he drove off at top speed and met the bridal procession on the highway, in a perfect downpour of rain.

Dripping wet, he burst open the door of his lady's carriage, stepped in, seated himself beside her, kissed her hand, her cheeks, her mouth, her throat. Then he held her at arm's length and looked at her. What he saw was a pink-and-white girl with round blue eyes, plump cheeks, and a full red mouth, which he kissed again. She gasped, and giggled, and then looked well at this most amazing person—this most irresistible lover. She touched the miniature which hung about her neck, and smiled.

"Your portrait does not do you justice, Sire," she said.

One year later, on the twentieth of March, 1811, the Emperor's son was born. Napoleon was beside himself with joy. Plans were begun at once for the formal christening and when it was held in June in Nôtre Dame Cathedral it was a gorgeous spectacle, and a masterpiece of perfect timing. Astronomers had calculated exactly when the sun would reach a certain window. Exactly at that moment Napoleon, splendid in royal purple, held the infant high in his arms before the altar. To the amazement of the people, like a blessing from heaven, the sun streamed in, and, spanning the nave of the great cathedral, fell directly upon the Emperor and his child! That ray of sunlight marked the peak of Napoleon's self-made glory but it also cast the shadow of his downfall. It was the last of his calculations that did not go astray.

In due time the baby cut a tooth, to the delight and amazement of his father, for Napoleon was a fond and doting papa. He idolized his little son and finally could not resist having him taken secretly to Josephine, that she too might see the wonderful child who was to be the next emperor of France. It was indeed a very beautiful baby boy that Josephine saw, one who would be called by his father's name for a few years, but who would never rule as Napoleon II.

Strangely enough, it was not Napoleon's son, but the grandson of Josephine who was to become the next Emperor of France. . . .

THE NEXT EMPEROR

Louis Napoleon loved his grandmama Josephine. She was soft and beautiful and smelled of violets. On every visit he threw his arms about her neck and covered her face with kisses. Then she would give him a sugar cane to suck, let him pick all the flowers he wanted in the conservatory, and choose sweet biscuits from the box. And when the visit was over she always said,

"Bring this pet of mine to see me oftener, Hortense."

Hortense was his mother. She was beautiful, too. Her skin was even smoother, and Louis could hardly tell which one he loved to kiss the most. He could never make up his mind to choose between other nice things, either. He couldn't tell whether he liked violets or roses best, or what he wanted to do when he grew up—sell violets like the boy who stood on the corner by the Tuileries, or become a soldier. Flowers made you quiver inside, but soldiers made you tingle outside. Especially soldiers of the imperial guard. Two of them always stood by the grand staircase in grandmama Josephine's palace. One day Louis tiptoed out of the drawing room and walked boldly up to them.

"I can do that too," he said. "I have a little gun."

One guard laughed. "The commands, can you give them also?"

"Present arms, shoulder arms, carry arms," said Louis proudly, while to his great delight the soldiers went through the motions with exaggerated gravity. Louis ran quickly to the box where the sweet biscuits were kept and brought one to reward each guard.

"Merci, Monseigneur," they said. . . . Thank you, YOUR HIGH-NESS! It was well, thought Louis Napoleon, that his mother had not heard them. She never let the servants call him by that title, and so she might also have corrected the guards. He should not want those fine soldiers to think they had made any mistake. Besides, he wondered, why shouldn't they call him that? His uncle Napoleon was the Emperor. His grandmother was an Empress, his mother was a queen. So why should to be just plain Louis?—nobody better than anyone else. Who was he, anyway, he wondered. This much was all he knew about it:

When his mother, Hortense, was a little girl, her father had died and her mother (his grandmama Josephine) had married his uncle Napoleon and become the Empress. When his mother Hortense had grown up she had married Napoleon's brother Louis and become a queen, because Uncle Napoleon had then made his brother Louis King of Holland. King Louis (his, Louis Napoleon's papa) had not ruled Holland to suit his brother Napoleon, so he had had to give back his crown, and had gone somewhere else to live . . . far away from Paris.

Grandmama Josephine must also have done something to displease his uncle, the small boy believed. She could not live in Paris either. One day it looked to Louis Napoleon as though she had been weeping. He ran to her, and that day she hugged and kissed him more than usual, told him never to forget that his uncle was the great emperor Napoleon. She hoped, she said, that her little Louis would never know anything but good fortune, and so be always happy.

"You would spoil him, mama dear," his mother said. "Far better to teach him to be able to meet either good or evil fortune with high spirit. That is worth more than a crown."

Josephine sighed. Little Louis Napoleon had stopped listening.

BECAUSE OF ENGLAND AND NAPOLEON

THOMAS JEFFERSON was still President of the United States when Abraham Lincoln was born, but he was tired and worn and utterly discouraged over a problem he had failed to solve. March 9, 1809, his last day in office, found him seated at his desk, an important document before him waiting for his signature. His Embargo had failed. It had to be repealed. He dipped his pen, then hesitated and sat gazing out of the window. His lean, bent figure in its slate blue coat and his sandy grey hair were outlined against small panes of glass upon which a wailing March wind blew thin slanting needles of rain.

Troubled thoughts swept him back over his eight years as President, eight years in which Napoleon had shaken the United States and changed its future both for good and evil. In 1803, needing money to start war on England, Napoleon had been willing to sell the great tract of land known as the Louisiana Purchase, and Thomas Jefferson had thus been able to double the territory of the United States. Satisfaction over that bargain, however, had been completely overshadowed, after the war had started, by the damage done to the ships of the United States by both France and England. A terrific problem had arisen of how to protect the rights of the United States and yet keep the country out of war. In March, 1809, the problem was still unsolved and the future looked black to Thomas Jefferson. Sadly discouraged, he turned at last from the window, dipped his pen again and signed his name. What would come next, he wondered. . . . Would it be war with England? . . .

John Bull defies Napoleon in an old English cartoon

War with the United States, if it came, could be but a minor issue to England, already engaged in a battle for her life. Napoleon for years had been determined in one way or another to conquer England, and England, equally determined, had managed so far to stand against him.

People said it was like a battle between an elephant and a whale. For while Napoleon's strength lay in his army, England's was in her navy. Napoleon was master of the continent, but England was mistress of the sea. And a channel of water lay between them.

"Let me be master of that channel for six hours only," said Napoleon, "and England is ended!"

In 1803–1804 therefore, Napoleon spent his Louisiana money on ships. He gathered fifteen hundred of them and twice as many men at Dunquerque and Boulogne, and made plans to cross the channel. The plans were fantastic. So too was his confidence in carrying them out. He even had Victory medals for his soldiers made in Paris ready to be given out in London. Meanwhile, the English people, terribly alarmed, kept up their courage by poking fun at Napoleon and the whole idea.

"You're coming? You be damned!" John Bull is seen shouting in the old cartoon. "Yes, damnye, Little Boney, why don't ye come out?"

Finally "Boney" did come out—that is he ordered his fleet to sail for England, but the English fleet, on the alert, forced the French ships back into a Spanish harbor. When they ventured forth again, it was to be defeated in the famous battle off Cape Trafalgar, in October, 1805.

Admiral Lord Nelson was commander of the English. From his flagship he had flown the words "England expects every man to do his duty." Then the four-hour battle began. Nelson died before it was over, but not before he knew that victory was won, the danger of invasion past, and England was still mistress of the sea.

After that battle, it was a different story, and a new kind of war. Napoleon talked no more about invading England. Instead he determined to defeat her by starvation. He struck at her commerce, and England struck back in the same way. It was then 1806. Napoleon declared a blockade of Europe from the Baltic Sea to the Mediterranean. All trade with England was forbidden. No ship from England was to be admitted to any port of France or any country under Napoleon's control.

"Blockade, indeed," retorted England. "Then it shall be a complete blockade. Any ship, of any nation, caught carrying goods to any port in Napoleon's Empire will be seized by the British as a prize of war."

Trade was crippled. Every country in Europe suffered. So did the United States. All during the war, up to this time, American ships had been active in the prosperous business of carrying supplies to Europe. Then suddenly ship after ship was seized by England. (England more than France, because England, of course, had the ships to do it.) Not only United States ships, but also United States sailors were seized and forced into the British service. England had always claimed the right to search American ships to find deserters from her navy, and, never having enough sailors, it was very easy to take along a few extra—by mistake!

A cry of indignation rose from the United States, but England, fighting for her life, gave no heed to it. So there rose a cry for war. "Not WAR," pleaded Thomas Jefferson. War was never a remedy. It was a last resort. Let them try to secure justice by other methods first, he urged. So . . . other methods were tried.

One was the EMBARGO. That was an act passed by Congress in 1807 which said that all ships of the United States must stay home and keep out of trouble. Not a ship engaged in foreign trade was to leave any port for any reason whatsoever. That did not work. England and France managed to get along somehow without American goods and paid no attention. The merchants of Boston and other American seaport towns were frantic. There in the harbors stood the ships, with barrels over the masts, and sails gathering dust and cobwebs, while they, the owners, went bankrupt. Counting houses shut up, clerks were out of work, grass was growing on the wharves. Even small fishing smacks could barely get permission to go out for mackerel. Indignation meetings were held in the town halls, and rebellion was mentioned. At last it had to be admitted by even those who had been most hopeful that to cure the ills of the United States by that method was likely to kill the patient.

That last dismal day in office, therefore, found Thomas Jefferson signing his name to the repeal of the Embargo.

Th Jefferson

What would come next? What would the United States do now to protect her ships and seamen? Would war be the answer? That was not for Thomas Jefferson to say. It was now up to the new Congress and the new President, James Madison.

Spaniards — European born
Fernando VII
Creoles — Spaniards born in Colonies

YOUNG CREOLES OF VENEZUELA

AND NOW, in the first year of Abraham Lincoln's life, Spain's colonies in the New World, jarred into action by Napoleon and the upheaval that he caused in Spain, began their fight for independence. Since the days of Columbus, Spain had ruled more of the two American continents than any other nation, always with the policy that the most profitable way to rule her colonies was to keep the people ignorant and oppressed. Native Indians and Negroes brought from Africa were slaves; Spaniards, no matter how high their rank, if American-born, were allowed to hold no important office in the government and were disdainfully spoken of as Creoles by the Governors sent out from Spain to rule over them. The situation had become unbearable to some of the younger men of South America. Fired by the success of the North American Revolution, they plotted secretly and continually for the day when their country, too, might gain its independence.

Young men of Caracas, the capital city of Venezuela, often met at the estate of their friend, young Simón Bolívar, now that he had returned from Europe. There they would lounge in the cool of the patio until the sun had set and the slaves had left the coffee and indigo fields. Going in at twilight, they would draw their dark, carved, high-backed Spanish chairs about the dinner table, lit by many candles, and talk on through the night.

Like the others, Simón Bolívar had been born in Venezuela, but in 1800 when he was seventeen, his uncle had sent him to visit Europe. There young Simón had done and seen everything that there was for a handsome, charming, carefree, fabulously wealthy young nobleman to do in the gay world of Paris or Madrid. At last, after almost ten years of playing, he had grown completely bored with his useless life. He was eager for something to do, something that would bring him glory!

It was then that Humboldt turned the attention of the young South American back to his native country. The great German scientist had just returned to Paris from an exploring trip in Venezuela.

"Ach," said he, "what possibilities lie in that wonderful land of yours! If it only could be freed from the yoke of Spain! But ah, the leader, the man who will do it—where is he?"

Some weeks later to that question that had been ringing in his ears, Simón Bolívar spoke the answer—not to Humboldt, but to his old tutor, Rodríguez, the man who had first pointed out to him the injustice with which Spain ruled her colonies. Simón had been but ten when Rodríguez had become his tutor. As they tramped the mountain paths of Venezuela together, the boy had been taught by him about man's age-long fight for freedom, and of his right to liberty, equality and justice. Memories of those teachings flooded Simón Bolívar's mind when there in Europe, ten years later, he met old Rodríguez again, and went with him on a walking trip to Italy.

Late one afternoon they sat on the Aventine hill, looking down on the ruins of old Rome—that city of great conquerors and emperors— but also city of slaves, oppressed by tyrants! Suddenly it became clear to Simón Bolívar what he wanted to do with his life. He rose to his feet and faced the red clouds of the western sky.

"Rodríguez," he said, "I swear before you that I shall never allow

16

my hands to be idle or my soul to rest, until I have broken the chains which bind my fatherland to Spain."

So Simón Bolívar had returned to Venezuela—to that land where a few young aristocrats talked of freedom, where most of the people, Indian, Negro and halfbreed, had not the vaguest idea what the word meant, and where the older Spaniards still believed as they had been taught to believe that "next to God they must honor the King of Spain."

It was by expressing this old loyalty to the King, and not by rebelling against him, that the war for South America's freedom began.

One day about a year after Simón Bolívar had returned from Europe, the startling news reached Caracas that Napoleon had invaded Spain. He had forced the old king Carlos IV to abdicate in favor of his son Fernando VII, and then tricked Fernando into giving up the crown, and had put his own brother Joseph Bonaparte on the throne as King.

At that outrage the people of Spain had rebelled. They had driven out Joseph Bonaparte, and formed a Junta or Congress, to govern until their rightful King Fernando was restored to them. The people of Venezuela were also loyal and also infuriated at the insult.

"Down with the tyrant Napoleon!" they cried, "Long live Fernando!" they cheered, marching the streets with flags and images.

The young liberal leaders had no use for Fernando, nor any wish to take orders from any Junta in Spain. What they wanted was independence, but, undecided how to gain it, they merely talked and waited. Months passed. Then came news that Napoleon had crushed the rebellion in Spain, put Joseph back as King, and wiped out the Junta.

"That means," cried the young radicals, "that, if there is no longer a Spanish government, VENEZUELA IS FREE!"

They spent an exciting night, about one hundred of them, in a meeting in Caracas. No more need now for the governor from Spain, was their decision. A Junta of their own citizens should now make the laws for them! Next day, just before High Mass in the cathedral, they marched to the Governor's residence, escorted him to the harbor, put him aboard a vessel and shipped him back to Spain. That day was Holy

Thursday, the highest, most solemn church festival of the year, the Thursday before Easter, 1810. It was a day the people of Venezuela were to have more than one reason to remember.

SHIPS AND TRIPS AND BUSINESSMEN

NEW YORK was a town of 60,000 people in the year 1809, and although it was growing, no one believed it would ever be as large as Philadelphia—almost no one, that is, except one sharp-eyed tight-fisted little man who had a hunch that it would keep on spreading up the island, and had just purchased another piece of property beyond the outskirts, a farm near the place where Broadway now crosses 52nd Street. This shrewd investor with the taste for real estate was John Jacob Astor, the first poor immigrant boy to land in America, start with a pack on his back and become a millionaire.

John Jacob Astor had made his money selling furs. In the beginning he had tramped the forest trails himself. Every summer he left home with a huge pack on his back filled with gunpowder, hatchets, knives, snuff, blue beads, tobacco, petticoats, rum and all kinds of cheap trinkets that he could trade to the Indians for far more than they were worth. By fall his pack would be full of glossy skins: mink, raccoon, muskrat, fox and, most desirable of all, the beaver.

Twenty years had passed since then. His American Fur Company was now a big concern. Other men tramped the trails, beat the furs for John Jacob Astor and sailed his ships to China. The Chinese wanted furs, the Americans wanted tea. So furs went to China and tea came back and there was profit, big wonderful profit at both ends of the trip. On one voyage alone Mr. Astor's ship the BEAVER made $200,000 for him. It was the year of the Embargo. Just because other merchants let their ships be tied up at the dock to gather dust was no reason why he too should be a *dummkopf*. So a trick played on the United States government got the BEAVER off for China. Now that the Embargo had been repealed, and all ships could go freely back and forth to the Orient, times were very good for Mr. Astor.

A new law had now been passed by Congress, which said that ships from the United States might trade with any country EXCEPT France or England. Troubles therefore were not over for merchants like Washington Irving's brothers, whose business was importing English hardware. They were much concerned about the future, and in the winter of 1811 decided to send their young brother Washington to report first hand on what new regulations, if any, were being made by Congress under President Madison.

Washington Irving shared an apartment with a young man who was also to be sent in the near future on a business trip, but in the opposite direction. He was employed, as it happened, by Mr. John Jacob Astor, and was to make a tour of the fur-trading posts along the Great Lakes to report any trouble that might have arisen with their rivals, the Northwest Fur Company of Canada, or with some of the Indian traders.

W. J.

Washington Irving left first, writing his friends about his trip, which he managed to enjoy from start to finish. Others might worry about business, but young Irving gave no thought to it whatsoever after he boarded the stagecoach. He was twenty-six years old, light-hearted and clever, but with no taste for business, so why think about it? A four-day journey by stagecoach in the dead of winter was none too agreeable either, if one's mind was on it.

"So I made up my mind," he said later, "to be pleased with everything, or if not pleased to be amused."

As good humor is contagious, the fellow passengers found one another surprisingly agreeable, and the journey not at all unbearable.

A very pleasant stopover was made at Baltimore, where a Frenchman was delighted to meet the author of that most amusing book, *Knickerbocker's History of New York* which he had recently translated into French.

"My first book," said Irving, also delighted, "published as you know about Christmas, 1809."

Two days out of Baltimore, the charming traveler, successful young author though very indifferent businessman, arrived in Washington. It was about dusk when the coach rolled into the muddy unpaved streets of the little town of only two or three thousand people, and drew up before the Inn. Too late it was for business, but not too late to attend the reception of Dolly Madison, America's most popular hostess, and wife of the President.

"I put on my pease blossoms and silk stockings," Irving wrote, "and in a few minutes emerged into the blazing splendour of Mrs. Madison's drawing room, and inside of ten minutes found myself hand in glove with half the people in the assemblage. Mrs. Madison is a fine portly buxom dame, who has a pleasant word for everybody—but as to Jemmy Madison—Ah! Poor Jemmy he is but a withered little applejohn."

Poor James Madison, indeed! He was in a tight spot those days. A man of peace, faced with declaring or not declaring war, and either way antagonizing one section of the country. For the country was divided. The south and west were for war, the northeast against it. Washington Irving heard both sides of the question, as he went about the Capital, met and dined with new and old friends in both parties.

"Let us keep peace," he heard the old Federalists of New England say, "we've our business to look after. What would we gain by war?"

"Just what we are losing by peace," retorted the young Republican-Democrats of the south and west. "Our commerce, our character—our honor! For those we must fight!"

"In both parties," wrote Irving, "I find worthy and intelligent men with honest hearts, enlightened minds and bitter prejudices." As the weeks went on he saw the bitterness increase.

Young men of the west accused the men of New England of being white-livered and cowardly. A New Englander called the young men of the west a pack of screeching war hawks. That was what they were, War Hawks. WAR HAWKS was a name that stuck.

Two of the leading war hawks, young men about Washington Irving's age, had entered the House of Representatives that year and were to play important parts in American politics for the next forty years.

JOHN C. CALHOUN of South Carolina and HENRY CLAY of Kentucky. Both were over six feet tall, otherwise not at all alike. John Calhoun, someone said, was a cast-iron man who looked as if he had never been born! He was deadly serious, never saw anything funny. His words were hard, flat and exact like footsteps on stone.

  Henry Clay was loose jointed and flexible in body and spirit, with a curved mouth like a jack-o'-lantern and a voice that had all the charm of a pied piper's flute. In his first speech in Congress he made it ring through the hall with an almost irresistible call to arms!

War feeling kept rising and by summer it looked as though Madison, although a man of peace, might be swept along with the ride.

By summer Washington Irving had returned to New York, to find his brother's business no better, his apartment empty and his friend gone on the trip west.

Letters from him soon came from Mackinac, telling how the Indians were suffering because the goods to which they were accustomed were no longer allowed to be imported from England.

"I am surrounded by a score of Indian Traders," he wrote, "who, cut off from their accustomed supplies from the Company, are as desperate as so many famished wolves. The whole blame will be thrown upon the Am. Govt. The British Government have a regular Indian department & distribute cloathing to upwards of Ten Thousand Indians annually. You may form an opinion of the popularity of the two governments and how easy it is to overrun the cup of bitterness.

"This letter will be accompanied by two genuine Indian Orations that convey a faithful picture of their present distress. Show old Astor the speeches if he wants to see them."

Old Astor now had his mind on another venture . . . another trading post much farther away than Mackinac was from New York City, but much nearer to China. A post from which his ships could go directly back and forth across the Pacific. The new post, named ASTORIA, was founded that year, 1811, near the mouth of the Columbia River in the far northwest. It was not to remain long in Astor's possession, but by this one and only business venture of his that failed, John Jacob Astor quite unintentionally was to render his country a service.

When the time came, the fact that Astoria had been founded by one of its citizens was to strengthen the claim of the United States to the territory known as Oregon.

TECUMSEH — THE FALLING STAR

THE SMELL of dying campfires hung in the night air. The haze of Indian summer folded the sleeping village of Tippecanoe, the last Indian village to be built in Indiana. Tecumseh, Shawnee chieftain, sat with his brother the Prophet on a high bank above the Wabash. As they watched the great orange circle of the harvest moon rise above the willows, they planned the future of their people.

"When day comes, I shall go," said Tecumseh, "on my journey. To the Cherokees I go, to the brave Creeks in Alabama, to all the tribes east of the Great River. Let us council together, I shall say to them, stand together—fight together against the treacherous white man."

"Also urge upon them the old wisdom of our fathers," said the

23

Prophet huskily. Gold hoops quivered in his ears, and his one eye glittered in the moonlight. "Urge them to forsake the White Man's evil way of living, to go back to the good way of the Red Man. Dress again in skins and hunt once more with bow and arrow, that the Great Spirit may smile again upon his chosen people. For out of his brain did he not make the Red Man, and out of his hand and legs the lowly White Man?"

"Lowly man—man of lying tongue is the White Man," said Tecumseh. "False promises they make—people of the white nation. With smooth talk they cheat us of our land. Our lone tribe against them can do nothing. Therefore until I return, keep peace with them, my brother."

As the moon slipped into the wide spaces of the sky, Tecumseh repeated the solemn words of warning, and the Prophet promised to risk no quarrel with Governor Harrison, the white chief of Indiana.

It was midwinter when, the long journey over, Tecumseh was hopefully returning from the Council Fire of the Creeks to the village on the Wabash. Near the Illinois he learned that he need go no farther. The village was gone. Tippecanoe had been burned to ashes.

The Prophet, his brother, told him the tale of misunderstanding and disaster. He told how Governor Harrison at Ft. Vincennes had sent for more soldiers—how he, the Prophet, had gone to assure the Governor that the Indians were friendly. How when he had left Vincennes, white settlers told the Governor that the Indians had stolen their horses, and when they rode after them with rifles, the Indians had fired back. How Governor Harrison had then marched on Tippecanoe with drums and many thousand soldiers, defeated the braves and burned their village.

And so when the next harvest moon rose above the Wabash, the high bank was deserted. No smoke from campfires mingled with the haze. No heads raised their dark hatchet shadows against the sky. Traveling north Tecumseh had found welcome in Canada, and offered his services to the British, hoping to gain a permanent homeland for his people.

It was not to be. The brave Indian's fate was forecast in his Shawnee name, Tecumseh, which meant "Falling Star." White men, from now on, not Indian braves, would sleep beneath the moon in Indiana.

SAM HOUSTON BECOMES "THE RAVEN"

THE GREEN CORN was planted, fish were plentiful in the river, peace and prosperity rested with the Cherokees in eastern Tennessee. Chief Oo-loo-te-ka also saw order in his Council House. Still his mind was troubled. Like shadows of clouds drifting over the foothills of the Smoky Mountains, he felt shadows of fear drifting over his contentment. Fear for the future of his people.

The Cherokees, his people, were a peaceful nation. They had no wish to join Tecumseh in war against the white man, nor did they believe with the Prophet that the old Indian ways were best. The Cherokees tried to learn all that the white man could teach them, and live in peace with the white nation. When the white nation was young and weak, it had made solemn agreements to respect the rights and boundaries of the Cherokee nation. Now that it was strong, the white man had forgotten his promises. White settlers were trying to crowd and drive the Cherokees from their mountain home. Oo-loo-te-ka's brother had lost faith completely. He had gone, taking "the Trail of Tears" across the Mississippi, to the far valley of the Arkansas, that the lodges of his people might be out of the white man's reach forever. The day might come when he, Oo-loo-te-ka, must do likewise. But not today. Today the sun shone warm, as he sat before his wigwam, and in the cool of the evening the young braves would dance for him the green corn dance.

That evening, while the braves were dancing, a white boy carrying a book came walking into the Cherokee village, and when the stars came out he slept in Oo-loo-te-ka's wigwam, with his book beside him. The book was *The Iliad*, and the boy was Sam Houston.

Sam had first read the wonderful book in the paneled library of the Houston homestead in Virginia. That was before his father the Major had died, and his mother had brought her family of nine out to Maryville, Tennessee. Sam had been reading the great poem again, just that morning in the village store when he decided that a storekeeper's life was no life for him, and made up his mind to run away.

> "Fellows in arms whose deeds are known to fame
> And you whose ardour hopes an equal name!
> Behold a day when each may act his part. . . ."

Those were the brave words he had been reading when—what did he have to do but come back from the Trojan War to pour out a jug of molasses and measure three yards of tape! It was unbearable! Without further ado, he marched out of the stuffy store, and down the grubby street to the edge of the town. Then off he went with a wide free stride in the tingling air, and keeping in step with the rhythm of

> "Fellows in arms-whose deeds-are known-to fame-,"

he disappeared over the brow of a hill and was gone.

It was not the first time that young Sam Houston had disappeared from home for a day or two, but this time when weeks went by his mother was worried. Two of his older brothers, who believed young Sam ought to be working the farm if not tending store, set out to look for him. Paddling down the river near the Cherokee village they spied at some distance a young Indian stretched on a shady bank beneath a tree.

"No sir, it's Sam, b'gosh," they said as they came nearer. Holding their dripping paddles, they yelled at him and told him to come home.

"NEVER!" quoth Sam rising to his feet dramatically. "Never—for I prefer measuring deer tracks to tape, and the freedom of the Indian to the tyranny of my own brothers." This said, he resumed his reading.

The brothers paddled off home again and Sam stayed on with the Cherokees. Chief Oo-loo-te-ka adopted him as a son, and gave him the name of Co-lon-neh, meaning the Raven. John and James, sons of the half-white counsellor, became like new brothers to Sam. He taught them to speak and read in English and they taught him the Cherokee tongue.

Only occasionally, during the three years that he lived as the son of Oo-loo-te-ka, did Sam "The Raven" return to Maryville, and then only to buy presents for his Indian friends and family. He piled up a debt that way of nearly a hundred dollars, and he was finally forced to go back and earn the money. He decided to open a school, and teach from corn-planting time in May to corn-husking in November.

That was the May of 1812, and Sam Houston, school teacher, was then nineteen years of age. One dull day in June, in the middle of Long Division, he heard horse's hooves come pounding down the road. Dashing by like greased lightning went a dusty rider, his hair and his horse's tail streaming behind him in the wind.

"War!" cried the rider. "War's been declared! Volunteers! Volunteers! Volunteers for war against England!"

Sam Houston finished his school term. Then he enlisted and marched off to camp with the company from eastern Tennessee. They went to put down an uprising of the Creeks in Alabama who, like Tecumseh, had taken the warpath for the British.

The Cherokees, on the other hand, were loyal to the United States. Sam's friends, John and James, and a band of Cherokee warriors also enlisted. That this loyalty was never to be rewarded makes theirs the saddest of the Indian stories. The Cherokee nation was also to lose its homeland. All would be sent westward over the "Trail of Tears."

1812

THE YEAR 1812—IN NORTH AMERICA

IT WAS TRUE. War had been declared. On the eighteenth of June, James Madison had reluctantly put his timid signature to the declaration. The "war hawks" were triumphant. They talked of a glorious victory in which all America's difficulties would be immediately settled. Seamen's rights and free trade upon the sea would be established, the fur trading posts along the Great Lakes forever freed of rival traders from Canada. They even spoke of invading Canada and possibly annexing the country. The south and west, indeed, were solidly for war!

A storm of protest, on the contrary, blew bitterly down from the northeast. The country was not ready for war, said people of New England. With a navy of not more than a dozen frigates, it was suicide to declare war on a nation that had a thousand warships. All over New England people gave voice to the most dismal forebodings. In the town squares they lowered the flags to half mast and tolled the meeting house bells as if for a funeral.

Young men of the south and west, however, who had grown up since the Revolution and didn't know what war was like, were full of enthusiasm and aglow with confidence.

"Let us not listen to counsels of timidity and despair," cried Henry Clay. "In such a cause as ours, with the aid of Providence, we are certain to come out crowned at once with victory!" . . .

28

The war opened with disaster. Hardly had it been declared than dismal reports began to trickle back from the northwest, where, some months before, a general had been sent on to be ready for the invasion of Canada. Now it seemed that, after cutting a road two hundred miles through the forests to reach Detroit, he had no sooner arrived than he had surrendered the fort to the British without firing a shot. It was incredible! Henry Clay, however, soon received a letter confirming the bad news and adding more. The letter came from General William Henry Harrison, who was then stationed in Ohio. It read:

Cincinnati, Aug. 29, 1812.
"I write you, my dear sir, amid a thousand interruptions. The rumored disasters upon our northwestern frontier are now ascertained to be correct. The important point of Mackinac was surrendered without an effort and an army captured Detroit after three shots; a fort (Chicago) in the midst of hostile tribes of Indians was evacuated and the garrison slaughtered; the numerous northwestern tribes of Indians in arms against us—is the distressing picture in this part of the country."

Fortunately there was better news from the east coast. There, three days after Detroit surrendered, the navy had a remarkable victory to report, one that was to become famous in American history. August 19, 1812, off the coast of Nova Scotia, the *Constitution*, one of the few good ships owned by the United States, met the *Guerrière,* a British ship. As this was recognized as one that had been very active in searching American ships, the battle between the two began at once. After twenty minutes of shrieking shells and smoke and crashing timber, the *Guerrière* was a shattered wreck without a spar standing, while the sturdy *Constitution* was almost unhurt. The shots had so bounded from the tough oak planks of which her hull was made, that from then on the sailors spoke of her fondly as "Old Ironsides." Oliver Wendell Holmes was only three years old when the battle took place, but years later when it was proposed to wreck the famous old ship, he wrote his poem which begins with the words "Aye, tear her tattered ensign down" and whose last verse begs for the ship a better fate than the wrecker's hammer.

> "Nail to her mast her holy flag,—
> Set every threadbare sail
> And give her to the god of storms,
> The lightning and the gale!"

Old Ironsides still stands today in the Boston Navy Yard.

The victory, hailed with delight by the Americans, was a shock to the British, and there were similar shocks to follow. That year five more English frigates were captured by the small but active American navy. A wave of enthusiasm swept the country. Henry Clay toured the states inspiring volunteers and raising money. He was the man of the hour, the pride of Kentucky. Even backwoods people like the Hankses and Lincolns felt right proud to belong to the same state as Mr. Clay.

Thomas Lincoln didn't enlist in the war of 1812. Some men from around those parts did, but Tom had a family to support. And a hard time doing it. The farm was no good: soil so poor he was figurin' on movin' that year. Before time to put in the crops he did move to another farm fifteen miles away. Same kind of land; same kind of a cabin, only the creek had a different name.

Abe was past three now and steady enough to wade in the creek. Sometimes Nancy, his mother, sat on the bank with her knitting. Sometimes he sat beside her, and she folded her hands and recited the Bible.

"Blessed are the peacemakers," she would say, "for they shall inherit the earth.

"Blessed are they that mourn, for they shall be comforted."

The boy listened, for his mother's voice was husky and low and the strange, incomprehensible words had a wonderful rhythm.

Massachusetts, meanwhile, decreed a day of fast, to pray the Almighty's forgiveness for going to war with England. All New England was as much opposed to the war as ever, opposed to the war and to the way it was being run. Until 1812, however, there was no strong New England man in Congress, but that year the Federalists elected a man who was to state the views of New England in no uncertain terms, and represent that part of the country in politics for forty years to come.

 DANIEL WEBSTER was his name. All Eyes, Black Dan, Indian Dan—those were some of the nicknames he had had at college. Huge solemn black eyes he had, set in deep caverns beneath a dome-shaped brow, and he had a huge chest like a drum, and when he spoke his eyes flashed and his voice came out like thunder rolling over the hills.

John C. Calhoun and Henry Clay saw at once in Daniel Webster either a powerful friend or an equally strong opponent. And so they were to look upon him for forty years to come. For they were to be together, those three—Webster, Clay and Calhoun, struggling with and against one another for the next forty years over the problems and government of the United States. Now in this, their first year together, it was Daniel Webster against Henry Clay and John Calhoun.

Republican-Democrats from south and west, Clay and Calhoun were enthusiastic over the war.

Daniel Webster, Federalist from New England, was dead set against it.

31

1812 IN SOUTH AMERICA

O N HOLY THURSDAY in the year 1812 a terrific earthquake
struck South America. It shook half of Venezuela, cracked
open the streets of Caracas and swallowed one-fourth of the
inhabitants into the earth. Panic-stricken, the natives who
still were alive fell on their knees beside their shattered dwellings, and
amid groans of the dying, prayed for mercy.

"Sodom and Gomorrah," cried a monk, holding aloft his cross.
"Pray for forgiveness! Two years ago this very day you banished your
governor, the King's anointed. Behold this holy day, God sends your
punishment! To your knees, then, and pray for His forgiveness!"

"No," cried Simón Bolívar, brushing the priest aside. Mounting a pile of rubbish, he swung his sword high in the air. "To your feet! I say if nature has joined forces with the tyrants, we will force her to obey. She stands in our way—but we will go forward!"

Simón Bolívar and the liberal leaders had reason to be bold. They had now a Republic to defend, for in the two years between Holy Thursday, 1810, and Holy Thursday, 1812, much had happened.

First of all, MIRANDA had returned to Venezuela. After years abroad, MIRANDA, the old soldier, the man who had dreamed and plotted longer than anyone else for South American freedom, had again set foot on his native land.

In January, 1811, he arrived. An English ship brought him from London, where for years Miranda's home had been the secret meeting place for young South Americans plotting for independence.

Simón Bolívar, slim and handsome, with a large gray hat shading his dark eyes, was at the harbor to meet Miranda. At first sight of the old soldier standing in the prow of the boat, he saw that he was wearing a cocked hat on his powdered hair, and his old French uniform of 1793, for Miranda had fought in the French Revolution. He had also been in the American Revolution of 1776, and for forty years had fought with armies here, there and everywhere. A lover of liberty he was indeed, but above all Miranda was a soldier.

"Where are the troops?" were almost the first words with which he greeted Bolívar. "Where is your army—the army that you wish me to command?"

Presented with the undisciplined group of volunteers, he snorted impatiently, then set to work relentlessly to whip them into shape.

The Junta meanwhile debated. Uncertain what attitude to take towards Spain, or what attitude Spain was going to take towards them, they continued to debate until it came to a torrid midsummer day, when they met in the ancient cathedral. That day, July 5, 1811, persuaded by the eloquence of Simón Bolívar and also frightened by Miranda's prediction that Napoleon might soon land an army on their shores, the delegates signed the Act of Independence.

33

July 5, 1811, is still celebrated as Venezuela's Independence Day, although the First Republic then formed was to have but a short life.

The following spring came the dreadful earthquake. In the confusion that followed, Miranda was made dictator as well as general. By some mistake in judgment, or believing himself outnumbered and helpless against the Spanish soldiers that had been sent to crush the new Republic, Miranda surrendered to Spain's general.

"Traitor! Traitor!" cried Bolívar, who was in charge of a small fort some miles away. "Miranda is a traitor!"

"Miranda has betrayed our cause and our republic," echoed the young rebels. Late one night, led by Bolívar, they went to Miranda's room, awakened and arrested the old man and threw him into a dungeon.

Next morning Spain's general moved into Caracas and took over the city. Simón Bolívar, made penniless, was banished to an island in the Caribbean. The First Republic of Venezuela was dead.

May 25, 1810, was Argentina's independence day, and in 1812 Argentina, unlike Venezuela, was still independent. There was no royal Spanish army in the capital of Buenos Aires.

In March, 1812, just before the great earthquake struck Venezuela, an English ship was sailing down the east coast of South America headed for the harbor of Buenos Aires. On board, in a sunny corner of the deck away from the wind, might have been seen a young man quietly playing checkers, or perhaps just moving the men and thinking. Had he been asked, he would have given his name as San Martín, just José de San Martín. And if anyone could have told him that he was to become Argentina's hero, he would probably not have been particularly impressed, for San Martín was not looking for glory. He was coming home, not to become a hero, but because there was work that he wanted to do.

San Martín, thirty-four years old, had been born in Buenos Aires, but when only a boy of eight had been sent to military school in Spain to be trained in the profession of his father. Since he was fourteen he had served in the Spanish army. When Napoleon had invaded Spain and made his brother Joseph king, San Martín had fought with the Spaniards in their rebellion against the invader.

Realizing then that the time had come for the Spanish Americas to strike for freedom, San Martín had felt that he must return and help gain independence for his native country. And by his native country he meant not merely Argentina, but all of South America.

"Toda la América es mi patria," San Martín often said.

All of South America was his fatherland. . . . Considering therefore South America as a whole, San Martín's thoughts naturally turned to the city of Lima in Peru, which had always been the headquarters of the Viceroy from Spain. Quite obviously, until Spain's government and royal troops could be driven from Peru, none of the other countries which had declared their independence would be entirely safe.

Take, for instance, Chile, which had also declared for freedom. Chile had already been invaded by Spanish troops, sent south from Peru, and was about to fall back into the hands of Spain. The high mountain ranges of the Andes separated Chile from the grassy pampas of the Argentine. Still San Martín planned to cross them and believed that the plan was possible and could be carried out.

Officials in Buenos Aires, he knew, would consider such a gigantic undertaking as he contemplated mad and impossible, so when he arrived he kept his plans secret and quietly thought out his moves.

He first asked to be made governor of a remote province just this side of the Andes from Santiago, the capital of Chile. There, driven out by the royalist army, came exiles from Chile, chief among them San Martín's good friend Bernardo O'Higgins. There in that remote province San Martín in his patient, practical manner set about raising and equipping an army of four thousand men, made up of all kinds of volunteers, from Chilean exiles to freed Negro slaves and wild gauchos, the cowboys of the pampas.

When all was ready to the last careful detail, San Martín was to attempt and carry out exactly according to schedule one of the great feats in South American history.

РОССИЯ!

TO MOSCOW AND RETURN

Moscow was burning! In September, 1812, a month after the *Constitution* had destroyed the *Guerrière*, and Simón Bolívar had been banished from Caracas, Moscow, Russia's ancient city, was in flames. It had been set afire by the Russians themselves, to save it from falling into the hands of Napoleon, for that summer Napoleon had invaded Russia.

The Czar of Russia had refused any longer to maintain the blockade against England. Russia needed the English market for her wheat and flax and timber, and suffered from the loss of it. Napoleon could afford no leak to weaken the trade wall against England. He demanded that the Czar hold to his agreement, but got no satisfactory answer.

"Soldiers!" cried Napoleon, "Russia swore everlasting alliance with France. Today she confronts us with dishonor or war. There can be no doubt about our choice. Forward!"

And forward they went, half a million soldiers. Carrying the imperial gold eagles, they crossed the Niemen River into Russia towards the end of June, 1812. And the Russian army lured them on. Instead of halting to confront the French in battle, the Russians kept retreating before them, destroying the crops, burning the villages and supplies. Five days of marching into Russia, and the huge invading army had no food. The supply wagons could not keep up with the marching men. But on they went. Nine hundred from one regiment died in a single day. The horses ate rank grass from the marshes and thatch from the roofs, and thousands of them died.

Napoleon grew nervous. It was seven hundred miles from the Niemen River to Moscow. He increased the speed of the advance. No sign of the Russian army on the burning steppes. No food in the charred wreckage of the villages.

Napoleon grew more nervous. Pacing up and down before his tent, he dictated letters to the Czar demanding an immediate settlement.

Finally, at Borodino, not far from Moscow, the Russians stopped and there was a most bloody battle. Seventy thousand men were killed. The Russians retreated again, and Napoleon entered Moscow, expecting to dictate a peace, but there was no one there to meet him. No one was there at all.

Moscow was a deserted city. Moscow, city of 250,000 people, was like a city of the dead. The houses were empty. The echoing streets were empty. Riding through the ghastly silence, Napoleon approached the white walls of the Kremlin, ancient palace of the Moscovy Czars. In through the open gates he went, and with resounding footsteps down the arched corridors and into the vast throne room. It too was empty.

Then came the fire! Only a red tongue here and there at first—then a few flames—then palace after palace caught fire and, whipped by the raging wind, it became an inferno of smoke, flames, blazing roofs and flaring timbers. At the end of four days most of the city was gone, and "beautiful magical Moscow," as Napoleon put it, "was no more."

"Everything has been destroyed," he wrote Marie Louise. "Enough is left, however, for the army. Much wealth of every kind to plunder."

To Alexander, the Czar of Russia, Napoleon wrote letter after letter pleading, no longer demanding, but almost begging him to arrange for peace. The Czar did not answer.

"I want peace," wrote Napoleon. "I must have peace. I absolutely insist upon it." Still no answer.

Week after week Napoleon waited, until there was no reason to wait any longer. With wagons, coaches and carts heaped high with plunder, topped by the gold cross from the Grand Ivan Church, the army trailed slowly out of Moscow. Less than one-fifth of the original number, they were, and only a small part of that number was ever to reach home.

Napoleon had waited too long. Earlier he might have saved his good soldiers, but now, in October, it was too late. The icy jaws of winter had snapped. Whirling blizzards caught them. Blinded by snow, the ragged troops, dressed for summer, were shot down by wandering bands of Cossacks or dropped to be swallowed in the drifts. Thousands, hurled through a broken bridge into an icy river, heaped it high with their dead bodies. Some were frozen sitting upright on their horses.

It was a journey of horror. Until December fifth, Napoleon, the man responsible for it, dragged along with the army. Then a despatch came from Paris. He, Napoleon, was reported dead! A new ruler was about to be elected!

What? thought Napoleon, aghast. What of his son? What of his empire? What of the dynasty he had founded? Conspirators were at work, he told his officers. He must leave for Paris at once. Under cover of night, huddled in a single sleigh, with a vial of poison tied about his neck in case of capture, he sped away . . . but "I shall be back again," he promised, "I shall be back in Russia in the spring!"

38

"DON'T GIVE UP THE SHIP"

ALL THAT WINTER, on the shore of Lake Erie, young Oliver Hazard Perry, oldest of four Perry brothers in the United States Navy, had been busy building ships. The snow was deep, the winter was cold, Lake Erie was far from any supplies. Iron, rope, rigging, all had to be hauled on sledges miles through the forest. It was a terrific job, but one that had to be done . . . that is, if the United States ever expected to regain Detroit.

Soon after Detroit had fallen, General Harrison had attempted to recapture it, but it was impossible, obviously impossible, unless the United States could control Lake Erie. The British had ships on the lake; the United States had none. Therefore a gang of ship's carpenters began felling oak trees, sawing planks, and pegging the green lumber together, and by summer had turned out five boats. As soon as Perry had enough men to man them, the boats were launched and sailed towards the western end of the lake.

A month later the Battle of Lake Erie took place. Just before it began, Commodore Perry called his crew together. And it was a motley crew, all kinds and ages of men, from old gunners stripped to the waist who had served on the *Constitution,* to Kentuckians in their fringed buckskin pants who had never been on a ship before.

Standing on a gun where all could see him, Commodore Perry spread open a blue flag, on which were painted in white letters five words: DON'T GIVE UP THE SHIP.

"My brave lads," he said, "on this flag are the last words of gallant Captain Lawrence, who died in battle, and after whom this vessel, the *Lawrence,* is named. Shall I hoist it?"

"Aye, aye, sir," shouted the crew. And the flag was run up.

When that blue flag came down, the *Lawrence* was fairly battered to pieces, and most of the crew were dead or dying. For a moment the British thought the battle was over. Then they saw the Stars and Stripes still flying, and caught sight of a rowboat from the *Lawrence* making for the *Niagara,* another of the American fleet. Though they reopened fire, the small boat reached its goal, the blue flag was hoisted again, and in fifteen minutes more the battle was won.

When the last British ship had struck her colors, Oliver Perry seated himself on a dismounted cannon, took an old dirty envelope from his pocket and, using his round sailor cap for a table, wrote this brief report to William Henry Harrison:

"Dear Gen'l: We have met the enemy and they are ours; two ships, two brigs, one schooner and one sloop. Yours with great respect and esteem." O. H. PERRY.

It was an absolute victory. Fort Detroit was recaptured and a battle or two won over the border in Canada. A wave of enthusiasm spread over the country . . . everywhere except New England.

Oliver Perry returned to his home state, Connecticut. There though he personally was lauded as a hero, he found that even the victories won had brought no change in the feeling of New England. People of New England were as bitterly opposed to the war as they had ever been.

ANDREW JACKSON THE INDIAN FIGHTER

OLD HICKORY was in bed with a bullet in his left arm and a wound in his shoulder, recovering from a duel, when he first heard that the Creeks were on the warpath. The Governor of Tennessee, who had ridden out from Nashville to Andrew Jackson's home, the Hermitage, found the general of his state militia haggard and yellow, and too sick to even enjoy a pipe of tobacco with his wife.

When he heard, however, the bloody story of how the Creeks had murdered or scalped or brained four hundred unprotected white people in Alabama, he was ready to be "up and at 'em!"

"Damned red-skinned villains," he said. "Give me a week, and by the etarnal, we'll blow those consarned scoundrels into etarnity."

41

Rachel Jackson, who knew her husband's pluck and loved him for it, made no annoying protest. When the day came she helped him onto his feet, into his boots and uniform and out upon the veranda, where two slaves lifted him into the saddle. He bent down and kissed her, then put spurs to his horse and was off, his left arm helpless in a sling but his thin body held erect as far as she could see him.

Andrew Jackson was headed for a meeting with his troops on the border of Alabama, but his plans carried him much farther. He planned a highway from Tennessee to the Gulf of Mexico. He wanted to see the Spanish colony of Florida invaded, and the British supply base at Pensacola captured. He wanted New Orleans made safe against attack. All this could be accomplished, once the Creeks were defeated and their towns wiped out. That ought not to take long, in his opinion, after he got supplies sufficient for his soldiers.

"Send me provisions," he wrote to his Governor, "and I will end this war in a month."

He got only a week's supply, but he started. Through the woods they went and over the Raccoon Mountains.

Already his Cherokee scouts had been threading their way through the Indian country, to see in which towns the crimson war club dangled and how many in number were the braves. Word that the Creeks were about to attack a white settlement, and discovery of a large band of painted warriors hiding in a ravine brought on the first real battle, which ended with the death of every brave.

"We shot 'em down like dogs," boasted Davy Crockett, after the battle was over.

The squaws and children of the dead braves were then lined up in front of the white "Tiger Man" (that was their name for Andrew Jackson). A soldier came up carrying one last papoose who had been found alive in the arms of his dead mother. The squaws shook their heads.

"Kill him, too," they said. They would not take him. Ugh-ugh. It would bring the Evil Spirit upon them.

The little round-faced fellow looked solemnly at the squaws with his bright black eyes, and then at the big general. Only a few minutes and he was sitting on the big knee drinking warm brown sugar water. That night he went to sleep curled up on an army overcoat, while the big general bent over a candle scratching out letters to any and everyone back in Tennessee who might possibly send supplies of food to his starving soldiers. He besought them to hurry.

Still the supplies did not come, and did not come until the soldiers, reduced to eating acorns, declared they would go no farther.

"Drink a jug of water with the akerns, that's what I do," advised the general, "and," added the old fire-eater, "the first one of you that takes a step back, I'll blow into etarnity!" And he meant it!

That night he wrote Rachel these discouraged words: "Pressed with mutiny of the volunteer army. Whether we have men enough to progress with the campaign I cannot say."

The campaign did go forward. Cattle and supplies and also re-inforcements of regular soldiers finally reached them.

To-he-peka was the scene of the last battle. It was a village which stood on a Horse-Shoe bend in the Tallapoosa River, well protected by a log barricade. Second over the barricade was young Sam Houston. A barbed arrow struck him and sank deep into his thigh. Other arrows flew about him. Arrows, spears, balls, flying swords, gleaming tomahawks, Indians black with paint and red with blood, screaming medicine men. . . . Then silence—with five hundred and fifty Indians dead upon the ground and more floating in the river.

Chief of the Creeks, a friend of Tecumseh, arrived a few days later and surrendered himself to Andrew Jackson.

"I have done you much injury," he said. "I should have done you more, but my warriors are dead. I cannot bring life to the dead."

Nor could the Creek Nation ever come to life again. The frontier of Tennessee and Georgia would never again be terrified by their war cry, nor ever again be "soaked by them in blood."

The war over, feeling their job well done, the soldiers turned home-ward. Andrew Jackson, now the hero of Tennessee, went back to the

Hermitage and Rachel. As a reward for his service he was commissioned Major General in the United States Army.

So came the spring days of 1814. While the new Major General was being measured for a full-dress uniform by the Nashville tailor, and little Andrew was playing with a warrior's bow his uncle had brought him from the battlefield, Rachel was making a place in the family circle for its newest member, a little brown-faced Indian boy.

A BOY AND A FISH

Tom Lincoln's cabin by Knob Creek was on the main highway leading north from Nashville, Tennessee, to Louisville, Kentucky. Soldiers often passed that way. One day, not far from the creek, a soldier met a small boy coming down the road carrying a fish. The boy looked at the man with a face as solemn as that of an Indian, and then handed him the fish. When the soldier thanked the boy and asked him what his name might be, he said it was Abe Linkum.

44

from an old English cartoon.

NAPOLEON DEFEATED

NAPOLEON'S DISASTER in Russia had banded his enemies together. It had given them hope that now, since the almost magic spell of his success was broken, this hitherto invincible superman could and would be defeated. And so he was. In the spring of 1814, surrounded by a ring of enemies, deserted by his trusted generals, betrayed by his tricky minister, Napoleon, the world's most famous man, "destroyer of the peace of Europe," finally fell.

Only, however, after a most brilliant campaign of defense. For two months by quick thinking, lightning swift action, striking here, there, right and left, Napoleon held back his enemies who came pouring over the boundaries, invading France from all directions.

Over the Pyrenees from Spain came Wellington leading 100,000 English, who several years before had been sent to help the Spaniards. Over the Rhine from the north and east came the army of Russia, and the army of Prussia under General Blücher. From the east came soldiers of Austria, all told 1,000,000 fighting men. Closing in upon Napoleon from all sides, the allies came marching towards him and towards Paris.

At the approach of the allied armies, Empress Marie Louise fled, taking with her the little son, now three years old, whom his father was never to see again.

Napoleon himself had not yet reached Paris when the allies entered the city. Hastening to its defense he met troops of cavalry on the road.

"Halt," he cried. "Why are you here? Where is the enemy? Where is the army? Where is the Empress? Who is guarding Paris?"

"The army? The troops? They have left the capital," was the answer. "The enemy is there."

It was too late, then. His most trusted general had delivered his army to the allies. The capital had fallen. The empire had crashed! He himself was ruined! He retired to the Palace of Fontainebleau.

from painting by DELACROIX –

There on April 4, 1814, after a night of deepest depression, Napoleon signed the abdication. Those who placed the paper before him saw a pitiable figure in a dressing gown crouched before the fire.

Napoleon—he scratched the name. The men silently took the paper and left. . . .

Napoleon stayed on a few more days. Once he asked for his pistols and found them unloaded. "To kill oneself," he said to his valet, "is the death for a gambler. I am condemned to live."

The island of Elba, he learned, was to be his future home, his miniature kingdom. Four commissioners arrived to escort him there, a Russian, an Austrian, a Prussian and an Englishman. There was nothing left to do then but bid farewell to the faithful soldiers who had remained with him to the end. Officers had deserted him, but many troops were faithful—soldiers of the Old Guard were there who had been with him in sixty victories or more, and wide-eyed boys of fifteen who had been drafted for this last campaign.

"Soldiers," he said. "Soldiers who have remained faithful to the end, receive my thanks. I cannot embrace you all, but I will embrace your general. Farewell, my children. Farewell, my friends."

Nothing but sobbing was heard as through their tears the soldiers watched him kiss the flag and leave the courtyard. Their beloved leader —their "Little Corporal" of old—their Emperor of yesterday was gone.

The journey to the coast was a different story, one of curses instead of sobs. The women of France had paid with the lives of their husbands and sons the terrific cost of Napoleon's glory.

"Kill the tyrant," they screamed. "Down with the fiend!" They stoned the carriage and tried to catch sight of him slumped down in a corner of the seat. "Kill the murderer!" was their cry.

The horses pressed on at full speed. Finally they reached the seaport. There Napoleon, disguised in the strange array of an Austrian uniform, a Prussian officer's cap, and the long green coat of the Russian army slung about his shoulders, left the great Empire of France for the tiny island of Elba. . . . And Louis XVIII became king of France.

(An Old Print)

Louis XVIII   Napoleon

His uncle gone, little Louis Napoleon found life more confusing than before. First he had been hurried out of Paris in the dead of night for fear of the dreadful allies. Then, suddenly, like the best of friends, two of those foreign kings came on a visit to his mother.

Louis Napoleon wondered who they were at first. "Are they some more of my uncles?" he asked his governess while she brushed his hair.

"No," said she. "One is the King of Prussia, the other the Emperor of Russia. The emperor is a generous enemy who wishes to help you and your mamma in your misfortune. Except for him you would have nothing in the world, and the fate of your uncle would be much worse."

"Then I ought to love him," said Louis. So later, when no one was looking, he tiptoed up to the good Czar and gave him a little present.

The King of Prussia had with him his two sons. Wilhelm, the younger, seventeen, looked very big and handsome to little Louis Napoleon who was only six. Fifty-seven years later, that big Wilhelm would be back to be crowned in France as the first Emperor of Germany. While little Louis, as Napoleon III, would be held by him as prisoner of war.

from a *Miniature*

THE VERY YOUNG WILLIAM GLADSTONE

QUITE NATURALLY the English, who had fought so long against Napoleon, were overjoyed when at last he was defeated and the war was over. Bells rang, guns were fired, towns illuminated with fireworks. All England celebrated. William Gladstone, who was not yet five years old, missed seeing the fireworks at home in Liverpool, because that spring he was with his mother, visiting her old home in Scotland. There in Edinburgh the victory had been announced by the boom and roar of the castle guns. And it was a wonderful booming that William heard. When he got home he stood out for guns as most exciting, while his older brothers argued that fireworks made a more thrilling celebration. No one could say just who won the argument, but it was a lively debate, and that was fun.

The Gladstone family, all of them, loved to argue and debate. At dinner they nearly always debated about some topic, great or small. As they were all very clever at it, each one had to think most logically what he was to say and how to say it, if he weren't to be caught up and made ridiculous.

"They would debate about everything," said a friend of the family, "whether the trout should be boiled or broiled, whether the window should be opened, and whether it was likely to be fine or wet next day. It was all perfectly good-humored, but curious to a stranger."

The only subject that was not open to debate that spring of 1814 was the victory over Napoleon. That they agreed upon as the finest thing that could have happened.

Mr. Gladstone looked for an immediate increase in trade, which was his great interest, for Mr. John Gladstone, William's father, was a very successful businessman. He was one of the wealthiest grain merchants in Liverpool. Ships of his loaded with cargo sailed back and forth from Liverpool to India, to the West Indies and to harbors everywhere. During the war his business had naturally suffered. One of his ships bringing back Russian wheat from the harbor of Riga on the Baltic Sea had been captured by French privateers.

Mr. Gladstone had been definitely opposed at first to the English orders which enforced the blockade against Europe, and had also indirectly injured American shipping, but as the war went on, he changed his mind and felt that the blockade was a necessary evil.

He also changed his mind about his political party. Believing firmly that a man's property should be safeguarded, he left the liberal Whigs who, he felt, were indifferent towards the matter, and became a Tory. So the Whigs took occasion to make up this squib about him:

"John Gladstone was as fine a man
As ever graced commercial story
Till all at once he changed his plan
And from a Whig became a Tory."

This may or may not have brought up the question at dinner as to whether it was not far better and more courageous for a man to change his mind, when he felt he was in the wrong, than to stick with stubborn pride to an opinion he had outgrown, or no longer held. Mr. Gladstone was very positive that it was, and this belief was most strongly impressed upon little William when he was old enough to understand it.

Mr. Gladstone had gone into business when he was quite young, and his education, like his fortune, he had been obliged to acquire himself. He was, therefore, especially eager to see his boys have the best schooling that the country afforded. As soon as they were ready, the older boys were sent to Eton. William wanted to go, too, when he was old enough. First, though, he must learn to read and write and "be prepared."

After they moved from Liverpool to a new home down the shore at Seaforth, the vicar of the church there became his tutor. William did very well with his Latin and English composition, but made such hard work of figuring that the good vicar almost despaired of teaching him arithmetic. After a most painstaking explanation, the boy would look up with an expression in his great brown eyes that showed he still had not the vaguest idea how to solve the problem.

Yet, strangely enough, this boy who had such difficulty learning to add and multiply and divide, was to become the greatest Chancellor of the Exchequer (Secretary of the Treasury) that England ever had.

Four times, also, he was to be Prime Minister and so virtually the ruler of the British Empire.

And, during his long career of over sixty years, William Gladstone was never to lack the courage to change his mind. Though he began life as a Tory, he was to end it as the great leader of the Liberal Party.

JUST BEFORE AND AFTER THE END

NAPOLEON'S DEFEAT left England free to pay more attention to war against the United States. Troops no longer needed in Europe were sent at once to America. At the same time commissioners were sent to the city of Ghent in Holland to discuss peace terms with commissioners from the United States. Since peace, however, was only to be discussed and war was actually going on, England intended to turn the tables now and invade the United States. An attack on Washington, D. C., came first.

One hot August day a post rider covered with dust dashed into the little city with news that the British fleet was in Chesapeake Bay! Washington, wholly unprotected, was thrown into wild confusion.

People scurried hither and yon to hide their valuables. A force of volunteer troops were hustled off to a village four miles away to try to protect the city, while James Madison turned this way and that. It was Tuesday when he left to inspect the defenses and assured his wife, though with a trembling voice, that there could be no immediate danger. Wednesday morning, expecting him back, Mrs. Dolly had ordered dinner to be served at three in the afternoon as usual.

"I set the table myself," said one of the servants later. "All of the Cabinet and several military gentlemen were expected."

"I was lookin' out the chamber window," said Sukey the housemaid, "jes' 'bout three o'clock it was when up the road come a man awavin' his hat. 'Clear out,' he cry, 'clear out!' "

Mrs. Madison ordered her carriage without delay and while waiting for it she jotted down a note to her sister.

"Wednesday 3 o'clock. Will you believe it, my sister, we have had a battle or skirmish—Two messengers bid me fly. I insist upon waiting until the large picture of General Washington is unscrewed from the wall. The process was found too tedious for these perilous moments. I have ordered the frame to be broken and the canvas taken out. It is done! And now my dear sister I must leave this house— Where I shall be to-morrow I cannot tell!

"Dolly."

She left not a moment too soon. As the galloping horses drew the swaying coach out of the town by one road, the enemy, entering by another, made straight for the "President's Palace." Drinking a toast to the absent host at the dinner table, they piled up the chairs, put a live coal to the pile, and so set the house afire. The fire spread through the town, till the sky was bright with flames.

Next day a hurricane added to the damage done by the fire, but when the storm of two days was over, the British had left. President and Mrs. Madison were able to return and find a new place to live. The walls of the President's Palace were still standing, but the sandstone was so streaked with water and smoke that it seemed best to paint it white. That done, it began to be called the "white house." One hundred years later "White House" became its official name.

Baltimore came next. From Washington the British fleet moved north up Chesapeake Bay to Baltimore, which, fortunately, was protected by a fort. All night of September 13 British guns bombarded the fort. All night citizens of Baltimore wondered anxiously if the fort could or could not hold out. All night also, from a British warship in the harbor, a young American who had gone aboard to see about an exchange of prisoners, listened to the noise of the booming cannon. So hopeful was he that in the dawn's early light he still might see the Star-Spangled Banner waving, that on a scrap of paper Francis Scott Key wrote the famous words of the song that years later was to become his nation's national anthem. The next night, in Baltimore, it was sung for the first time.

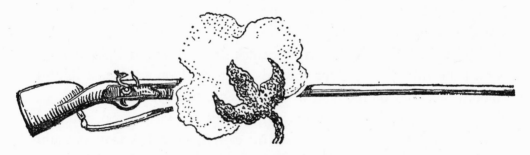

Attack on New Orleans was expected next

"Hasten your militia to New Orleans," James Monroe, Secretary of State, wrote to the governors of all the southern states.

General Andrew Jackson, the man who was to save New Orleans, was one who didn't wait for orders. He was already on the way. He had reached the Gulf of Mexico in August, and driven the British from the harbor base in Florida which the Spanish governor had loaned them.

Then in late November he had turned his horse westward and in ten days arrived with his men in New Orleans. He took one look about.

"What," he swore, "no arms? . . . No soldiers? . . . No supplies? Nothing done to defend the city! . . ."

Then here and there he went, in a fever of activity, storming, persuading, threatening—getting things done. Whites, blacks alike, pirates from the harbor, convicts from the jails, anybody who could carry a musket was put into line. Two days before Christmas the British landed, 1,600 of them, seven miles below the city. One mile away, between a cypress swamp and the river, Andrew Jackson took his stand. A barricade was made of cotton bales.

On Christmas day in the cold foggy delta land the two armies faced each other, ready for battle, not knowing that the day before, December 24, the peace treaty had been signed in Holland and they were no longer at war. News could travel over the ocean no faster than a sailing ship could carry it, so it took three weeks or more to reach America. In three weeks many men can die unnecessarily in war.

Many men fell at New Orleans on January 8, 1815.

"Give it to them, boys!" cried Jackson as his sharpshooting backwoodsmen loaded their rifles behind the cotton bales. "Let's finish the business in one day."

And they did. The Americans, crack shots with their rifles, mowed down the British who came towards them as if on parade. Frightful bloody heaps lay on the field when the battle had been won.

New Orleans went wild with joy over the victory. So, too, did Washington when the news reached the eastern coast, but as news could travel over land no faster than horses could run, it was one month before they learned of the victory in Washington. Or in New England.

New Englanders had come to the conviction that it was high time for them to take a positive stand about this despicable war.

Therefore they had held a convention at Hartford, Connecticut, and actually proposed withdrawing from the United States, seceding from the Union. Delegates from five states. Connecticut, Massachusetts,

Rhode Island, Vermont and New Hampshire, drew up the resolution.

"A sentiment prevails," it stated, "that the time for a change is at hand. Events may prove that the causes of our calamities are deep and permanent. If so a permanent separation will be preferable to an alliance among (so-called) friends but real enemies."

Three New Englanders were on their way to Washington to lay the sentiments of their Convention before Congress when they were met with the glorious news of Jackson's victory in New Orleans. Ten days later came the even more welcome news from Europe that the treaty had been signed and there was PEACE. That news made the New England delegation unnecessary, and thus saved the Union.

So the war of 1812 was at an end. The grievances which had caused it were also ended—not because seizing American ships and seamen was mentioned in the treaty (for it wasn't) but simply because Napoleon had been defeated, and England had no more need to continue the unpleasant practices. The treaty didn't settle much. Mr. John Jacob Astor was disappointed that no settlement had been made regarding Oregon, where, during the war, his new trading post Astoria had been taken by the British.

A few years later, however, the agreement was made. Oregon was to be held and occupied by England and the United States together for ten years to come. At the same time it was agreed that neither nation should ever again build any fleets on the Great Lakes nor forts along the boundary (which was then marked out as far west as the Rockies).

Today that borderline, still unprotected, is pointed to with pride by both nations as the longest unfortified boundary in the world.

BACK TO THE KINGS AGAIN

Now at last had come the glorious moment, so long awaited by the kings of Europe, when they could put back the continent the way they wanted it. Napoleon, destroyer of their peace, was safely stowed away on the island of Elba. Louis XVIII, fat and lazy and almost sixty, brother of the Louis who had been beheaded in the revolution, had been brought back from twenty years of exile to be king of France. Now had come the glorious moment to redivide the continent of Europe and give each king his share.

It was in Vienna, Austria's capital city, that the kings, invited by the Emperor Francis, met to perform the pleasant duty. There they came; emperors, kings, archdukes and princes, attended by such a following of celebrities, diplomats, representatives, guards, and musicians as had never before been seen in a single city. Never had there been seen so much gold braid, so many sparkling jewels or waving plumes as at

56

that CONGRESS OF VIENNA. The populace stood agape at the spectacle.

One man there was, however, in Vienna, that September of 1814, who was not dazzled by the glitter of royalty, nor humbled by it.

"Kings must give way to us—not we to them," he had once told the poet Goethe. And truly. Today when the names of kings and princes who met at that famous Congress of Vienna are all but forgotten, his name lives on—Ludwig van Beethoven.

A short, swarthy, homely, unkempt man, he was living that year next door to the herring-seller and up three flights of stairs. His neighbors called him the "Mad Musician." They told how he had been known to hurl eggs at his housekeeper when he was angry. When he was writing music, they said, he would often sit and pour water over his head until it ran through the floor onto the people below.

By the Emperor Francis, however, and the kings who were his guests and by all the celebrities attending the Congress, the herring-seller's *Närrischer Musiker* was recognized as a genius.

Since 1809, when his Fifth great Symphony had been published, Beethoven's fame had been steadily growing. His *Fidelio* was the first opera performed for the royal visitors at the Congress. Two concert halls were furnished him by the government that the royal guests might hear his symphonies performed, and also enjoy the Cantata, composed especially for the occasion, entitled "The Glorious Moment."

Concerts, dinners, banquets, dances and fireworks filled the evenings. The days were less glorious. Greed and envy sat with the sovereigns at the conference table. Polite discussions soon turned into disagreeable arguments, and before long had degenerated into downright squabbling. Austria and England were actually talking of going to war with Russia and Prussia . . . when suddenly, like a bomb shell, came the news that NAPOLEON HAD ESCAPED FROM ELBA!

The squabbling among the allies had led Napoleon to attempt this boldest and most exciting adventure of his life. The escape had been carefully planned. He landed on the coast of France on the first day of March, and appealed to his still loyal soldiers.

An Old Print..
Contains profiles of Napoleon Marie Louise and their Son

"Soldiers," he cried, "we are not conquered! . . . We were betrayed. Soldiers, come! For your interests, your glory. Come! March to victory!" Marching, they met a regiment sent by the royalists to stop him.

"Stop me! Here I am," Napoleon cried. Throwing open his coat he stood before them. "You know me. If there is a soldier among you who wishes to shoot his Emperor, let him do it!"

Dead silence. Then "Vive l'Empereur!" came the cry. The soldiers rushed towards him. Tearing off the royal colors, they put on again the red, white and blue cockade. Regiment after regiment fell in, town after town met them with cheers until it became a triumphal procession—that march from the seacoast to Paris.

The night before Napoleon arrived, Louis XVIII fled from the Tuileries, escaped from the city in a small black carriage. The next day the newspaper, which had begun by talking about "the escape of the ogre from Elba" announced that "His Majesty the Emperor made his public entry and arrived at the Tuileries amid universal joy."

True, Napoleon had entered Paris, but the joy was far from universal. There was faint cheering in the streets. Many faces he had hoped to see were not there to greet him. Marie Louise and his little son were gone. His brothers were scattered. The Empress Josephine was dead. But her grandson, little Louis Napoleon, was still there, and since it was spring, the boy who sold violets was also standing on the corner.

"Uncle Napoleon came back with the violets," thought little Louis as he went with his mother to the Tuileries. That was a great day for him, standing on the balcony beside the Emperor and looking down upon the people. But it was a sad day when he went again in June to bid his uncle goodbye before he went to war.

"Don't go. Don't go to war!" sobbed Louis, hiding his face on his uncle's knees. "The naughty allies will kill you."

That day Napoleon started on his last campaign. The English army,

58

commanded by the Duke of Wellington and the Prussian army under General Blücher were in Belgium. Hoping to prevent their meeting and to defeat each army separately before the Russians and Austrians also took the field, Napoleon entered Belgium. On June 18, 1815, he met his final and complete defeat at Waterloo.

Victor Hugo was only thirteen then. Many years later in his great novel *Les Misérables* he was to describe that terrific battle, in which the English stood firm with desperate courage, until the Prussians reinforced them and made possible the utter annihilation of the French.

Three days after the tragic news reached Paris, the boy Victor Hugo wrote in his school book this bitter verse against Napoleon:

> "Tremble thou despot, the avenging hand of fate
> Down to its doom thine odious empire shakes;
> But now alas! thy fall for France
> Still costs her blood, still makes her tears to flow!"

While the boy was writing, not far off, in the Chamber of Deputies, patriotic Frenchmen were demanding Napoleon's abdication. Among them was General La Fayette, one of the great leaders in the early days of the French Revolution, who for twenty-five years had remained faithful to his belief in liberty of the people. Now it was his firm conviction that Napoleon must abdicate.

"In ten years, three million Frenchmen have perished for that man," he cried. "It is enough. Our duty now is to save France, to rally around the old tricolor flag of 1789, the flag of liberty and equality."

Napoleon abdicated. Undecided where to go, he boarded a British ship and from Portsmouth harbor sent this appeal to the English king:

> "Your Royal Highness . . . I have closed my political career, and I come to throw myself upon the hospitality of the British people . . . and beg Your Royal Highness, as the most powerful, the most persistent, the most generous of my enemies, to grant me this protection."

Napoleon

It was a dignified appeal, but it came from a dangerous enemy. England could afford to take no chances. Napoleon was sent to a rock in the South Atlantic, the island of St. Helena, there to be kept constantly under guard for six, black, barren years until his death.

"No one but myself can be blamed for my fall," he said. "I have been my own greatest enemy, the cause of my own disastrous fate."

Napoleon on St. Helena, Louis XVIII back again as King of France —and the Glorious Moment after one hundred days' delay had come again for the kings of Europe. More determined now than ever, they were, to reestablish the good old substantial order of things whereby kings ruled and people obeyed and peace was maintained.

"To that end let us as brother monarchs form a Holy Alliance," suggested Czar Alexander of Russia. "Let us as Christians be guided wholly by the principles of justice and mildness. Let us look upon our subjects as children, and in the spirit of brotherhood help one another on all occasions and so maintain a lasting peace."

Alexander was the grandson of Catherine the Great, and a well-meaning man of high ideals, but as it worked out his Holy Alliance was holy only in name. In actual practice the members—Russia, Prussia, and Austria—were guided not by justice and mercy, but by the cold-blooded ideas of Prince Metternich, chief adviser to the Emperor of Austria, and one who admitted that he had never made a mistake in his life.

Metternich believed in monarchy absolute and infallible. He hated parliaments, constitutions or anything that suggested self-government by the people. Dangerous movements towards freedom anywhere he would see stamped out like a contagious disease. Likewise all change—all disturbing new ideas. Thus he advised the kings, and the kings were all quite ready to follow his advice.

Europe, therefore, in 1815 entered the "Era of Metternich," an age when liberty, education, free speech, all things taught Europe by the French Revolution were to be suppressed. For the next forty years the kings would be supreme, Europe would lie in the shadow of the Austrian crown, and Liberty would live only in the hearts of the people.

PART TWO : WHEN
Abraham Lincoln
WAS A **BOY** IN
Indiana

Other People who were living

NOAH WEBSTER
wrote his first American Dictionary of the English language.

HANDS OFF

JAMES MONROE
5th United States President stated the

"MONROE DOCTRINE"

HANDS OFF

FREE

HARRIET BEECHER
was hunting something to read among her father's sermons, born 1811

SIMON BOLIVAR
became the "Liberator" of South America
(born 1783)

SEQUOYAH
a Cherokee Indian made an alphabet for his people.

JOHN JAMES AUDUBON
was drawing the last of his "BIRDS of AMERICA"

(born 1767)

"KIT" CARSON (born 1809)
rode to Mexico over the newly opened Santa Fe trail.

Ex-president **JOHN ADAMS**
90 years old in 1825, saw his son **JOHN QUINCY ADAMS** as President

U.S. GRANT
was born in 1822

(born 1783)
WASHINGTON IRVING
popular American author was travelling in Europe,

BENITO JUAREZ
Mexico's great Indian patriot was born in 1806

and some Events that took place

when Abraham Lincoln was a Boy

CHARLES DICKENS
a poor boy of London was working
in a shoe blacking factory (born 1812)

VICTORIA was born in 1819
one year before the death of
her grandfather George III

(also born Feb 12, 1809)

CHARLES DARWIN
to be one of the world's greatest scientists
was collecting toads, crabs, shells etc

WILLIAM GLADSTONE
one of England's great statesmen
was a school boy at Eton (born 1809)

RAILROADS
came into use in 1829 - because of

inventions by
GEORGE STEPHENSON
(born 1781)

(born 1813)
DAVID LIVINGSTONE
explorer of Africa was
working in a cotton mill

(born 1815)
II NAOSUKE
who was to open Japan
was studying for the future

(born 1807)
GARIBALDI
a boy of Italy was
sailing the sea

Victoria's German uncle
LEOPOLD
lived in England until in
1831, he became King of a
new nation - Belgium.

LI HUNG CHANG
future statesman of China
was learning to write (b.1823)

between the Years 1815 and 1830

The UNITED STATES & Territories

Year 1815

ENGLISH

ASTORIA
FORT VANCOUVER
COLUMBIA

LOUISIANA PURCHASE

MISSOURI

MISSOURI

MISSISSIPPI

Spanish

SANTA FE

RIO GRANDE

MEXICO

ST. LOUIS

MISSISSIPPI

X Lincoln's Home

OHIO

OHIO

ERIE

ST. LAWR.

Where ERIE
CANAL was
to be dug
1817-25

HUDSON

NEW YORK

POTOMAC

WASHINGTON

First National
Road connecting
Ohio and Potomac
was to be finished 1817

18 States

Territories

NEW ORLEANS

Spanish

.... Path of LEWIS & CLARK

+++ SANTA FE Trail
(to be opened about 1822)

《《THEY FOLLOWED THE RIVERS》》

TRAILS TO THE WEST

ON JULY 4, 1816, the United States was to celebrate its fortieth Independence Day. It was then, with the second war for independence from England fairly won, that people of the young nation turned their faces to the west and the era of the pioneer, the frontiersman, the common people of America began.

Daniel Boone, famous old pioneer of early days, was still alive. He was eighty years old, and living in the Missouri Territory, which was as far west as settlers had ventured so long as hostile Indians were still powerful east of the Mississippi. Now, however, with the defeat of the Creeks by Andrew Jackson, all the eastern half of the Mississippi's broad fertile valley was safe for white settlers and their families.

So by hundreds and thousands from all parts of the country people began moving westward, and it looked to old Daniel Boone very much as though civilization was catching up with him again. Every spring when he took his furs down the Missouri River to St. Louis and saw a town of eighteen hundred people he thought he should be moving on.

Usually, though, as he sat mending his fur traps or scraping away on a new powder horn, his thoughts carried him not into the future, but over trails that led into the past. He recollected the days when he was young, and the Allegheny Mountains, not the Mississippi River, had been the western frontier. The United States was just a colony of England then, and Kentucky was Indian battle ground. The King had forbidden settlers to go over the mountains, but by the time war came in 1776, there were several log forts in Kentucky like the one at Boonesborough.

1776

1783

1803

In 1783 when the war was over, all the land east of the Mississippi belonged to the United States and more settlers began to find homes beyond the mountains. So he, Daniel Boone, had moved on to where there was "more elbow room"—out to this Louisiana territory that then belonged to Spain. Spain had turned it over to France. In 1803 the United States had bought it. The next year, as Daniel Boone remembered, two young men, Lewis and Clark, had been sent by President Jefferson to explore the new territory. They had paddled up the Missouri River, past his home. Old as he was, he would like to have gone with them—out to Oregon. Some day he'd also like to see that Spanish colony, California. . . .

But here halfway across the continent was to be for Daniel Boone the journey's end.

Other pioneers would now pick up the trail. Settlers would follow the trappers and traders across the desert and over the Rocky Mountains until they had carried the United States to the Pacific Ocean and spread the Stars and Stripes across the continent.

66

ABE GOES TO INDIANA

THE LINCOLNS moved from Kentucky to Indiana the winter that Abe was seven. Just a mite older, Thomas Lincoln said, than he was himself when his paw, Abe's grandpappy Abraham, had brought the family from Virginia to Kentucky, following after his friend Daniel Boone. Kentucky was full of Indians then. One of them had killed his father, Tom said, and would have killed him too, if it hadn't been for his big brother Mordecai, who shot the Indian just in time. Hadn't been Indians to bother folks in Kentucky for a long time now, but there were other worries, these days.

Times were hard, and crops were poorly, and too many folks were moving in who had slaves to do the work. That made it hard for plain folks who worked their own land to get along. Besides that Thomas Lincoln couldn't get the deed to his farm straightened out, so as soon as he got his money back, he made up his mind to move from Kentucky.

Indiana, he figured, was the place to go. Folks said there was rich land not so far north of the Ohio River. The Indians had been cleared out and Indiana had enough settlers to be made into a state that year instead of a territory. It was going to be a free state, with no slaves. Every man was to vote, and it looked like there'd be a chance for a poor man to make a real home for himself in Indiana.

Abe wished his mother didn't feel so sad about going when the time came. She didn't say much, just brushed her hair out of her eyes with the back of her hand and kept on getting ready. His father said that the place he had picked out near Pidgeon Creek was a hundred miles away, and if they wanted to be there before snow fell they'd have to hustle some.

There wasn't much to take, just some kiverlids for the bed, a few pots and pans, the axe and hoe, his father's carpenter tools, and such like—no more than the two horses could carry with Abe and his father on one and Sarah and his mother riding the other.

When they finally reached the place in the deep woods where the log house was to be, it took the rest of the winter to build it. Abe helped. He hacked the branches off the logs and cut the notches in them. When it was up at last, it seemed so fine after the three-sided open-faced shed in which they had been living all winter, that they moved right in, and Tom never did get around to laying a floor or making a window. He didn't trouble to tear down the pole shed either, so when Uncle Tom and Aunt Betsy Sparrow and Dennis Hanks came the next fall they had it to live in, too, till their cabin was built.

The next year how his mother had grieved when Tom and Aunt Betsy had died of the "milk sick" that was going the rounds! Before long she, too, had flushed cheeks and a burning tongue. Abe did what he could, bringing her cups of water, but one day he saw his mother lie still, quite still forever. With tears streaming down his face he went outside, and while he helped his father make a long box for her to lie in he thought of words she used to say to him:

"Blessed are they that mourn, for they shall be comforted."

He wished that there had been a preacher to say those words above her grave the day when they laid her away in that lonely spot by the salt lick, where the deer came down.

Abe couldn't eat anything when they came back to the cabin that night, just the four of them, his father and Dennis Hanks and he and Sarah. He couldn't sleep much, either, when he climbed up the pegs and lay down on his pile of cornhusks in the loft. Wide-eyed for hours, he watched the stars pass by an opening in the logs.

The next winter Thomas Lincoln went back to Kentucky. He didn't say why he was going or when he was coming back. It was pretty bad for them, then, but they managed. Abe was ten, Sarah was twelve, but Dennis was nineteen and could shoot all the food they needed. It was dreary, though, terribly dreary . . . until one morning Abe thought he heard the creak of a wagon. They ran to the door, he and Dennis and Sarah, and listened again. Then they saw it—a great big wagon, piled high with furniture, drawn by four shaggy-footed horses, come round a clump of sycamore trees. On top sat two girls and a boy, and on the driver's seat beside Tom Lincoln sat a woman.

"This is your new mammy," said Thomas Lincoln to his children.

"And these are your new sisters and brother, John and Sarah and Matilda Johnston," the woman added. As she spoke she smiled.

So Abe smiled a little, too. Then the new mother looked deep into the eyes of the dirty neglected little boy, and drew him to her. Abe had only to feel her warm arm about his shoulders to know that it would not be lonely in the cabin any more.

That night, because Sarah Bush Lincoln had come to be his mother, Abe slept for the first time on a feather bed instead of a pile of corn-husks. And he went to bed washed and clean, with no grit in his black hair. Before long he was even learning to read and write. This is a piece torn from his homemade copy book, written with a pen that Dennis Hanks made for him out of a wild turkey buzzard's quill:

69

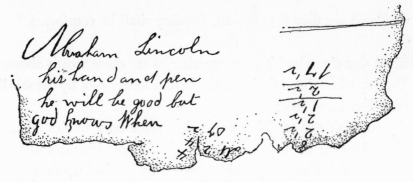

The good stepmother couldn't read herself, but whenever a teacher kept school for a few months nearby, she saw that her children went. Abe was so eager to learn that even going to school "by littles" he soon learned to read and write and cipher and spell.

Less than a year in all he spent in school, but every day of his life he worked, the way poor boys in the backwoods had to work, first for his father, and then as "hired boy" for some neighboring farmer. Clearing brush, chopping trees, plowing, pulling fodder, husking corn—it didn't matter to him what work he did so long as he had a book tucked in his shirt, time to snatch a page of it now and then, and a chance to read it all by the fire at night when he got home.

And here, too, Sarah Lincoln saw that he had a chance. His father complained he was wasting his time, but she liked to watch him. Things he wanted to memorize she saw him writing down on the back of a wooden shovel. Sometimes he laughed out loud at what he was reading —*Æsop's Fables,* perhaps. Then he might turn and share it with her.

Years later, looking back, she would often say, "His mind and mine, what little I had, seemed to run together."

A life of George Washington was the first book Abe ever owned. It was a borrowed book, but when at night the rain came through the logs and spoiled the covers, he shucked corn three days to pay for it. It was well worth it to him. It was a book that made him think.

"I'm not always goin' to grub and shuck corn and split logs and such like to earn my livin'," he said one day.

And Sarah Lincoln, his stepmother, the "best friend he had in this world," believed in him.

ROBERT LEE OF VIRGINIA

ROBERT E. LEE was eight years old in 1815 and of course, because
he was a Lee, he was living in Virginia. At Stratford, the old
Lee plantation, in the room where Robert was born, three generations of his family had been born before him. Two had
signed the Declaration of Independence—their portraits hung in the
great hall. Families without position or property might move from
Virginia, but to the Lees, Virginia was home and mother country.

Robert E. was not living on the plantation when the war of 1812
was over but with his mother in a small house in Alexandria. By that
time dreadful misfortune had befallen his father. He had lost his money
and his health and been obliged to leave the country. With his two older
brothers away at college, Robert felt that his mother needed him, so
nearly every afternoon he hurried home to go driving with her. As he
ran up the steps of the red brick house, and opened the white door, he
would call to her from the hall:

"Mother, I'm here. I'm here, Mother. Are you ready?" Then as he
laid his school books on the table, he listened for her answer.

"I'm ready." The words were always the same, but Robert could tell
from their tone whether she felt better or not so well that day. If her

voice held a quiver of sadness, he thought up something to tell her that would make her smile, while he held her coat and bonnet. And always, as she saw him standing there so courteous and so handsome, Ann Carter Lee was thankful that the fire and charm he had inherited from the Lees was balanced by the sterling qualities of the Carters.

Then, as she rested her slim hand lightly on his arm, he matched his step to hers, and they walked slowly down the short path between the snowball bushes to the carriage. There old Nat the coachman in his green uniform threadbare at the seams, but with his black face shining, stood beside the door. When they were seated he would close it gently, climb to his seat and start the horses at a leisurely trot down the cobbled stone street.

Sometimes they chose to turn eastward towards the Potomac, ride along the river and look across to Washington, where the government buildings destroyed by fire were now being rebuilt.

If the day was pleasant they might go as far as Arlington, where little Mary Custis lived in a home that looked like a Greek temple. There her father George Washington Parke Custis, the adopted son of George Washington, welcomed all guests with an elaborate hospitality.

Other afternoons they took the road leading towards Mount Vernon. As they rode, Ann Carter told her son how his father, "Light Horse Harry," had been one of George Washington's favorite generals in the Revolution—how he had been in Congress when the great commander died, and how in a memorial speech he had spoken of Washington as "First in war, first in peace, and first in the hearts of his countrymen."

Only the good qualities of his charming father did Ann Carter want Robert to remember, so she said nothing of the foolish extravagance and speculation by which Light Horse Harry had squandered all his fortune. Robert, with understanding, did not question her. So the two shared happy days until Robert was eighteen and ready for college.

"How can I ever live without him?" said his mother, trembling at the thought of parting. "He has been both son and daughter to me!"

However, when he was ready for West Point, and Mr. John C. Calhoun had secured the appointment for him, Ann Carter Lee bade her son a brave farewell. Robert had always been a splendid student, and she felt sure that he would also make a faithful and courageous soldier.

At West Point, four years later, he was graduated, ranking second in his class, and with a record that "failed to show a single demerit against Cadet Lee." That summer, back in Virginia just before his mother's death, Robert was at her bedside with his Lieutenant's commission in his hand and wearing his new blue uniform.

In that uniform of his country Robert E. Lee was to serve faithfully for more than thirty years. He would lay it aside for one of gray only when the broader loyalty to the United States challenged that narrower but more personal loyalty to his mother state, that deep love of Virginia, which was born with him in his heart.

HARRIET BEECHER, THE PREACHER'S CHILD

IT WAS a Sabbath morning in Connecticut, about 1820. The last church bell was tolling in the village of Litchfield as the Beecher family, ten or so of them, hustled along the elm-bordered streets and up the meeting-house steps. Then gasping for breath in the vestibule, they filed sedately down the aisle to their regular pew. Harriet was next to the littlest, so she went in first. Henry Ward was younger, but he wiggled so that he had to sit where one of the older sisters could keep a hand on him.

Meanwhile father Beecher, who had caused all this regular Sunday panic, quite calm now and collected, was taking his place behind the pulpit. Only ten minutes ago they had seen him come tearing down from his study, with his hair on end, his necktie behind his ear and a bunch of notes for the morning's sermon pinned to his coat lapel.

Harriet's cheeks were still pink from the rush, and her soft brown curls were moist beneath her bonnet as she peeked from under it. There were three more empty pews this week. Her father would not be pleased with that, she thought. It meant that three more families had gone west to live. Her father "deplored" the fact that so many Connecticut people were "willing"—that was the way he said it—"willing to leave towns of culture and refinement for the wild lands of the west and the still wilder society." He feared for the good of their souls.

Harriet wondered about her own soul, too, sometimes. She was especially worried when her father preached about Hell. What if she should be one of those sinners whose souls were not saved and would burn forever? She sincerely hoped her father would not preach a hell-fire sermon that morning, because if he did she could not help but listen to every horribly fascinating detail. Yet if he didn't, if he talked about "Predestination" and words like that, she would not be able to keep her sinful mind from sailing off on a magic carpet to the land of Aladdin. That would be dreadful on the Sabbath. Tomorrow, though, just as soon as she finished the stint on her sampler, she would run right up to her father's study and see what was going to happen on the next page when Aladdin rubbed the lamp.

Many days little Harriet Beecher spent in that study of her father's at the top of the "old windy castle" of a parsonage. "Lined from floor to ceiling with the friendly faces of books" it was her favorite retreat. There she would curl up in a corner, quietly reading, while her father sat in his great writing chair at work on his sermons. She was a tiny thing and as quiet as a mouse. She never disturbed him with any questions, so he liked to have her there.

He liked to have her around, too, when there was work to be done. Then she flew about like a busy little wren. One day when they were all out carrying in wood, he praised her and also spurred on her brothers by saying how much faster she worked than they did. Father Beecher was a genius at making the family work together and enjoy it. At apple-paring time, when a barrel of applesauce had to be made for the winter's use, there was work for everyone in the kitchen.

"Tell you what we'll do," he'd say, "to make the evening go off. Let's take turns and see who can tell the most out of Scott's novels."

That pleased Harriet. One summer she and one of her brothers read *Ivanhoe* through seven times, and could recite many scenes from memory. Some day Harriet planned to write a novel of her own.

"The main thing," her teacher at the Academy told their English class, "is to have something you really want to say."

The year that Harriet was twelve, the three best compositions of the term were read at the school exhibition. Harriet watched her father's face while hers was being read. Then she heard him ask the principal who was the author, and when the principal answered, "Your daughter, sir," and she saw his face light up, it was the proudest moment of her life.

It made up a little for the days when she felt that she "was fit for nothing and wished she could die young and let her faults perish in the grave." Stories of the Pilgrim fathers, however, filled her with courage. Wonderful words like the Declaration of Independence made her long to "fight for her country, or make some declaration on her own account . . ." do something—she didn't know what . . .

As nothing seemed to need her help at once, she decided wisely that perhaps people cannot plan ahead too far or too precisely. Perhaps all that was expected of her now was to make the most of the talents God had given her and the time and place would come for her to use them.

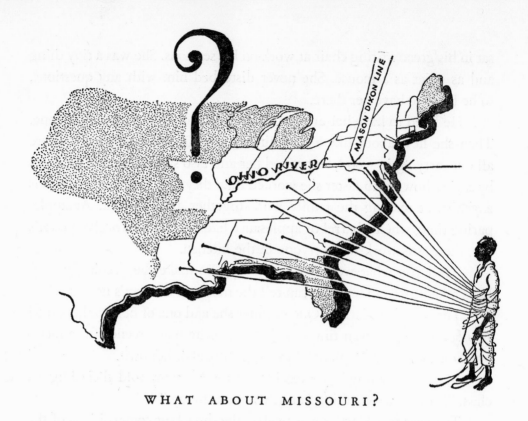

WHAT ABOUT MISSOURI?

AMES MONROE was elected President of the United States in 1817. The vote was almost unanimous. After the war, differences of opinion between the sections of the country had melted away into a period of peace and harmony later known as the Era of Good Feeling. Everyone hoped that it would last forever, but suddenly it was gone. In 1819, a question came up that roused the country from one end of it to the other. "Like a fire bell in the night" it sounded to Thomas Jefferson at Monticello, and dismal too "like the death knell of the union." It was the ugly question of slavery and it had come up in connection with Missouri.

Missouri Territory wanted to become a state. It had now the necessary 65,000 settlers. The question was: Should Missouri be a state where only FREE men might live, or one where SLAVERY was to be allowed?

Indiana had entered as a free state, the year the Lincolns moved there, because it was north of the Ohio River. As far west as the Mississippi, the Ohio acted as a continuation of the Mason and Dixon line dividing the free states to the north from slave states to the south.

"That line should be extended across the river," said the northerners. "Missouri lies north of the Ohio and therefore should be free."

"Missouri should be a slave state," said people of the south. "Most of the settlers are slave owners from Kentucky and Tennessee. They want a slave state. They should be allowed to have it."

"Besides," they added, "if Missouri should come in a free state it would destroy the balance between the slave states and the free."

From the map it is easy to see what they were talking about. Of the twenty-two states in 1819, eleven were slave and eleven were free. Each state was allowed two senators, so there was a deadlock when the question of Missouri was first brought up in Congress. Before the next vote, all over the country, people were discussing the question.

At a meeting held in Boston, Daniel Webster protested earnestly against allowing the evil of slavery to spread. Little Harriet Beecher heard her father preach a sermon against it that moved even the men in the meeting house to tears.

Never before in the history of the country had there been such excitement over slavery. Petitions poured into Congress. The debate raged for two years, until the gentleman from Georgia shook his fist at the gentleman from Illinois and threatened that "if he persisted the Union would be dissolved!" Some of the southern members threatened to withdraw from Congress. Daniel Webster was alarmed, forgetting how recently New England had been making the same threat.

Henry Clay was distressed. He saw that something must be done at once to satisfy both sides, for Henry Clay saw both sides. He considered slavery "the deepest stain on the character of our country." He was a leader in the movement to give freed Negroes a home in Liberia, but he owned slaves himself, and realized that slaves were valuable property to their owners. Therefore, when a compromise was suggested that he thought might settle the matter harmoniously, Henry Clay begged, schemed and pleaded until finally the Compromise was made.

Missouri was to be admitted as a slave state, BUT from then on slavery was to be barred from all territory north of its southern boundary line, as far west as the Rocky Mountains. Maine was to be admitted as a new free state, thus making free and slave states equal again. The country heaved a sigh of relief. The Union had been saved. The dangerous question of slavery, they hoped, had been hushed forever.

"Hushed it is, indeed, for the moment," said Thomas Jefferson dismally, "but this is not the final sentence." The day of reckoning, he knew, would come.

The Missouri Compromise had but postponed that evil day.

U.S. + Florida

And now to the United States, growing like a young giant in population and land, not only new states but a new territory had been added. The peninsula of FLORIDA. That land of sun and flowers which belonged to Spain had become in recent years a breeding ground for trouble. Pirates, robbers, runaway slaves, hid in its swamps and everglades. Joined with the Seminoles, the native wandering Indians, they continually made raids on the people of Georgia, killing the planters and their families and stealing their property.

Andrew Jackson finally was called upon to put a stop to this outrage, and in his usual fashion "Old Hickory" made quick work of his assignment. Within three months he had beaten the Seminoles, hanged a few troublemakers, and practically taken possession of the country and again made himself a hero!

Spain protested, naturally.

John Quincy Adams, Secretary of Foreign Affairs, replied that Spain must either keep order in Florida—or sell it.

It seemed better to sell than lose it, especially as it was lost already. So Spain took $5,000,000 and the United States took Florida.

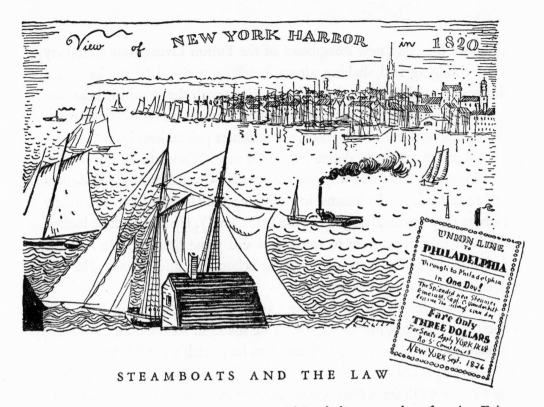

STEAMBOATS AND THE LAW

IN THE YEAR 1817, the first shovelful of dirt was dug for the Erie
Canal. That year Cornelius Vanderbilt changed his mind about
steamboats, and so began to build up his tremendous fortune. What
was more important, he brought to light a bad situation, which, if it
had not been stopped by law, might well have split apart the fast growing United States, and destroyed the Union.

Ten years before, in 1807, when Robert Fulton had first launched
his steamboat on the Hudson River, "Corneel" Van der Bilt was just a
thirteen year old tow-headed kid, who lived on a farm on Staten Island.
By the time he was sixteen, he was rough and tough and as able to fight
for his rights as any man in New York harbor, and he was in business for
himself. He had a sailboat of his own, and ferried passengers across from
Staten Island to the city for eighteen cents apiece. Every day he went
sailing back and forth like mad, crowding in as many trips as possible,
proud of his profits and his sailboat.

"Who in heck'd want to ride on one of them rattletraps," he'd say

79

as one of the eight new steamboats of the Fulton Livingstone Company went chugging and shaking along, belching a cloud of smoke and a shower of sparks and cinders. True, sailing with the wind his boat was faster and smoother, but sailing against the wind was a different story. No matter how hard he worked, the steamers passed him by.

"Let 'em get there, damn 'em," he'd say. "Who cares?" But he did.

He cared. That was why one day in 1817 Corneel paid seven dollars and took a ride on the steamship *Fulton* up the Hudson River to Albany (where they were starting to dig the Erie Canal). Up and back he looked the boat over from stem to stern, and did some figuring. He had the ferryboat business, three ocean-going schooners, and $9,000. He was doing well—but not well enough.

"Goin' to sell all my sailboats and go into steamboatin'," he said one day. "The big money's goin' to be made in steamboats." And big money was what he wanted. Wanted to be as rich as "Old Astor" was.

So he packed up the wife and kids and moved to New Jersey. There he went to work for a man named Gibbons, running his steamboat ferry between New Jersey and New York. Now if Corneel had left the cranky little boat the way he found it, probably nothing would have happened, but Corneel was a worker. He got the boat in good shape, running on regular schedule and paying a profit. Then a warrant was issued in New York for his arrest! For what? He knew for what—for operating a steamboat to New York harbor without paying for the privilege.

Fulton and Livingstone Company had the sole right to run steamboats on the waters of New York State. Anyone else who wanted to start up for himself had to pay them for the right—or be arrested.

"Arrested?" said Cornelius. "Let 'em try."

They did try. Again and again. But the warrant officers couldn't arrest him because they couldn't find him. He always managed to be under the gangplank, or down in the hold, somewhere out of sight when they came aboard. Finally in desperation to get rid of the Gibbons competition, the monopoly tried to bribe this impudent fellow who had been able to make it a paying business. Ogden offered him a good salary and command of his largest steamer. Corneel refused. He was no quitter.

This man Ogden had formerly been a partner of Gibbons, but had gone over to the monopoly, and helped it bring suit against him. It was called the Ogden-Gibbons or Gibbons-Ogden case.

Before long the State of New Jersey took up the fight, and forbade any officer of New York to arrest any citizen of New Jersey for not having a license. Connecticut was incensed also, and forbade any vessel owned by the monopoly to come into her harbors. The idea of one state making laws against another spread. Out on the Ohio River, Kentucky made a law against Indiana, and Abraham Lincoln was arrested.

Abe then had a job as a ferryman. He took passengers on a flatboat from the Indiana shore out to steamers going up or down the Ohio River. One day two brothers who ran a similar ferry from the Kentucky shore had him arrested and taken before the Justice of the Peace. Abe testified that he had taken passengers out to the middle of the river, but *not* to the Kentucky shore. The case was dismissed.

"Mighty handy to know the law about any business you're in," thought Abe. After that he hunted up law books to read, and sat up half the night. Days when the Justice of the Peace held court he went, whenever he could, to listen. In the Louisville newspaper he liked to read what new laws were made by Congress, and what decisions had been handed down by the Supreme Court of the United States.

So in time he must have read of the famous Gibbons-Ogden case, for in 1824 (just the year before the Erie Canal was finished) that lawsuit, tried and retried, had finally reached the Supreme Court. Gibbons was defended by the young lawyer of New England, Daniel Webster.

John Marshall, the great Chief Justice, handed down this decision that abolished the monopoly: ALL THAT ANY MAN NEEDED WAS A FEDERAL LICENSE AND HE WAS FREE TO USE ANY RIVER OR LAKE OR HARBOR IN THE UNITED STATES. This was one nation—not twenty-four. John Marshall made many important interpretations of the Constitution, but none more important than this, in helping cement the states into one united nation, guaranteeing justice and equal rights to all of its citizens.

81

"KIT" RIDES TO SANTA FE

Daniel Boone died in 1820, and not many years later, a reward of one cent was offered for the return of a boy, a distant kin of his, who was to become the great guide west of the Mississippi, and whose father had followed Daniel Boone into Missouri. On October 6, 1826, this advertisement appeared in print:

> NOTICE: Christopher Carson, a boy about 16 years old, small of his age but thickset, light hair, ran away from the subscriber, to whom he had been bound to learn the saddler's trade, on or about the first day of September last. One cent reward will be given to any person who will bring back said boy.   (Signed) David Workman, Franklin, Missouri.

And where was Kit Carson when that reward was offered? He was on the trail to Santa Fe. He had to go. The hankering of the pioneer was in his blood. Besides, how could any boy sit at a bench boring holes in leather and stitching harness when the very air was full of tales of the two great paths that led beyond the sunset?

Back from the northwest came trappers and traders with bundles of furs and tales of rivers and mountains. Back from the southwest came men in broadbrimmed hats with gold dust and silver nuggets. Even more fascinating were their tales of desert and prairie, of buffalos and Comanche Indians—of caballeros and señoritas who danced the fan-

dango, in a far off Mexican city called Santy Fe! So when the next wagon train left for the west by south, Christopher Carson was on it.

There he was, riding along at the end of a string of extra mules and horses, while on ahead, swaying and creaking, rumbled the long line of covered wagons, heavily loaded with goods to trade. Like ships through a sea of grass they crossed the prairies of Kansas. They forded the Arkansas River and trailed through the sun and dust of the Cimarron desert. Fifty nights or more they stood wheel to wheel beneath the sky, before the trail began to climb, and finally brought them out one fine day onto the edge of a red rock eight hundred miles from home.

There the old-timers threw their hats in the air and shouted,

"Thar she be! Thar's old Santy Fee!"

And there in the valley below the red violet mountains on the opposite sky line, Kit saw for the first time the low flat-roofed adobe houses of the old Spanish city. Down then into the town they went, past the market full of red peppers and melons and grapes, past the church with its gold cross and ancient bell, on into the open plaza. And everywhere were the dark-haired, dark-eyed people, in gold-embroidered coats and broad sombreros, in bright striped blankets, brilliant skirts and shawls. It was a strange sight for the yellow-headed boy. And he was a strange sight to them. A boy. *"Un muchacho."*

"Un muchacho Americano," they cried and pointed.

It was always a great day for Santa Fe when the caravan arrived. Only four years had the trail been open. Before that Mexico had belonged to Spain and strangers who ventured over the border soon found themselves in jail. Now they were welcome. Mexico was free.

BENITO JUAREZ, A BOY OF MEXICO

YES, MEXICO was free in 1826 and a Republic. Vittoria, the first President, was serving his second year. He was an upright man abiding by the Constitution and enforcing its laws, one of which provided for free education. That was why in the city of Oaxaca, so full of monasteries and cathedrals, a new school of Arts and Science had now been opened, free to all—including the Indians.

Benito Juarez could go at last to a school where he was welcome. All five years in the old Seminary, although the kind Señor had paid for his tuition, he had been jeered at by the white pupils and slighted by the teachers. Often he had overheard visitors say:

"An Indio here? Indians cannot be educated. They have no sense."

Fortunately Fra Antonio had not agreed with them. Good Fra Antonio! To him Benito Juarez owed everything. A poor waif, unable even to speak the Spanish language, Fra Antonio had taken him in and given him a home. He had taught him to repair and clean the books for the monastery and then to read in them. Fra Antonio was much feebler now. Benito often watched him nodding over his prayer book, and

84

thought of his first days with the kindly old man in this little bookshop.

How like a feast those first meals of tortillas and fruit and beans had tasted after years of not having had enough to eat! He remembered how hungry he was the day he arrived in the city of Oaxaca, hungry and tired, for he had walked a long way from the home village in the mountains. Since that day he had not seen his uncle, but he could never forget his cruelty. His dead parents? They were a dimmer memory. After the old grandmother too was dead, there had been no one left but the uncle. That was why Josepha, his sister, had gone to find work in Oaxaca and why when he was twelve he had followed her. He remembered well the day he left. How cool the mountain air was. How red and beautiful in the sunrise had been the ruins of the old Zapotec temple. How clear the reflections in the mirror-like surface of the enchanted lake. He had thrown a stone into it and watched the ripples follow one another in ever-widening circles until they died away.

That was the way sound traveled, he thought, coming back to the present. It was wonderful to study physics now and the other sciences, and to learn of the great laws which ruled the universe.

In a year or so, the instructors told him, he might begin the study of Social Laws, the laws by which men try in their feeble way to keep order in their lives with one another. Ancient laws and modern laws he would study. The laws of Spain, the laws of the United States and its Constitution, after which Mexico had now patterned her own. All the laws of this new republic he would study, laws which were now to insure justice and equality to all the people. His people, too, the Indios, he hoped, after three hundred years of oppression might now take their rightful place in their homeland. Had not the Republic chosen for its flag an ancient Indian symbol? The eagle with the serpent in its mouth, according to legend, was the sign which led the Aztec Indians to found their first capital on the site of Mexico City. Now old Mexico City was the capital of the new republic.

Benito Juarez had been but four years old in 1810 when the first cry for freedom from the rule of Spain had been raised in Mexico by the

creole priest, Hidalgo. Now the famous cry, called *El Grito de Dolores,* and the story of Hidalgo were part of Mexican history. Hidalgo was a poor parish priest who had been made to feel humiliated because he was a creole, for in Mexico, as in all Spain's colonies, Spaniards born in the new world were oppressed by their overlords who had been born in Spain. So it was "Down with the Spaniards!" "Down with those who wear the spurs!" Hidalgo cried. Rousing the Indians of his parish, he marched with them from village to village adding to his forces, carrying as their standard a painting of the Indian virgin, "Our Lady of Guadalupe." Hidalgo was no general. His army was soon overpowered by the royal forces, and he was shot.

MORELOS, another poor parish priest, took up the cry and bravely carried on the fight for freedom, but he too was captured, carried to Mexico City and shot. Within the next few years all the other rebel leaders were either killed, imprisoned or driven into hiding in the mountains. By the time Benito Juarez came to live with Fra Antonio, the first rebellion was over, and Spain again was in control.

Soon, however, rebellion was begun again, and this time not by poor parish priests and Indians, but by the wealthy creoles. They were alarmed for the safety of their wealth and property by news from Spain of certain liberties that the king had been forced to grant the people. Fearing similar liberties might be given the poorer classes in Mexico, the wealthy creoles determined to separate from Spain, to set up a kingdom of their own over which they would have control.

ITURBIDE, General Augustín Iturbide, was their leader. He united the rebel forces, and by September, 1821, had entered the capital and declared Mexico independent. Gathering courage, the following year he had "pronounced" himself the Emperor, Augustín I. His empire had but a short life. In six months he found himself "pronounced" against by one of his former officers, and a year later exiled.

As for Mexico. Mexico was then a REPUBLIC —declared so in 1822 by the same officer who had "pronounced" against the Emperor—a wiry, sallow-faced, clever little man with a tricky tongue and a gaudy uniform, whose ambition was to seize the power in Mexico and make himself "the Napoleon of the West." His name was SANTA ANNA.

Benito Juarez could not have seen Santa Anna before 1828. That year President Vittoria had finished his four-year term, and another election had been held. The candidate backed by Santa Anna had been defeated. It was the same candidate for whom Benito Juarez, now twenty-two years old, had voted. He also was disappointed, but he respected the law and so he respected the verdict. Not so Santa Anna.

In defiance of the law, Santa Anna attempted to "pronounce" against the newly elected candidate, in favor of his friend. This time he spoke up too soon, and things got so hot for him in the capital that he had to scuttle out of Mexico City. He turned up in Oaxaca. There he barricaded himself and his soldiers in one of the monasteries, until the pursuing army of the opposite party gave up the chase and left.

Then he appeared again. And Juarez saw him, the center of a spell-bound crowd, dazzling their eyes with his red and gold uniform, while he filled their ears with oratory, highly spiced and as colorful as his dress.

Somber young Benito Juarez, garbed in the solid black considered suitable for a lawyer, was the exact opposite of the highly colored orator in character as well as appearance. To him it was treasonable, that idea of trying to overturn by force the president who had been elected according to the law. The law? Santa Anna cared nothing for the law, or Mexico either, except as Mexico or its laws could be of use to him. That was the man who was to hold Mexico in his ruinous power for more than twenty years. Yes. Mexico was free, in 1828 . . . free from Spain, but not free, alas, from Santa Anna.

87

"TODA AMÉRICA ES MI PATRIA"

SPAIN had now lost all her colonies in the New World—Florida, Mexico and also South America, for on December 8, 1824, Peru, that last stronghold of the Spanish forces, had fallen. Neither Simón Bolívar nor San Martín took part in the final battle, although for twelve years both men had been working towards that victory. Twelve years it was since the spring of 1812 when San Martín had returned to Argentina, the earthquake had struck Venezuela, and Simón Bolívar had been banished to an island in the Caribbean.

From that island, penniless but hopeful still, Bolívar had returned to accomplish wonders. Like a bandit chief he had raised an army of ragged volunteers against the forces of Spain. Down dark rivers he had led them, through steaming jungles, up rocky and freezing mountain heights and down again into the tropic plains, fighting battle after battle until he had won through to success and his well-earned glory.

Then under arches of flowers and flags, beautiful girls of Venezuela had drawn him in a chariot into Caracas, the capital city. Later in flowery triumph he had also entered the capitals of New Granada and Ecuador. Those three countries he had then united into a republic, which he named Colombia, in honor, of course, of the first explorer.

Simón Bolívar himself had been hailed as the "Liberator of Venezuela, New Granada, and Ecuador," and was the President of Colombia.

Meanwhile San Martín had become known as the "Liberator of Chile" and "Protector of Peru," for while Simón Bolívar had been setting free the northern parts of the continent, San Martín had been working up the west coast from the south. In his quiet manner San Martín had also accomplished what he set out to do. Back in the secluded province of Argentina he had raised and equipped his army. In 1817, in January, which is the middle of summer, when the mountain passes are free of snow, he took his army, cannons and all up over the tortuous heights of the Andes Mountains and down into Chile. There, with the help of Bernardo O'Higgins, he defeated the royal army of Spain, entered Santiago and established Chile's independence.

San Martín had then sailed to Peru. There he again defeated the royal forces, besieged and entered the city of Lima, and declared Peru independent. Peru's independence had been only declared, however, in 1822, not entirely won. The Spanish forces had left Lima, but were still strong in the highlands to the east. So, very sensibly, San Martín looked to the great leader of the north, Bolívar, hoping that they might plan to join forces and complete the work together.

A meeting was arranged. And so, on a day in July, 1821, a ship sailed into a harbor in Ecuador, with a quiet man aboard watching the shoreline eagerly for his first glimpse of the "great Liberator." On shore watching the ship approach stood a graceful man in full dress uniform, with fluttering ribbons and a helmet topped with plumes. He was surrounded by an excited crowd, glad of an excuse to celebrate.

San Martín, therefore, as he walked modestly and rather shyly down the gangplank, found himself caught up at once in a public embrace, and showered with flowers, huzzahs, laurel wreaths and lavish compliments to the point of embarrassment. Riding to headquarters he kept his eyes on his boots, while Bolívar, on the contrary, flashed his charming smile to right and left in gracious recognition of the applause.

The interview between the two men was secret. They were two very different men. At the end of the conference, Bolívar escorted San Martín to the harbor and he sailed away. Rather than make a division between the patriots before the fight for freedom was won, he preferred to withdraw and resign his command to Bolívar.

So Bolívar, without having to share either the glory or the responsibility, finished the fight in Peru, although it was his general, José de Sucré, who led the troops at the final battle. High in the Andes on a plateau surrounded by snow-capped peaks, the last representative of Spain in the New World surrendered. The victorious commander sent this report to Bolívar—"General: The war is over and liberty of Peru assured. The only reward I ask is to retain your friendship.
The Battlefield of Ayacucho   Antonio José de Sucré."
Dec. 8, 1824.

Meanwhile the United States and England had been watching with great sympathy the fight for liberty in the Spanish colonies. Metternich and the Holy Allies, Russia, Prussia and Austria, had watched it with alarm. To them liberty of the people was a dangerous fire to be stamped out, whenever or wherever it put in an appearance. They had stamped it out in Spain. When the Spanish people had demanded a Constitution from Fernando VII, they had sent an army into Spain and restored Fernando at once as an absolute monarch. Well pleased with that success, the Holy Allies now thought to set things completely back in order, by restoring to the King of Spain his rebellious colonies in America. Here they met with opposition.

"Hands off," said England firmly.

"Hands off," said the United States even more firmly, and so came into being one of the famous documents in American history.

On the advice of John Quincy Adams, President Monroe, in his message to Congress in December, 1823, declared that, just as the United States did not intend to meddle in European affairs, they did not intend to allow any European nation to meddle in the affairs of the Americas.

"Any attempt on their part to extend their system to any portion of this hemisphere," so read the words, "we should consider as dangerous to our peace and safety and as the manifestation of an unfriendly disposi-tion towards the United States."

America for Americans, that was the MONROE DOCTRINE.

Toda América es mi Patria was what San Martín always said. A united South America had also been Simón Bolívar's dream. The first Pan American Congress was his idea and undertaking. In his mind were principally the countries of South America, but, because of the Monroe Doctrine, the United States had also been invited.

"The day when our representatives meet will begin an immortal epoch in the politics of America," were his enthusiastic words.

The Congress of 1826 was a dismal failure. At the opening meet-ing, of all the nations invited only four were represented, Colombia, Peru, Guatemala and Mexico. Some didn't even answer the invitation. One of the delegates from the United States died on the way, and the other arrived after the Congress had been adjourned. Bolívar's great hopes were dashed. He was bitterly disappointed.

"Life is a torment," he moaned. "I have ploughed the sea."

Such moods, however, alternated with joy such as he felt one day on opening a small package from the United States. It was accompanied by a letter from the French general La Fayette, a man who had fought for freedom in America before Bolívar had been born. He was sending Simón Bolívar, he said, this miniature of George Washington.

"And I believe," he wrote, "that there is no one to whom my pater-nal friend would have preferred offering it than to the great citizen whom South America has greeted with the name of Liberator."

CITIZENS OF THE WORLD

ENERAL LA FAYETTE was in the United States when he sent the miniature to Simón Bolívar. It was his first visit to America since he had bidden farewell to his beloved friend George Washington the year after the American Revolution. La Fayette was now in his late sixties, but hale and ruddy and with a heart young enough to enjoy every moment of this very gala occasion. He was coming as an especially invited guest of the United States.

On June 15, 1825, the fiftieth anniversary of the Battle of Bunker Hill was to be celebrated, and Congress had felt that it would be most fitting to have present the generous and beloved Frenchman who had given so largely in money and service to the American Revolution.

From the day he arrived in August, 1824, to the day he left in September of the following year he was feasted and fêted in such a round of dinners, receptions, balls and speeches as would have been the death of a less hardy guest. La Fayette enjoyed it all, traveled in all the twenty-four states, had a smile for the thousands who wanted to shake his hand and went out of his way to visit old friends.

John Adams, now almost ninety, he found very feeble and bearing up with difficulty under the suspense of the coming presidential election in which his son was running against Andrew Jackson and Henry Clay.

92

La Fayette was glad for the old gentleman's sake when Henry Clay withdrew and secured to John Quincy Adams his election as the sixth president of the United States.

Early in the fall La Fayette had visited Mount Vernon, and had spent a few sunny autumn days with Thomas Jefferson at Monticello, recalling old days spent together in France.

James Madison also received a visit and interested La Fayette by saying that he thought his plantation failed to pay because of the difficulties of slave labor. Slavery was a great evil, in his opinion, but how, pray tell, could it ever be done away with? More slaves were being used each year, because of the great cotton plantations that were now spreading over the south.

For La Fayette's visit to the western states, the rivers were used as much as possible. From New Orleans America's guest went by steamboat up the Mississippi, spending one night at the house of the leading fur trader of St. Louis. After turning aside to visit Andrew Jackson at the Hermitage just outside of Nashville, La Fayette went on up the Ohio to Pittsburgh. Completing the circle by coach, he was back in Boston in time to lay the cornerstone of the Bunker Hill Monument.

Daniel Webster was the orator of the occasion, and in his booming voice made a great address, long remembered by all those who heard it.

Memorable, too, was the toast proposed by La Fayette at the banquet that followed. It was a toast that showed his unwavering faith in the future—a faith that all must have whose hearts stay young.

"To Bunker Hill," he said, raising his glass, "and to the holy resistance to oppression which has already freed the American hemisphere. May the next half century's toast be to a liberated Europe."

There in free America, La Fayette thought sadly of France and of all Europe, where liberty for the time being was crushed.

While La Fayette was visiting old friends and making new ones in America, an unofficial ambassador of good will from the United States was making friends for himself and his country in Europe. It was that happy traveler and now well-known author of *Rip Van Winkle* and many other popular stories. It was Washington Irving.

Washington Irving had gone to Europe directly after the war. The very day he landed in Liverpool in 1815, mail coaches had just dashed in with the news that Napoleon had been defeated at Waterloo.

Six years later, after a visit in Paris, he was back in London just in time to see the coronation procession of the new King of England, George IV. George IV, although not crowned, had been acting as King or Regent for many years, because his father, George III, had been insane. At last in 1820, after sixty years of stubbornly "being King," old George III had passed away.

Washington Irving stood with the crowd watching the new King arrive and leave Westminster Abbey, but he did not enter the church. He modestly hesitated to ask permission.

"Hoot, mon," exclaimed Sir Walter Scott, the following day, "you should have told them who you were; you'd have got in anywhere."

Washington Irving laughed. So did Sir Walter Scott. They liked each other immensely. Irving had paid a visit to Abbotsford, Scott's famous home in Scotland, where he said that "the golden-hearted old worthy had completely won his heart."

In 1825, the year of the Bunker Hill celebration, Washington Irving was in Spain, hunting material for a life of Columbus. There he met a handsome young American about half his age who had just arrived in Europe to complete his education. His name was Henry Wadsworth Longfellow. He was delighted to meet the favorite author of his boyhood.

The English students also loved Washington Irving's books, and made the halls ring with their cheers for him when, a few years later, he was at Oxford to receive the honorary degree of Doctor of Laws.

The first American author to win recognition abroad, Washington Irving and his books helped to make a better understanding and friendlier feeling between the United States and England.

Like La Fayette, Irving had that generous tolerant spirit that makes the native of any country a citizen of the world.

VICTORIA IS BORN

MAY 24, 1819, almost a year before her uncle George IV, not at all a pleasant person, became King of England, Victoria was born. That her father died the following year caused the king no sorrow. George IV had never had any use for his brother, the Duke of Kent, nor for his brother's wife whom he considered a disagreeable and meddlesome woman. When the baby daughter was born to them, therefore, George took great pains to be present at the baptism and to see that she got a name her father would not like.

The Archbishop of Canterbury, holding the pink-and-white baby girl before the font, inquired what he should name the child.

"Alexandrina!" spoke up the Prince Regent in a loud tone.

"Elizabeth," said the baby's father, glaring at his brother.

"Alexandrina, I say," repeated the Regent in a still louder tone. "She's to be named for her godfather Czar Alexander of Russia, and for a second name let her have her mother's name, Victoria."

So while her father grumbled under his breath that it sounded too foreign for a future Queen of England, Alexandrina Victoria became the baby's name. Never daunted by difficulties, her mother said later:

"It iss a long name, yes, but ve vill call her 'Drina."

REVOLUTION
N N
FRANCE

grandfather of   Louis XVII lost   (brothers of Louis XVI)
Louis XV Louis XVI Marie Antoinette PEOPLE Napoleon Louis XVIII Charles X

MONARCHY • REPUBLIC • EMPIRE • MONARCHY

HARD TIMES AND BAD KINGS

LA FAYETTE SO LOVED freedom that when he left the United States a
chest filled with its earth went with him. It was his wish that
when his last sleep came, he might be laid to rest beneath the
"sacred soil of liberty." He was returning, he knew, to find conditions worse in France than when he left.

Louis XVIII had died during the year, and his brother, Charles X,
had been crowned King. There was no doubt in La Fayette's mind as to
what Charles X would try to do, and no doubt in the mind of Charles X
as to La Fayette's opinion. The two old men, now nearing seventy, were
old acquaintances. They had known each other since they were little
boys in riding school, and as Charles X himself said, they "had had
many a fight." As firmly as La Fayette believed in liberty of the people,

Charles X believed in the divine and absolute right of kings. As far as possible he intended to turn the calendar back fifty years or more and rule as his grandfather, Louis XV, had ruled, in those good days before the Revolution.

His coronation, at which he was anointed on seven parts of his body with sacred oil to show his divine descent, was like a spectacle of the Middle Ages. It was disgusting to the people of France. They had beheaded his brother in their fight for freedom.

How long, La Fayette wondered, would they tolerate Charles X?

Conditions were bad in France and they were also bad in England. George IV, the king, was a waster and a good-for-nothing. "A bloated old sensualist" was what Washington Irving called him, and that was no exaggeration. His debts were enormous, and alas for the poor tax-payers, Parliament was obliged to keep on paying them until he should do England the favor of dying. Aside from that, no more about George need be said, for happily England was not an absolute monarchy—happily, that is, for one-tenth of the people, those who held the power.

England was not under the rule of an absolute king, but neither was it a democracy. The government was in the hands of the Lords and a few wealthy businessmen, who controlled Parliament and so ruled the country. Tories and conservatives, they had been so alarmed at what had happened in France during the Revolution, when the common people had seized the power and beheaded aristocrats by the wholesale, that they were determined to let nothing of the kind occur in England. A government by aristocrats and property owners was the best of all governments for them and for the country. There must be no change.

Under this upper crust were nine-tenths of the people. They had no voice at all in the government. Even lawyers, doctors, teachers, small businessmen—people of the middle class—were not allowed to vote, to say nothing of the very poor, for whom life was far from right.

Factory workers were paid starvation wages. Children, half-starved, were hired for even less and made to work ten and twelve hours a day in the cotton mills. Men could be thrown into jail for debt and hanged for stealing a fish, and some two hundred other trivial offenses.

"You have no idea of the distress and misery that prevails in England," Washington Irving wrote home. "It is beyond description."

Peace after the war had made bad matters worse. Munitions factories were closed, men no longer needed in the army and navy were also thrown out of work. Taxation for the war was terrific. Meetings of people to discuss their troubles were broken up by troops. They were desperate, but what could they do?

"Get the right to vote!" answered William Cobbett, who was a bold leader of the masses, and published for them a weekly paper. "If you want better conditions," he kept telling them, "you must get the vote."

Get the vote! That was far easier said than done, when those who opposed any change controlled not only the House of Lords, but also the House of Commons, where representation had now reached a most peculiar state. Six hundred years ago when the council that became the House of Commons had been formed, each town then in existence had been given the right to send two members. Now, though many of the old towns had disappeared, the arrangement still held good. There might be not one house left where once had been a town; nevertheless, the Lord who owned the land could still send two representatives to Parliament. Cities, on the other hand, might have 20,000 inhabitants, but if less than six hundred years old would not be represented.

The Whigs, or Liberal Party, had long realized the need of reform but had been powerless, because for many years the Tory Party, who were afraid of change, had been in power. But reform, revolution, change and adjustment to it were bound to come. Life does not stand still.

"The great cause of the world will go on," wrote Washington Irving. "What a stirring moment it is to be alive!"

VICTORIA—WHO WAS SHE?

'D RINA HAD no idea when she was five that she would ever be
Queen of England. She had never been to visit her Uncle King,
and knew very little about the world outside of Kensington
Palace. She didn't know, of course, that there were any children in England who were starving. If she had, it would have made her
very unhappy, for 'Drina loved so to eat. She loved strawberries and
cream and tarts and cakes, but Mamma never let her have anything but
the plainest food. Mamma was very strict. So 'Drina had troubles every
day. Sometimes she had to stamp her foot, they made her so angry.

One morning in bright October, she opened her blue eyes, and
closed them tight again when she saw her governess, Lehzen, moving
about the room. She buried her round pink cheek in the pillow and pre-
tended she wasn't awake. It was just another day, she thought, of having
to learn her lessons or listen to Mamma scold. Then she remembered!

This was no ordinary day. This was a wonderful day. This was the
day they were going to visit dear Uncle Leopold, Mamma's brother, and

see Grossmutter who was coming from Europe. At that thought she sat up her small round self in a hurry and jumped out of bed.

"Lehzen," she said, "vy didn't you call me? Ve vill be late."

But they were not late. Lehzen never allowed anyone to be late, and although it seemed long after breakfast before they were on their way, they reached Claremont, Uncle Leopold's home, before those who had gone to meet Grossmutter had returned. 'Drina was in her fresh white dress and blue sash when she heard the wheels of the carriages on the gravel, and ran on tiptoe to meet the travelers at the door. There was dear Uncle Leopold, whom she loved so well, and there was darling Grossmutter, whose face folded into charming little wrinkles when she smiled. There was Mamma, of course, who hoped as usual that "her 'Drina had been a good little girl." And Feodore. Feodore was her precious sister who was seventeen and so beautiful, but for some reason not treated by people with half so much honor as she was herself. Lehzen had told her that that was because Feodore was a half-sister only, and not a niece of the King, but still she wondered about it.

With so many uncles and aunts and relatives, it was hard at times for 'Drina to keep them straight, but she remembered all she had heard about her cousins Ernest and Albert, who lived with Grossmutter in Germany. Their father, like Uncle Leopold, was a brother of Mamma's. Ernest was older, but Albert was just her age, and looked like her too, Grossmutter said. He kept a diary and had a new goat. Three goats, those boys had, Grossmutter said, and a wagon to ride in.

"Oh please, please," Victoria begged, "couldn't Albert and Ernest come to visit me too, some day, and bring the goats?"

Victoria. That was the name by which she was going to call herself now instead of 'Drina. That's what Grossmutter called her and she liked it. So after that visit the little girl was called Victoria by all who knew her, EXCEPT Uncle King!

George IV would persist in calling her Alexandrina, as she found out on her first visit to him.

That unexpected invitation to visit the King came about two years after the visit to Claremont. The idea of going to Windsor at last threw the little family at Kensington into a flurry. Though Mamma had little money to spend, Feodore must have a new bonnet, and Victoria had fresh rosebuds put under the brim of her last year's hat. And it was a new white organdy dress that she was wearing, a new blue sash and new stockings without even the tiniest darn when the King first saw her and she first saw him.

An enormously fat old man he was, wearing a greasy brown wig, a wrinkled dressing gown, and nursing a gouty foot.

"Come, give me your little paw," he growled. Then he called for a box and presented her with a miniature of himself encircled with diamonds, which made him look far handsomer indeed than he did that day.

Uncle King was looking much better the next afternoon, too, when Victoria, riding with Mamma and Feodore, met his phaeton in the park.

"Pop her in," said he, pointing to his small niece, and to her delight she was removed from Mamma's side and popped in beside her uncle. Off they dashed towards the lake where the band was playing.

"What is your favorite tune?" he asked. "The band shall play it."

"God Save the King," said Victoria quickly and also honestly.

George IV laughed and raised his eyebrows. The minx has tact, he thought. Well, she'll have need of it. At that moment some of the people, recognizing his small companion, cheered: "God save Her Royal Highness!" Victoria smiled and waved to them. Once again she wondered.

No one actually answered that question in her mind, until she was eleven. Then perhaps it was Lehzen, perhaps it was Mamma, or perhaps it was Dr. Davys, her tutor. Only the day before he had asked her to make a list of the kings and queens of England, and she had left the last line blank, though she supposed her own name should be written there.

For a long time she had suspected it, but when they told her, when she actually heard it said in words, that she, little Victoria, would become the Queen of England, it was almost overwhelming.

"I will be good," she managed to say bravely, but that night in the small bed beside her mother's there was a pillow wet with tears.

Old Cartoon of Factory Children. by Cruikshank

CHARLES DICKENS—OR DAVID COPPERFIELD

IT WAS a foggy London morning in April, 1824, the year Victoria was five. Far from Kensington Palace, down by the slums and warehouses where the tide washed up the Thames, the smoky air was pierced with the acid smell of dye. It was sharp in the delicate nostrils of a small boy of twelve who was descending slowly step by step a flight of narrow crooked stairs that led to a tumble-down old blacking factory. A gray rat slid from a hole in the wall and down the stairs ahead of him. The boy shivered, and choked back his tears.

It was all horrible. He was completely miserable and forlorn. Even the characters from books who used to keep him company had deserted him. Going down these slimy stairs, he could not even imagine he was a brave Knight descending into a castle dungeon, much less Aladdin about to enter a magic cave. No. Here he was nobody but himself, Charles Dickens, the most miserable, forlorn and utterly wretched boy in London, whose father had been put into prison for debt, whose books had gone to the pawnshop, and whose heart was broken.

To think that he, Charles Dickens, a gentleman's son, who had once lived in a decent house in Camden Town, with a little garden, and had gone to school and was planning, when he grew rich and famous, to buy the big house on Gads Hill—to think that he had come down to this! But gentleman's son he was and he intended to act the part. And no one, no one should ever know where his father was! He turned into the dingy room, with a crowd of boys from the neighboring slums, to begin the long day's drudgery.

" 'Ere comes our little gent," said one of them—the one who was proud of being a fireman's son. "Wot was it ye said your gentleman father worked at now—or didn't ye say?" he queried.

Charles did not answer, only reached for another bottle and label.

"Nothin' eh?" jeered the boy. "D'ye hear that, guys? He says nothin'. Maybe 'is old man's such a swell 'e don't 'ave to work."

"Shut up, will ye," said Bob Fagin, a boy whose heart was as big as his fist. "Might be a sleight o' hand artist judgin' from the quick way his son 'ere's learned to tie paper on these 'ere bottles."

For Charles had learned. Much as he hated the job, he hated more not to excel at whatever he did. So hour after hungry hour during the long day his slim deft fingers flew rapidly amid the bottles and paper and string.

One day, taken ill, he crumpled down limp and white on his bench. Bob Fagin made him a bed of straw in the corner, filled empty blacking bottles with hot water to put at his side, and when closing time came insisted on helping him home to his family.

"No, no!" protested Charles. For nothing on earth would he have Bob find out that the family lived with his father in prison, while he slept in an attic near by. After trying in vain to get rid of the good-hearted boy, he finally shook hands with him on the steps of a strange house, making believe he lived there. Then, with Bob fairly out of sight, he crept down the dark streets to his attic.

Early next morning, as usual, he was waiting outside the tall gates of the prison until they were opened and he could go in for breakfast. Waiting as usual, too, was the orphan girl who came in to cook for the family over the open grate in their room. And while they waited Charles

103

made up wonderful fairy tales to tell her about the towers and buildings, which still looked mysterious in the pink-gray mist through which the early morning sun was breaking.

A strange life went on inside the prison. Ashamed as he was to be part of it, Charles couldn't help enjoying with a sharp relish all the peculiar characters who were there. Prisoners in for debt were allowed to move about and associate with one another, and with their wives and children they made a noisy, motley company. Some laughed unnaturally to hide their shame, some drowned their tears and sorrows in the bad ale sold for a few pence by the turnkeys. Others were hopefully waiting for "something to turn up"—none more optimistically than John Dickens, Esq., whose spirits were uncrushable. Expanding in a lordly manner, he enjoyed fully his place of honor among the inmates, as orator, literary man and scribe. As president of a committee, he took particular pride in one flowery petition he drew up, begging His Majesty the King for extra bounty that "His unfortunate subjects in prison might drink to His Majesty's health on His Majesty's birthday."

Before His Majesty's birthday came, however, a small legacy turned up that enabled Mr. Dickens and family to move from the prison. Not immediately, alas, but in due time, with an elegant gesture on the part of his father, Charles was also removed from the blacking factory and sent to school. There as merry as he had been miserable, he was soon doing his lessons, directing the plays and dodging the blows of the head-master, all as part of a glorious game. A year only, and he was at work again—this time as office boy for a firm of lawyers.

Years later, Charles Dickens's books would bring to life again all the queer characters he had known, and by arousing sympathy for them, help to better the lives of the overworked, hungry children of the poor.

It was then that his father (who was the model for the improvident but lordly Mr. Micawber, in *David Copperfield*) was to be often asked what had been the education of his famous son.

"Well, in a manner of speaking," he would reply, clearing his throat impressively, "he may be said to—ah—to have educated himself!"

WILD TURKEYS AND WASTE TIME

THIS IS the WILD TURKEY as John James Audubon painted it, when wild turkeys were a common sight in the backwoods of America. One day, when little Abe Lincoln was about eight years old, he had propped his father's rifle in a crack in the log house and shot his first wild turkey. When he felt its warm brown feathers, he never wanted to kill anything again. His father saw no sense in a boy who wouldn't go hunting but wasted his time reading books.

Neighbors in Kentucky saw no sense either, in a man wasting time painting birds, when he'd better be tendin' store and lookin' after his business. But Lucy thought the drawings were beautiful. Lucy Audubon had married John James and come down the Ohio River from Pennsylvania to a new home in Kentucky two years or so before Abraham Lincoln was born. They were still there when the Lincolns moved to Indiana, but a few years later that "crazy Frenchman, the bird painter," had come to grief just as the neighbors knew he would, and had been put in jail for debt. Then, the debts paid somehow, John James Audubon had gone down the Mississippi to New Orleans, taking his drawings with him.

In the spring of his nineteenth year Abe Lincoln made that same trip down the Mississippi River to the great southern market. They floated down on a flatboat, he and another young fellow, a boat that they had made themselves and loaded with bacon, ham, corn, flour, apples to be sold. Abe managed the forward oar, and kept the blunt nose of the sixty-foot barge squarely in the current and free of rocks, snags and treacherous sandbars. It took about three weeks to go the thousand miles, floating along through bright days and misty days, and days when the coppery gray water was dappled with warm summer rain. They watched the familiar trees of oak and sycamore give way to fields of sugar cane and cotton, to cypress swamps, and live oaks hung with silvery moss.

Then came New Orleans, the first city the tall boy from the backwoods had ever seen. Old New Orleans with its signs in French, and its strange foreign houses with their shaded courtyards and balconies of iron lace. The levee piled with cotton bales—the ships anchored in the harbor, three-masted schooners and frigates from all over the world—the Negroes in the slave market where they were being sold—all these gave that boy from the backwoods a great deal to think about as he rode on the steamboat up the river home again to Indiana.

John James Audubon had never gone back to live in the wilderness again. Instead he had sailed one day for Liverpool on a schooner loaded with cotton for the mills in England. Under his arm he carried the drawings of his birds, and Lucy had slipped into his pocket gold pieces she had saved from teaching. He had been gone more than two years when Abe Lincoln reached New Orleans, but Lucy was still living there, and teaching, and very happy now.

Every packet from England was likely to bring her another letter telling more of the great enthusiasm with which her John's bird drawings were being received in Europe. Lucy had always known how beautiful they were. Now her faith in them was more than justified. One letter told how they had been exhibited in Liverpool and the hall was crowded. Another, how the crowds more than filled the rooms at the Royal Society —how John had gone to Scotland and Sir Walter Scott had asked to meet him. And the WILD TURKEY? It was to be Plate I in a book, BIRDS OF AMERICA, and was valued by experts at 100 guineas, more than $500!

One December night in 1826 Audubon was speaking in Edinburgh, Scotland, about the American wild turkey and its habits. In the audience, listening with rapt attention, was a seventeen-year-old English lad who was also interested in stuffing birds. He was Charles Darwin, and because he could observe carefully and think clearly he was destined to become one of the world's great scientists. But then, if anyone had told him so, he would have thought it "as ridiculous and impossible as if he had been told that he would be elected King of England."

So, too, would the old headmaster of the school back home in Shrewsbury. He had rebuked the boy publicly for wasting time collecting bugs and beetles and rocks and minerals or making strange smells in his chemistry laboratory, when he should be learning his Greek and Latin.

Dr. Darwin, therefore, trying to find a suitable school for his son, had sent Charles to Edinburgh to study medicine, but that didn't suit the boy either. He couldn't bear to watch operations done in those days of no chloroform or ether. So he made friends with the zoology professor and busied himself collecting sea animals and stuffing birds.

"You can't just waste your time that way," said Dr. Darwin. "Why not leave here for Cambridge and become a clergyman?"

So Charles, willingly enough, brushed up on his Greek and Latin, and went to Cambridge for three years, all the time adding to his specimens and taking geology and botany excursions during the holidays.

Then one August came the thrilling invitation that was to make good all the time that he had "wasted" and determine his career. It was an invitation to go as the naturalist of a party that the English Government was sending to chart the coast of South America!

Back in Indiana a tall boy, born on the same day of the same year, was still splitting logs to earn his living, but still reading and studying at night and hoping maybe some day his chance would come. . . .

THE STORY OF BRAZIL

THE SHIP on which young Charles Darwin sailed to South America in the autumn of 1831 headed directly for Brazil, and in due time passed under the shadow of the Sugar Loaf Mountain and into one of the most beautiful harbors in the world—the harbor of Rio de Janeiro. Only six months before, from another English ship anchored there, and awaiting orders to sail, Dom Pedro, former Emperor of Brazil, was looking for the last time at that beautiful harbor.

Across the sparkling water, above the rich green tropical foliage, he could see among the white buildings of the city, flags and festoons of yellow and green flying in the breeze. There the crowds were cheering their next Emperor-to-be, Dom Pedro's own son, five-year-old "Pedrinho" who was now to become Emperor Pedro II of Brazil.

The little boy looking out across the water, from the palace balcony, could see the top spars of his father's ship. Dressed in his best white satin suit he was standing on a chair, bowing and smiling at the cheering people as he was told to do. But he was wishing that he could go to see his father or be down in the courtyard playing with his sisters.

The sisters with their black eyes and dark curls resembled their handsome Portuguese father, Dom Pedro. Pedrinho had fair hair, pink cheeks and big, blue eyes, like his Aunt Marie Louise. She had been the Empress of France, the wife of Napoleon, and a sister of Pedrinho's mother. So the Emperor Francis of Austria was his grandfather.

Pedrinho could not remember his mother, for she had died when he was only a year old. Now he had also lost his father, though for many, many days he could still see his father's ship standing in the harbor. With the help of his nurse, the little boy wrote his father a letter, and in reply received one that he was to cherish all his life:

"My beloved Son and Emperor:

I deeply prize the letter you have written me. I had trouble reading it, because of the tears in my eyes. As long as there is life in me, my concern for your welfare and happiness will not end. Now the time has come for me to retire to Europe; this is necessary if Brazil is to have peace so as to work out God permitting the degree of progress and prosperity of which she is capable.

Goodbye my dear son! Receive an embrace from your father who leaves in sorrow and without hope of ever seeing you again.

Dom Pedro de Alcantara

April 12, 1831   On board the ship *Warspite*."

Dom Pedro was thirty-three years old. Though he had been born in Portugal, he had come to Brazil when he was only nine. Since then it had been home to him, and he had seen Brazil change from a colony of Portugal into an independent Empire.

Like the independence of the Spanish colonies in South America, the independence of Brazil had also been brought about by the actions of Napoleon. Back in the days when Napoleon had tried to hold Europe blockaded against England, he had not been able to control the coast of Portugal. Portugal had always been friendly towards England, and through her harbors a continual stream of goods from spices to war supplies leaked out. So Napoleon decided to invade Portugal and whip that troublesome little country into line.

At word of the proposed invasion the Portuguese royal family had been terror-stricken. Not knowing what else to do, Dom Pedro's father, Dom João, as Regent of Portugal, decided to take the whole court to America, and establish the seat of government in tiny Portugal's giant colony, Brazil. Crown jewels, therefore, state papers, family archives, chamberlains, ladies-in-waiting, valets, secretaries, priests—all people and things attached to the court, including the horses from the royal stables, were prepared for the journey. When the ships left the rocky coast of Portugal behind, there were 15,000 people headed for America.

The voyage was "a nightmare." There were not enough beds, blankets, food or water. And by some mistake the trunks filled with clothing had all been left behind, so the same clothes had to do for eight weeks. At the end of the journey no one was fit to go ashore until clean garments had been borrowed from the people of the town. In addition the ladies had all had to have their hair shaved off to get rid of lice. Dom Pedro could never forget how funny they looked nor how furious it made his ill-tempered mother, who never was to forgive her husband for bringing her out to what she considered a God-forsaken jungle.

Dom João, on the other hand, grateful for the enthusiastic welcome given him by the good people of Brazil, took genuine interest in the country, and did all he could for its improvement. Seven years passed and though Napoleon was defeated, Dom João stayed on in Brazil. Five more years, and the people of Portugal concluded that they might as well have no king at all, and become a republic. Far off in Brazil warnings of this reached Dom João. One was put in verse:

"Se tu depressa não vais
  Para oteu pais natal
  João alha que perdes
  O Brazil, e Portugal."

"If you do not speed
  To your native land
  John, you will lose
  Both Brazil and Portugal."

So in the spring of 1821, Dom João prepared to return to Portugal. Not Portugal, however, but Brazil was home to young Dom Pedro, and he had chosen to remain. The last day Dom João spoke to his son of the future of the country!

"The day is not far off, Pedro," said he, "when I believe Brazil will refuse to be governed by Portugal. When that time comes, my son, throw yourself with the revolutionary movement, declare Brazil an Empire and make yourself emperor. I would prefer to see you, of whose respect I am certain, take it rather than some unknown adventurer."

A little over a year and, as his father foresaw, independence of Brazil had to be granted, and Dom Pedro became the first emperor. It was an imperial democracy, an Empire with a constitution and a Parliament. Members of the Parliament, however, were appointed by the Emperor, and four years later the liberal leaders were again dissatisfied.

"Down with the aristocrats appointed by the King," they cried. "We want a Parliament made up of the people."

One night Dom Pedro tried to speak to them from the balcony of the palace, but they jeered at him and, carried along with excitement, cried, "Down with the Empire. Long live the Republic."

Dom Pedro went inside, then sat down at his desk, and signed the abdication in favor of his very beloved and honored son the Senhor Dom Pedro de Alcantara Braganza—five-year-old Pedrinho.

The people, sorry that they had pressed him so far, after begging him in vain to reconsider, gladly accepted his child as Emperor.

That was why on that April day of 1831, Dom Pedro on board ship in the harbor was gazing intently towards the city, and the little boy Pedrinho, standing on the palace balcony, was being cheered by the people as the next emperor of Brazil.

No country was ever to have a more honorable or democratic ruler. Pedro II was to be emperor for fifty-seven years, for not until 1888 would Brazil, the largest country in South America, cease to be an empire. Then Pedro II would also abdicate, and more sadly than either his father or his grandfather he too would sail away.

THE DRAMA OF GREECE

DURING the 1820's, when Brazil, Mexico and South America were gaining their independence, Greece, the oldest civilized nation in Europe, was also fighting for freedom—from the rule of Turkey. The struggle was watched with keen sympathy and interest by all the people of Europe, especially the English.

Greece began the struggle the year that William Gladstone, twelve years old, entered the fourth form at Eton. Schoolboys of Eton studied Greek and so they were interested, because to them Greece was the great land of Ulysses, Menelaus, and the heroes of the Trojan War. Lord Elgin, too, the father of one of the boys, had traveled in Greece, and had brought back to England many very beautiful marble statues from old Greek temples that were lying in ruins. They had been purchased by the British Museum and visitors who saw them there also imagined Greece as being still the nation of Pericles and the Golden Age.

Three English poets living in Italy were particularly in love with all things Greek. Keats, who had written the beautiful *Ode on a Grecian Urn;* Shelley, who retold in verse the myth of Prometheus, and Byron, who sang of Marathon, lying between the mountains and the sea:

> ". . . And musing there an hour alone,
> I dreamed that Greece might still be free. . . ."

Lord Byron did more than muse and dream. He entered the bloody desperate struggle and lost his life in the fight.

The Greeks of 1821 were far from being the people they had been in ancient times. They were mostly rough sailors and mountain herdsmen. Oppressed and downtrodden for four hundred years under the rule of Turkey, they had sunk to a sad state. Few of them could speak or even understand the pure Greek which the boys at Eton were learning.

Since the French Revolution, however, the Greeks had begun to take a pride in their glorious past. Poets retold the stories of the Trojan War, and of the famous victory at Marathon. Parents named their children after the old heroes, and wealthy merchants founded schools in which pure Greek was to be taught again. Before 1800, a Greek poet, exiled in Vienna, wrote a national hymn for his country, beginning "Rise, Sons of Hellas, the day of deliverance is nigh." He was seized by the Austrian police, and drowned by the Turks in the Danube. But

"I have sown the seed," he said, "and the day will come" . . .

"Rise, Sons of Hellas"—that was the opening chorus of the bloody, tragic drama between Turkey and Greece with the world as audience.

Act I began with the first revolt led by Prince Ypsilanti, another Greek exile, who was a major general in the Russian army. As Russia had always been the enemy of Turkey, he had written to the Czar, hoping that Czar Alexander would help Greece. Metternich, however, would have none of it. He persuaded the Czar that it should be none of his affair. When Ypsilanti's feeble army was defeated by the Turks and he fled to Austria, Metternich threw him into prison and smiled.

Act II saw a wild uprising of the Greeks all over the peninsula of

Morea. "Not one Turk shall remain in Morea!" was their cry, and 12,000 Turkish inhabitants, men, women and children, were slain in cold blood. The rest fled the country. In January, 1822, in an ancient open-air theater, a "National Assembly" met and declared Greece independent.

Act III. In Constantinople, the Turks returned murder for murder. Innocent Greeks were strangled. On Easter Sunday, the Greek patriot priest Gregorious was hanged in his sacred robes before the door of the cathedral, and then dragged through the streets.

Then came the atrocious massacre of some 20,000 Greeks on the Island of Chios and the violent revenge taken by others who managed to set fire to the Turkish fleet anchored off the island and blow the villain who had started the massacre and the rest of his Turks to bloody bits. The audience shuddered.

Then came a short intermission, while Turkey gasped for breath, and the Greeks began to fight among themselves. Turkey was weak. No longer the empire that had once terrified Europe, it was sick and decaying. The Sultan was obliged to call upon the ruler of Egypt, another part of the Turkish Empire, for help. So Mehemet Ali sent his powerful fleet and well-trained soldiers under his son Ibrahim, to Greece."

Act IV. The Egyptians recaptured town after town in Morea. They captured Athens. They besieged and captured Missolonghi, at which siege Lord Byron died. And the audience was shocked . . . sufficiently shocked at last to rise from their seats and run to the rescue.

England, France and Russia sent their fleets to the Bay of Navarino, where they attacked, destroyed the Turkish-Egyptian ships and left them mere wrecks floating on the bay. That since famous battle of Navarino was the last ever to be fought by SAILING vessels. The next year the Russians marched on Constantinople, the French drove the Egyptians out of Morea, and in 1829 the Sultan was obliged to recognize the independence of Greece. So in 1829, the drama ended.

The poor little country now invited Victoria's Uncle Leopold to be their king, but he refused. So in 1833, seventeen-year-old Prince Otto of Bavaria became the first king of modern Greece.

ULYSSES GRANT, NAMED AND RENAMED

SYMPATHY for Greece and interest in its struggle had spread through the United States as well as Europe. Money and volunteers had been raised to help, Greek study clubs formed, new towns given Greek names like Athens, Ithaca and Ypsilanti, and even children named for the Greek heroes.

Mr. and Mrs. Jesse Grant's first boy got his Greek name by chance. He was born in the spring of 1822, the year that Greece declared itself an independent nation, and he was six weeks old before they picked a name for him. Then they drew it out of a hat. The relatives gathered for the lottery in the kitchen of their small frame house, in Point Pleasant, Ohio, a village fifteen miles up the river from Cincinnati.

All winter Grandmaw Simpson had been deep in a fine story about the Greek hero Ulysses and his son, so it was the hero's high-sounding name that she wrote hopefully on her slip of paper. When it was the first to be drawn from the hat, she beamed with satisfaction, but Grandpaw snorted. He had written down the good plain commonsense name of Hiram. What was the matter with that? It happened to be the next name drawn—so they put the two together and the boy was named!

"HIRAM ULYSSES GRANT!" exclaimed the proud father. "Fine smart name for a smart baby. Look at him smile at his paw, would you."

"That's no smile," said the mother flatly, "just a bubble of wind in his stomach." Boasting of any kind embarrassed Hannah.

But Jesse was proud of his son, and boasted about him continually. He moved to Georgetown soon and started a new tannery there. Every farmer who sold him hides and every merchant who came to buy leather had to hear about Ulysses and how smart he was. Soon he had turned the son of whom he was so proud into the town's standing joke.

"D'ye hear the latest tale Grant's telling about that boy of his?" grown people would ask each other over the supper table. The young ones listening in would snicker and then tell how stupid they thought Ulysses was and how they had nicknamed him "Useless."

That undue mixture of praise and ridicule was torture to the boy who was neither "smart" nor stupid, just slow-going and shy. He would have been utterly miserable, if it hadn't been for horses.

Horses were his friends. Almost as soon as he could walk he was playing around a horse's feet or swinging by its tail. When only eight years old he was the teamster on the wagon, hauling bark to the tannery. He was no more than ten when he drove a team all alone forty miles to Cincinnati and back with a load of passengers.

One summer a circus came to town, and he managed to ride a trick pony that had thrown every other boy who tried. Round and round the ring he went, clinging on tight until he won the prize. Everybody had to admit that it was "a wonder how Lys Grant could hang on."

Hang on—that was one thing that Ulysses Grant could always do— stick to whatever job he tackled until it was finished. Years later, to Robert E. Lee, that quality was to spell surrender.

Lee was fifteen years older than Ulysses. In June of 1831, the summer before Lys rode the circus pony, Robert E. Lee was married to Mary Custis, daughter of George Washington Parke Custis. The wedding was at Arlington in the house that always looked to Robert like a Greek temple, when he used to drive there with his mother. He was Lieutenant

Lee now, for two years before he had been graduated from West Point.

Hiram Ulysses Grant was also to enter West Point when he was seventeen, only under a changed name. He made the first change himself, when he saw the letters H.U.G. in brass nails on his trunk. Shuddering for fear he might be nicknamed "Hug," he reversed the names and became Ulysses Hiram. The Congressman who sent his application to the War Department made another change. He was in a hurry when he wrote it, couldn't recall the boy's middle name, guessed it was Simpson after his mother's family and wrote it that way: Ulysses SIMPSON Grant, quite unaware that he had rechristened a future President.

"Ulysses Grant going to West Point!" exclaimed the Georgetown people when they heard of the appointment. "Why on earth didn't they appoint somebody with brains enough to do credit to our district!"

Poor Ulysses felt about as they did. Aboard the steamboat, when the whistle blew and the wheels began to turn, he was positively ill with fear of failure. If only something would happen, he thought, a collision, anything to prevent his reaching the Academy! Nothing happened, and he arrived, a short stubby country boy in a suit of homespun clothes dyed with butternut juice, and rough round-toed shoes that squeaked as he walked up to sign the register.

The Adjutant looked at the signature and scowled. The boy's ears grew red and his hands grew cold. What was wrong now, he wondered.

"There's some mistake," said the Adjutant finally. "Our records call for Ulysses SIMPSON, not Ulysses HIRAM Grant. The papers will have to be returned to Washington."

"No use going to all that trouble," thought Ulysses. He took the pen and wrote his name again, this time as short as possible:

U. S. Grant—U. S.—the cadets at West Point dubbed him Uncle Sam. In the end, however, his ability to "hang on" was to translate those initials into a final and suitable nickname of "*Unconditional Surrender.*"

IN 1829, the year Victoria was ten, and Abraham Lincoln was twenty, George Stephenson made his famous engine, the "Rocket" and railroads were born. Ever since James Watt had perfected the steam engine, sixty years before, men had dreamed of putting that engine onto wheels. Many men had tried a hand at it, and gradually one by one the difficulties that baffled them had been solved.

Trevithick

Richard TREVITHICK, a superintendent who handled the stationary engines used in mines, made the first engine ever hitched to a carriage to draw passengers. It ran on Christmas Eve, 1801, but it ran on the streets, and not on rails. What he called a "tram wagon" that did run on rails, he built at the request of a Welsh mine owner who had made a bet that he could haul ten tons of iron over certain tracks then used for horse-drawn cars. The engine won the bet for him but it was too heavy for any practical use and no one knows what became of it.

GEORGE STEPHENSON, whose name and locomotive were to become famous, also had charge of engines used in mines—coal mines north of Newcastle. His employer, wishing to keep abreast of other mine owners whose engineers were experimenting with small locomotives, furnished the money for Stephenson to build the one he had in mind. From then on for some fifteen years he worked on locomotives. Meanwhile a group

Rocket

of merchants had built a railroad between Liverpool and Manchester, and having decided not to use horse cars, advertised that in October, 1829, there would be a competition held for the best steam locomotive for that thirty-eight-mile line. It was a festive day, with bands playing, ten thousand people gathered at the course, the directors with white ribbons fluttering in their buttonholes, and the Iron Horses which were to compete painted in the brightest colors and puffing clouds of steam. Stephenson's entry, the *Rocket,* yellow and black with a "tall white chimney" was the first to run. Back and forth it went over a mile and three-quarters of track until it had covered the mileage between Liverpool and Manchester. The others did the same. After a test of three days the award was given. The *Rocket* was judged to combine all features necessary to a successful locomotive. So it won the day and made its maker famous.

The *Tom Thumb,* the first locomotive made in the United States, was built by PETER COOPER of New York, for the first railroad in the United States, the Baltimore & Ohio. He wanted to persuade the directors who were in favor of horse cars that steam engines such as were being made in England were the thing to use. *Tom Thumb,* only intended as a model, was so small that it looked like a toy when it appeared on the track for the trial run in August, 1830.

Tom Thumb

People laughed and called it a "teakettle on a truck." But it ran! And to their amazement fourteen miles in an hour and a quarter! Yes, it had

ON THE MOHAWK & HUDSON . . .

speed, owners of the stage coach line agreed to that, but in the long run, they said, it couldn't stand up against one of their good horses. To prove it, they drove a gray mare out to a place where there were parallel tracks, and had a race. The horse got off first, then *Tom Thumb* forged ahead, until snap! a belt broke connecting the wheels—the gray mare caught up, passed and won. The directors of the Baltimore & Ohio, however, had been won over to steam.

At first, as in the case of most inventions, opposition to the railroad was furious, both in England and America. Some people of course oppose changes of any kind. Some, like those interested in stage coaches, for instance, were afraid the railroad would put them out of business. Others were just afraid. They were appalled at the very idea of flying through space at such a terrific speed.

"Twelve miles an hour!" exclaimed the editor of a London magazine. "As well trust oneself to be fired off on a rocket!"

To have engines dashing about the country, asserted others, would scare sheep, stop hens from laying, poison the air with gas, kill the birds and animals, and drive people mad with fright."

"Suppose, Mr. Stephenson," said a member of Parliament who thought he had an unanswerable objection, "suppose a cow should get on the track in front of your locomotive. What then? What about that?"

"That," replied the inventor, "would be very bad for the cow!"

Directors of the Erie Canal raised the most strenuous objections because they saw that the Baltimore & Ohio would rob them of some of their passengers and freight. On the other hand, it was because the traffic on the Erie Canal was making New York City grow larger than Baltimore that citizens of Baltimore had decided to build the railroad.

And the railroad was here to stay. In 1833 the Charleston-Hamburg, built in South Carolina to carry cotton to market, had 137 miles of track and was the longest railroad in the world owned by one company. By 1840 there would be 3,000 miles of track in the United States.

Nothing could stop the spread of the railroad. Nothing—for never can greed nor fear nor narrow self-interest stop the spread of a new idea that means progress in the world.

July 1830

an old Print

A THREE-DAY REVOLUTION

AN EXPLOSION, the first railroad accident, occurred on the South Carolina road, when a Negro fireman who didn't like to hear steam escaping tied down the safety valve and the boiler blew up! About that same time Charles X, the King of France, had a similar shock. He tried to clamp down on the French people's freedom of speech and their right to vote, and produced an explosion that blew him off the throne.

Wednesday, Thursday, Friday of the last and hottest week in July of 1830 there was a three-day revolution. It took place in the streets of Paris. The people tore up the paving stones and built barricades of wagons, barrels, boxes and furniture across the narrow crooked streets. There they successfully defied, trapped and fought off the royal soldiers until Charles X, seeing that his cause was lost, gave up the throne, left France and fled to England.

Now what form of government? Empire—monarchy—republic?

"A republic," said those who had done the fighting.

"No," said the wealthy bourgeoisie. "No more republics." They remembered too well the Reign of Terror and anarchy of the last one. A monarchy would be best, they said, not with a king like Charles X who favored aristocrats and tried to become an absolute monarch. No. A king who would observe the charter, and uphold the rights of the middle classes, was what they wanted. Louis Philippe, a prince who was known to be democratic and to hold liberal opinions, was suggested.

The final decision rested with La Fayette. All things considered, La Fayette felt that a limited monarchy under a democratic king would most nearly unite the many parties in France—Bonapartists, monarchists of all kinds and republicans. So he favored Louis Philippe.

Louis Philippe, therefore, became King of France. For fifteen years the Congress of Vienna had held good. Now revolution, so feared and hated by the kings, had triumphed again. The royal family they had restored to France had been driven out forever, and in Belgium more work of the Congress of Vienna was undone, for the revolution spread.

In 1815, in rearranging the map, Belgium had been given to the Kingdom of the Netherlands as a province, but the Belgians, who were Catholics, were not happy under the rule of Protestant Holland, so now in 1830 Belgium rose in rebellion and drove out the royal Dutch troops and declared itself an independent kingdom.

Upon invitation of the people, Victoria's Uncle Leopold left England in July, 1831, and went to Belgium to become the first king of the new nation. The next year he married Louise, the daughter of Louis Philippe, and so became son-in-law of the King of France.

Meanwhile what of Metternich? Where were the Holy Allies? Why had they allowed these changes to take place? Not from choice, you may be sure. Metternich had been opposed to recognizing either Louis Philippe as king, or Belgium as a nation, but it had been unavoidable. Sparks from France had started revolutions in still other countries, and given the kings troubles nearer home to settle. Russia had to stamp out an uprising in Poland. Austria was faced with rebellion in Italy.

YOUNG PATRIOTS OF ITALY

AND ITALY? What *was* Italy in 1830? Nothing but a divided land. "Nothing," said Metternich, "but a geographical expression." Italy, once the heart of the great Roman Empire, was only a name, forbidden, in some parts of the peninsula, to be spoken aloud even by actors on the stage, a name that could be whispered only in dark cellars and secret meeting places of those who loved their country and planned for the day when it would be free.

Piedmont, or the Kingdom of Sardinia, was the only independent state in 1830. The center of the peninsula belonged to the Pope, and the rest was broken up into small states ruled over by foreign Archdukes and Princes. Northern Italy belonged to Austria, and so was under the despotic rule of the Emperor Francis and his henchman, Metternich.

Ten years before an Italian uprising against Austria had failed. Now, in 1830, the rebellion was also quickly stamped out by Austria's

123

troops and the revolutionists killed, imprisoned, or driven into exile.

The year after the uprising in a house in Marseilles, France, one of the young Italians, driven into exile, bent earnestly over a desk piled high with books and papers. He was writing a letter—one that was to become as famous in Italian history as his own name, MAZZINI. His slim, sensitive fingers guiding the pen sped across the paper; otherwise his slight figure was tense and motionless, almost a thing of spirit as his thoughts swept through it. Against the shadows his beautiful face was outlined like a delicately carved Italian cameo. Curling black hair hung to his shoulders, and he was dressed in black—all black in mourning for his country, which was dead.

Dead, yes, but not for long, Mazzini prophesied, for after death came resurrection! And Italy would rise again to a new life. "Radiant," he visioned her, "and, purified by suffering, moving as an angel of light among the nations that had thought her dead." All that the patriots needed to bring that vision to life was faith and a leader who could unite them. Members of "Young Italy," the great secret organization Mazzini had started, were not lacking in faith, he knew, and in the King of Sardinia he hoped to find a leader for them. It was to the King of Sardinia or Piedmont that he was writing that letter:

"Sire," he wrote, "there is a crown more brilliant and sublime than that of Piedmont, a crown that awaits the man who dedicates his life to winning it. Sire, have you ever cast an eagle glance upon this Italy, girt round with barriers so strong that it needs but a firm will and a few brave breasts to shelter it from foreign rule?

"Place yourself at the head of the nation, write on your flag Union, Liberty, Independence, and we will bring the little states of Italy under your flag. Unite us, sire, and we shall conquer."

The King of Piedmont hesitated, then crumpled the letter and threw it into the fire. He, too, loved Italy. He, too, wished to see Italy free and united, but he lacked self-confidence or the courage to try.

The King of Piedmont, however, had a young son, VICTOR EM-MANUEL, who was now but a boy of eleven years, but who was not to lack the courage when his time came to show it. Besides the young king and the idealist Mazzini, two other men from Piedmont would take part in that final liberation of Italy. One, the statesman CAVOUR, was now just a young nobleman living the obscure life of a gentleman farmer on his country estate. The other was an unknown sailor who was to become the most romantic hero of Italy, her William Tell, Robin Hood, or knight of the Holy Grail—bold, pure-hearted, lovable GARIBALDI.

It was on board ship, said he, returning from the Black Sea on one of those "transparent eastern nights beneath a sky all spangled with stars" that he, Giuseppe Garibaldi, first learned about Mazzini, about "Young Italy," and of the men who were working to free his country.

"His country!" Not Christopher Columbus, said he, could have been more overjoyed to hear the cry of "Land" than he had been to hear those words. From that night on his life was dedicated to "his country."

Garibaldi had been born in Nice in 1807, in a house by the sea. He loved the water, swam like a fish when he was little more than a *bambino*, and was long waiting for the day when he could become a sailor like his father. Domenico Garibaldi, however, wishing for his son a safer life than that of a mariner, spent much of his hard-earned money on an education for the lad, hoping to make of him a lawyer, a doctor, or, best of all, a priest. It was of no use. The boy's heart had gone to sea.

So when he was fifteen Rosa, his mother, packed his outfit and, with tears and prayers, saw him off on his first voyage—that big handsome boy of hers with the sunlit hair.

He sailed that time to a Russian port on the Black Sea, and after that made many voyages full of danger and excitement to the eastern lands along the Mediterranean. On a day in 1832 the ship on which he was returning from the East was sailing towards the harbor of Marseilles.

A few days later young Mazzini, seated at his desk, raised his dark eyes from his writing, to see two men standing in the doorway. One was an acquaintance, the other a stranger and a sailor with gold wind-blown hair and eyes the color of the sea. His name was Garibaldi. He had come, he told Mazzini, to join the association of "Young Italy," and stood ready to consecrate his life to the service of his country.

Suiting action to his word, he took part in the next uprising against the Austrians, which like the others failed. In 1834 Garibaldi was an exile condemned to death and fleeing from the country. Escaping from Genoa disguised as a peasant, he made his way through the mountains guided by the stars. Swimming swollen rivers, living for days on chestnuts, and once leaping fifteen feet from a balcony to escape pursuers, he finally reached Marseilles. A few months later he sailed as second in command on a ship leaving for South America.

Early in 1831, the year that Mazzini escaped to Marseilles in France, another young man in his early twenties, who had joined in the Italian uprising, was also fleeing from the Austrians. To him Marseilles offered no refuge, for he was Louis Napoleon, and like all of the Bonaparte family was forbidden to enter France. He was an exile.

Fifteen years he and his mother Hortense had been living in Switzerland. Now, however, that Louis Philippe was King, and had restored the tricolor flag in France, Hortense hoped that she and her son would be allowed the rights of French citizens again. Daring to cross the border in disguise, they made their way to Paris and appealed to the King. Louis Philippe, personally, would have been willing to let them stay, but dared not, with Louis Napoleon bearing the name he did. So the two, mother and son, returned to exile in Switzerland.

Soon they learned that Napoleon's own son had died in Austria, and with his cousin's death, Louis Napoleon considered himself heir to the throne. Never doubting that one day the Bonapartists would be able to restore the Empire, he spoke of the future with surprising confidence.

"On that day when I shall preside over the destinies of France," he promised the members of Young Italy, "I shall support with all my strength the claims of Italy to become a nation."

Even partially fulfilling that promise in years to come was to hasten unexpected and overwhelming disaster upon himself and France.

"A BLOODLESS REVOLUTION"

THE YEAR that France got rid of Charles X, England was relieved of her burden, George IV. He died in June, and Victoria's uncle William, a bluff old fellow who had spent his early life in the navy, became king, and with a "heigho-my-hearties" manner began to steer the ship of state.

The Duke of Wellington, England's most popular hero since the battle of Waterloo, was Prime Minister, but not for long. A new king meant a new election to Par——nt, and in that election the Tory party, of which the Duke —— which had been in power for almost fifty years. —— he control of Parliament passed at last ——

—— ll proposed his first Bill, for the —— to Parliament. He proposed to —— ten boroughs" and divide the —— with some degree of fairness. —— proposal, but it opened a bitter —— the Halls of Parliament for fifteen months —— violent opposition from the Tories.

—— Gladstone was twenty-one, in his fourth year at Oxford, —— active member of the Debating Society which met in a room over the shop of the pastry cook.

The earnest members held a three-night session over the Reform Bill, and announced as their profound conclusion that the present ministry was incompetent to conduct the government of the country!

"Moreover," added young Gladstone, "they have unwisely and unscrupulously introduced a measure which threatens not only to change the form of our government but ultimately to break up the very foundations of the country. What is that—but a symptom that the chill and damp of death are creeping over England's glory? May God avert it."

The Bill did not pass. The ministry was defeated, Parliament dissolved and a new election called for.

"The Bill, the whole Bill, nothing but the Bill!" cried the people, and the reformers were re-elected. Lord John Russell introduced the Reform Bill for a second time in the House of Commons where, despite stiff opposition, it was passed and sent on to the House of Lords. There the Lords (who profited by the old arrangement) killed the Bill at once.

The country was enraged. Riots broke out in London. Members of the House of Lords were booed and hooted at on the street. Stones were thrown at the carriage of the Duke of Wellington, who had opposed the Bill, and the windows of his town house were smashed. Ten thousand workers besieged St. James's Palace and the troops had to be called out.

At the next session of Parliament, Lord John Russell rose for the third time and for the third time proposed the Reform Bill. After endless speeches against it, it again passed in the House of Commons, but again it appeared certain to be defeated in the House of Lords.

There was one way to force it through. The king could create new noblemen—enough to pass the Bill and give them seats in the House of Lords. At first William IV blustered about and refused to do it, but finally gave in and made the threat. The threat alone was sufficient. The Lords saw that the game was up and passed the Bill in June.

That Reform Bill of 1832 widened the circle of voters from less than one out of every fifty to about one out of thirty.

Still, as in France, the workingmen and the poorer middle classes were left out. They still had no share at all in the government. A great revolution, however, had taken place, and the most important step made in six hundred years towards making England a democracy.

Old Cartoons

"UNION AND LIBERTY"

ANDREW JACKSON—"Old Hickory," the Indian fighter, hero of New Orleans, sharp-tongued, hard-hitting, warm-hearted Andrew Jackson left Tennessee for Washington in 1829 to head the nation as its President, and also by his high-handed way of going at the job to gain from his enemies the new nickname of "King Andrew." Westerner, a man of the common people, he was the first President who was not the son of well-to-do, cultured parents of either Massachusetts or Virginia.

During all of its early years the United States, like England, had been governed entirely by its wealthy citizens. No man who did not own a certain amount of property was allowed to vote. Now, however, in many old states and all new western ones, every man over twenty-one had the right of voting and they had elected Andrew Jackson.

129

On the day he was inaugurated, they thronged to Washington to see him. Into the White House they pushed, a scrambling mob of men, women and children, jostling one another. Pioneers in their coonskin caps went tramping in on the good carpets with muddy cowhide boots, and even stood on the beautiful damask-covered furniture to catch a glimpse of their hero. Cut-glass and china, several thousand dollars' worth, were smashed as they pushed for the ice cream and lemonade. When all was over, it looked as though there had been a stampede of cattle. It was disgraceful, and not surprising that cultured people of the east were horrified and moaned that the country was "going to the dogs!"

Andrew Jackson himself did not approve, but he understood. The people were rough, and had lost what manners they had in their excitement, but they were sound at heart, had their rights and were entitled to them. In the first place he was going to see to it that the little man as well as the big man who had voted for him was rewarded. So out went hundreds of postmasters, deputies and clerks whether they had served faithfully or not, and into their jobs went Jackson men. "To the victor belong the spoils" was the famous excuse given for this wholesale sweeping in and out of government officials. It was a senator who gave that answer—not the President.

"Old Hickory," was no man to offer explanations for doing what he thought was right. He was used to snapping out orders and taking no back-talk. That was his way, and the way he intended to be President.

Also, no sooner was he in office than he started to veto one bill after another passed by Congress. If, for one moment, he suspected a bill of being unfair to the common people he vetoed it! Veto followed veto, while his enemies gasped and his friends applauded.

"Good Old Hickory," cheered his followers. "He'll stand up for the common people. He'll see to it that we get our rights." Every act of his they upheld with a loyalty only equaled in vigor by the violence of his enemies' attacks.

"What does he think he is?" they stormed, "KING of the United States? Congress, not a king, is ruler of this country."

Joining together against the Democrats who stood staunchly behind their leader, the opponents of Andrew Jackson formed a new political party and called themselves the WHIGS. The name WHIG they borrowed appropriately from the party in England which stood for the rights of Parliament against the power of the King.

So now, sharply divided were the people of the United States over Andrew Jackson into Democrats and the Whigs—but that did no harm. There was no danger to the Union in having the Nation divided into two parties, so long as each party was composed of people from all sections of the country. Only a question that divided one section of states against another could ever endanger or break up the Union.

But now such a question arose. And, as in 1814 New England threatened to secede because of the way the War of 1812 was being run, so now in 1830 South Carolina threatened to secede because of the question known as NULLIFICATION, which in simple words was this:

Did any state have the right to disobey, declare NULL and void any law passed by the national government of the United States?

South Carolina said "YES."

New England said "NO."

South Carolina said "YES" and furthermore threatened to secede if not allowed to set aside certain tax laws that, as it happened, had been passed to benefit New England.

"Why should we Southern planters let ourselves be ruined," they argued, "just to help a few Northern factory owners?"

This is the story from the beginning:

During the War of 1812 when supplies of manufactured goods from England had been cut off, people of New England had been encouraged to start factories of their own. After the war when English goods could be imported again the factories in New England were hurt by the competition, because English goods could be sold at lower prices. (Workers in English factories were paid lower wages.) So a tax had been placed on goods from England to make them as high in price as the same articles manufactured in America. That was fine for the factory owners of New

England who had goods to sell, but hard on the Southern cotton growers who had to buy every manufactured article they needed from steam engines and plows to calico and pins.

Times were especially hard in South Carolina. The land was old and worn out, and the crops comparatively small. Some planters could scarcely afford to buy even the most necessary articles. Every time John C. Calhoun went back to his native state on a visit, he saw that many of the fine old plantation homes he had admired as a boy had grown shabby both inside and out, and their fences and stables were sadly in need of repair and paint.

"It's those taxes, Mr. Calhoun, sir," the planters told him. "That last tax is outrageous, abominable! We should rebel at paying it."

That opinion was shared, it seemed, by John C. Calhoun himself. He passed it on to a committee appointed by the Governor to investigate the matter of how much power the national government had over each individual state. Into their report went the bold theory that South Carolina or any state had a right to do away with any law of the national government that it did not like!

Which was ridiculous, of course. As Daniel Webster said, if every state could set aside any law it wanted to, there would soon be twenty-four little separate nations instead of one United States. He was speaking about it before Congress on a winter afternoon in January, 1830, long remembered as the beginning of the famous Webster-Hayne Debate. Senator Hayne had presented in his speech the theory of states' rights held by South Carolina, to which Daniel Webster replied in one of his greatest orations, coming to a climax in these closing words:

"LIBERTY AND UNION, NOW AND FOREVER, ONE AND INSEPARABLE!"

Daniel Webster stood firmly for the power of the National Government. John C. Calhoun stood for the power of the state. Where did President Jackson stand? Jackson had been born on the border between North and South Carolina and was a cotton planter. Would he uphold the South? That was the question every one was asking. Andrew Jackson gave his answer at a banquet.

Thomas Jefferson had now been dead four years, but on April 13, 1830, a banquet was given by the Democrats to celebrate what would have been his eighty-seventh birthday. Many speeches had been made favoring Nullification when, as a climax, President Jackson was called upon to propose a toast. All eyes were fastened on him, while the guests waited expectantly for him, as the President, as a Southerner, as head of the Democratic Party, to indicate his sentiments. He rose, a tall thin figure in the candlelight, raised his glass, paused a moment, then cut the silence with the positive words:

"OUR FEDERAL UNION. IT MUST BE PRESERVED."

That was all, but his meaning was unmistakable.

South Carolina, nevertheless, plunged madly ahead, refused to pay the federal tax, and threatened to secede if the government tried to put through the law by force.

"Let 'em make threats to their hearts' content," said Jackson, "but if one drop of blood be shed in defiance of the laws of the United States I'll hang the first man I get my hands on to the first tree I can find."

And he meant it. Immediately, with the permission of Congress to use force, Jackson sent units of the army and navy to South Carolina to be ready to act if action was necessary. It was not.

Just in the nick of time, just the very day before the new tax law was to take effect, Henry Clay again came to the rescue with a Compromise. He proposed to gradually reduce the tax. South Carolina was satisfied, and gave up the idea of seceding. Once more the country heaved a sigh of relief over the grave danger so narrowly escaped. They hoped the question of states' rights had been settled forever. But again the final settlement had only been postponed.

"Liberty and Union, one and inseparable." Those were the words that Daniel Webster had sent resounding through the Hall of Congress on that January afternoon in 1830. Repeated, and reprinted in every newspaper, they had gone echoing across the country.

And so they had reached the ears of the tall, gaunt, lanky fellow who was plodding along beside a wagon drawn by two yoke of oxen, heading northwest from southern Indiana.

It was the middle of February, 1830, and the Lincolns were moving again. After fourteen years in Indiana they were going into Illinois. Before they left home Abe had read the speech of Daniel Webster in the Louisville paper, and as he walked along he pondered on the meaning of the words, and said them over to himself—those words in whose defence he should be called upon to lead the final battle.

Through the forests of Indiana they went, over its hills and hollows out onto the level prairies of Illinois, to a place on the Sangamon River that their relative John Hanks had picked out for their home.

Sangamon was an Indian word meaning "land of plenty to eat." Tom Lincoln hoped it would be. In possessions and wealth he was leaving Indiana no richer than he had been when he had gone there from Kentucky, fourteen years before.

It was much the same kind of cabin as the one from which they came that they now built in Illinois—just a house of logs. Abe helped build it. He plowed the land, put in the crops and split rails to fence the fields. Didn't seem like too good a place, though, so when spring came they moved again—southeast to Goose Nest Prairie. There again Abe helped to build another cabin, split rails and get the family settled.

Then he laid down his axe, and said goodbye to them, to his father, his stepbrother and sisters, to Dennis Hanks, who had married one of the sisters, and, with a lump in his throat, to his mother. Then he turned, picked up his little bundle of clothes and strode away. Off he went through the tall grass of the prairie, that grew almost as high as his head.

He was twenty-two years old. He no longer owed his services to his father. He was a man now—free to go and do with his life whatever he would or could. The winter of 1831 found him keeping store in the village of New Salem.

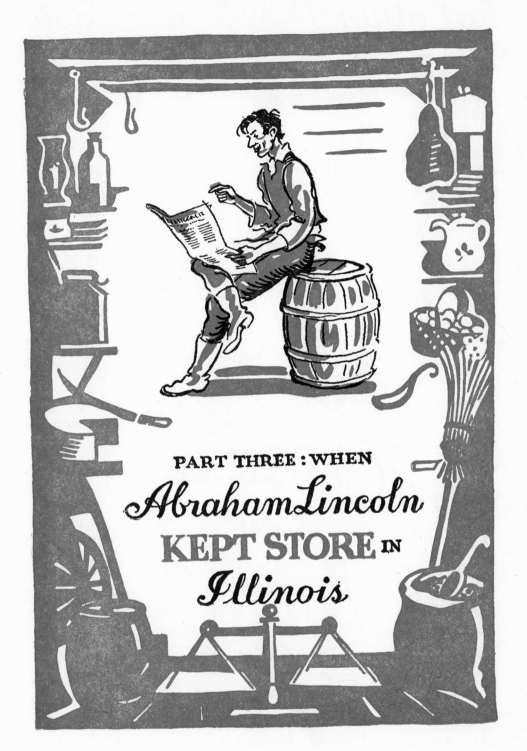

PART THREE : WHEN

Abraham Lincoln

KEPT STORE IN

Illinois

What other People were doing

ANDREW JACKSON was President of the United States until 1837

He upheld the Union when S. Carolina threatened to secede

1833, CHICAGO, youngest of the world's large cities, became a town

CHARLES DICKENS wrote his "Christmas Carol" 1843

POSTAGE STAMPS came into use: Eng. 1840 U.S.A. 1847

Wm LLOYD GARRISON Abolitionist, was fighting Slavery.

LIBERATION

BLACK HAWK and his tribe were defeated and driven from Illinois

COLORADO OKLA NEW MEXICO TEXAS

TEXAS won its independence from Mexico in 1836 and became part of the United States in 1845.

The store failed. **LINCOLN** became a soldier in the Black Hawk War — then Postmaster,

DAVID LIVINGSTONE began his exploration into the heart of Africa

WASHINGTON IDAHO OREGON

The OREGON TRAIL was opened, (1846) and Oregon became part of United States.

Surveyor, Member of the Illinois Legislature, and ... in 1837, a lawyer

and some Events that took place

when Abe Lincoln kept Store

1842
CHINA was defeated, and England got **HONG-KONG**.

VICTORIA became Queen of England (1837) (1840) wife of Albert, and mother of the next King (1841)

LOUIS PHILIPPE, the last King of France, reigned from 1830-48
1848 (France became a Republic)

CLIPPER SHIPS designed for speed were sailing the seas.

RUBBER came into use.

The **TELEGRAPH** was invented

Through "Daguerreotypes," **PHOTOGRAPHY** was introduced

STEAMSHIPS first crossed the Atlantic Ocean **1838**

ETHER was first used to deaden pain. **1842**

MATCHES were made

BATHTUBS were considered dangerous, and in some states laws made to limit their use

1848
WAR with **MEXICO** and payment of $15,000,000 added this territory to the United States

CALIFORNIA · NEVADA · UTAH · ARIZONA

ZACHARY TAYLOR
WINFIELD SCOTT were the commanding Generals

1848 !
GOLD was discovered in **CALIFORNIA**

between the Years 1830 and 1848

ROUTES TO THE FAR EAST

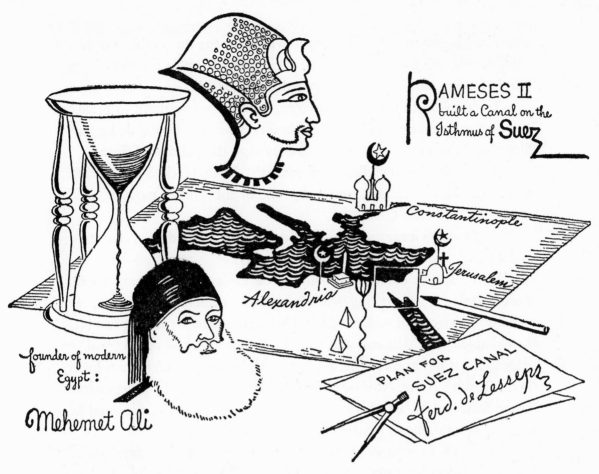

RAMESES II built a Canal on the Isthmus of Suez

Constantinople

Jerusalem

Alexandria

founder of modern Egypt:

Mehemet Ali

PLAN FOR SUEZ CANAL
Ferd. de Lesseps

TIME MAKES AN OLD IDEA NEW

TRADE ROUTES to the East! Routes to India and China—overland by camel-caravan, and down around the end of Africa by water. For centuries, European traders had been traveling those old routes to bring back the priceless treasures of the East. Now times had changed. European traders still sailed the old routes to India and China, but now they went in search of foreign markets. Their ships were loaded down with products of their own to sell.

Since the steam engine had been invented and machines made to take the place of handwork, factories, especially in France and England, were turning out more products than the people at home could use, and gobbling up more raw materials than they could supply. So manufacturers had begun to send all over the world for the things they needed, and were shipping out quantities of their machine-made products to be sold in foreign lands—to India especially and to China.

Trade routes to the East, therefore, were more important to France and England than they had ever been before, when Ferdinand de Lesseps first thought of cutting a shorter route through the Isthmus of Suez.

Across the narrow ribbon of sand that then blocked the eastern end of the Mediterranean, runs today one of the world's most traveled waterways, the Suez Canal.

And though it may seem ridiculous, a germ and a dish of macaroni had a part in making it, according to the story.

In the spring of 1831, Ferdinand de Lesseps, a charming young French diplomat, was sailing over the Mediterranean on his way to Egypt to become vice-consul in Alexandria. He had heard much of Egypt and its remarkable ruler, Mehemet Ali, from his father who had been consul in Alexandria thirty years before. Mehemet Ali had then been but a colonel in the Turkish Army. Now he had made himself practically independent of the Sultan of Turkey, his former overlord, and was to be regarded by coming generations as the founder of modern Egypt.

Young De Lesseps was at last to meet Mehemet Ali, and as the lighthouse of Alexandria came into sight across the blue waters of the harbor, eagerness to land was uppermost in his mind. Then he learned that no one would be allowed to land! A germ had been at work. A case of cholera had broken out on board, and the ship had to be held in quarantine for several weeks. So there he was—an impatient young man left with nothing to do for all that time but lean on the rail and look at the water. At least, so he was thinking one morning when a parcel arrived for him, sent out by the thoughtful consul general . . .

BOOKS! What a relief! One of them caught his eye at once. The title? *A Canal of Two Seas.* The author? An engineer who had been with Napoleon on the campaign in Egypt thirty years before. Napoleon? Had Napoleon thought of cutting a canal through the Isthmus of Suez? So it seemed. This amazing book gave all the plans and measurements.

Fascinated, De Lesseps read on for days, absorbed by the idea.

A canal across the isthmus! An outlet from the Mediterranean into the Red Sea! What a marvelous help to commerce that would be. No more would ships have to make the long, slow journey down around the end of Africa to Asia. India and China would be five months nearer to Europe. The whole world would be brought closer together.

Perhaps he, Ferdinand de Lesseps, was the one meant to revive and carry out the plan for that wonderful man-made river. Rivers—how he loved them! Years ago, when he was a small boy in Paris, he remembered walking along the banks of the Seine with his father, and saying that he wished some day God would let him help Him build a river. Here was the answer to his wish! He would build this great international river, that all the people of the world might use.

Three weeks later, when the quarantine was over and he was at last established in Alexandria, De Lesseps spoke of the canal to Mehemet Ali. Egypt's ruler was interested, as he was interested in all public works, but the canal, he said, was not a new idea, even with Napoleon. There had been a canal there in the days of the Pharaohs. Traces of the ancient banks were still visible in the sand. And as to a canal today—his country might suffer from becoming an international highway. The nations of Europe were apt to fight for control of the canal. There were many things to be considered. At the moment he was concerned about his favorite son, Mohammed Said.

Said was too fat. He ate too much. Punishment did no good. Each week he was punished if he did not lose. Each week he gained a pound or two. Monsieur de Lesseps was a splendid horseman. Would he as a special favor be willing to teach fat Mohammed Said to ride?

De Lesseps was willing, but Mohammed Said was glum. Bumping up and down on a horse's back held no attraction for the fat boy, but he had to try it. At the end of a week he weighed in a few pounds lighter as a reward for his perspiring efforts. For additional reward De Lesseps, as a friendly gesture, invited his reluctant pupil to dinner.

It was a delicious dinner, but the high spot of the meal in Mohammed Said's opinion was that dish of Italian macaroni. What a food was that! What a delicacy! What a flavor! How his round face shone as he relished every savory mouthful with almost rapturous delight!

Many dinners followed, but it was that first plate of macaroni that marked the beginning of a lifelong friendship. Years later when De Lesseps needed help for his long-cherished plans of starting the canal, Mohammed Said, the new ruler of Egypt, would not fail him.

THE SULTAN'S GUEST

MACHINES, factories, railroads—all of those inventions of the last sixty years had brought a new way of living into Europe, while life in the Far East had gone on unchanged. Gradually, though, all the proud old lands of Asia were to be invaded by the new ideas of the west, and their leaders made to realize that they must adjust their ancient ways to fit a changing world.

The Empire of Turkey, quite naturally, was the first in Asia to be touched by the European ideas, for Turkey, circling the eastern end of the Mediterranean, belonged both to Europe and to Asia. Constantinople, her capital city, lay like a jeweled link, joining the two continents.

There in Constantinople, on an afternoon in December, 1830, while outside pale winter sun shone on gold-topped mosques and minarets, inside the Sultan's palace two men sat facing each other in the perfumed shadows. One was clad in conventional English clothes, the other was wearing a turban, blood-red shirt, fringed girdle, blue-striped trousers and pointed crimson slippers. One was the Sultan, the other his guest, a young author from England, who seemed quite at home in a Sultan's palace, although this was his first visit to the East.

A faint smile played about his lips as he raised to them the amber tip of a Turkish water pipe, and watched the Sultan's face through the curling smoke that rose between them. He found the situation amusing —as fantastic as a scene in a play in which the leading actors had changed costume by mistake. For it was he, Benjamin Disraeli from London, England, who was wearing the turban, and the Sultan Mahmud II who was dressed in English clothes! And both men, like this city in which they met, were a blend of East and West.

Benjamin Disraeli, now on a pleasure trip around the Mediterranean, had been born in England, but his ancestors had come from the Orient, by way of Spain and Italy. For he was of that oriental race which is at home in nearly every country. He was of the people of Israel. That was the meaning of his Italian name D'Israeli.

Mahmud II, though son of a Turkish Sultan, was half French. As a young girl his mother had been captured by Algerian pirates. Sent as a present to their overlord the Sultan, she had become the favorite of his harem. From her Mahmud as a child had learned to speak good French. From the time he had come to the throne in 1808, he had been trying to graft European customs, and especially modern methods of warfare, onto his backward country, but with little success. His Mohammedan subjects cursed him as a foreigner—a "Giaour" Sultan who was betraying them with the teachings of unbelievers. From him, when they turned their prayer rugs to the east, they prayed to Allah for deliverance.

Benjamin Disraeli knew this, and in spite of the Sultan's cruelty, of which he also knew, he felt a certain sympathy for the man beaten at every turn by stupid prejudice. Still vivid and sharp in his memory were scenes in which he had first learned that such prejudice existed.

The first scene was in a schoolroom. A small, puzzled boy of five on his first day at school was being made to stand alone while the other pupils stared at him curiously as they knelt in opening prayer.

Scene two. The same schoolroom. A rabbi with his long beard was standing in the doorway. The small boy was being singled out to take his lesson in Hebrew while the other children nudged one another and giggled.

Third scene. The library of a London home. A man with pink cheeks, silver hair and a small black skull-cap sat at his desk surrounded on all sides by books. Before him stood a boy and his sister who had brought to their father the puzzling question as to why they should be blamed and scoffed at for their race or their religion.

"Because of superstitions, my children," answered their scholar father in his gentle manner, "superstitions and prejudices which should have died out long ago just as some practices and beliefs of our people the Jews should also have long since been discarded. Both belong to a by-gone age—not to the age of reason."

The next scene. The Church of St. Andrew on a Sunday in 1817. The boy, thirteen now, was being baptized into the Church of England. Many careers were closed to all but members of that church by the English law. Isaac D'Israeli therefore, believing that a man's true religion is tested by his life, not by his form of worship, had been persuaded that it would be best for his children to conform to the established church.

So the young man who was visiting the Sultan that winter afternoon was both a Christian and a Jew, as he was both an Oriental and a European. To his natural sympathy this first visit was to add undying interest in the mysterious East. Later as a great Prime Minister of England, Disraeli's chief concern was to be in foreign affairs, and in promoting England as a world power and an Empire.

It was he, Benjamin Disraeli, who would one day bestow upon his Queen the additional title of Empress of India.

तैन्धव देश

The British first landed here and then went to Calcutta & on up the Ganges

INDIA

INDIA belonged to England in the 1830's, for England held Delhi, and there is an old saying that "whoso holds Delhi holds India." From the beginning of history India's conquerors one after another sweeping down from the north had taken possession of that ancient city. Outside its sun-baked walls amid tangled weeds could be seen crumbling back into the yellow dust the relics of six other Delhis. One upon another they had risen and fallen into ruins there beside the Jumna River, before a Moghul Emperor had built the present city.

The Moghul (or Mongol) Emperors who were Mohammedans from Central Asia had been India's last conquerors before the English. More than three hundred years they had lived in lavish splendor in Delhi, and for a time had been supreme over half of India.

In 1830 Shah Mohammed, last of the Moghul Emperors, an aged man of seventy, was still permitted by the English to live in his rose-red palace overlooking the river, but he was no longer powerful and no longer rich. The old brown fingers twisting the end of his chalk-white beard were loaded with jewels, but no longer had power to squeeze unlimited streams of gold from the Indian people.

145

It was the white conqueror from the north who now collected the taxes. Shah Mohammed lived on a pension from the English government, which though far from meager, was not generous enough to supply the wants of the 12,000 members of his family who filled the palace.

So resentment, hatred of the British, ate like green poison in the seventy-year-old heart of Shah Mohammed and glittered in his eyes.

Two hundred fifty miles from Delhi on the river Ganges, river sacred to the Hindus, there was also living at this time a seven-year-old Hindu prince by the name of Nana, in whose hard little heart was likewise instilled a hatred of the conqueror. Nana was but seven, but Nana had strangely set, uneasy eyes that saw everything. . . .

Every day he saw worshippers bathing in the sacred river. Every night he saw the smoke from funeral pyres burning on the sacred ghats. Once he had seen a widow wail and beat her breast because she could not throw herself upon her husband's funeral pyre and burn with him. The English conquerors had forbidden her to pay him that last honor. The English! Ssss! Nana had seen them too. He had seen them come riding down from Cawnpore—those foreign people, those animal-eaters, who would eat even flesh of the sacred cow! And he had seen his foster-father's eyes grow hard at the sight of them and his nostrils tighten when he thought of the wrong that they had done to him.

Twelve years before as leader of the native rajahs, he the proud Peshwa of Poona had led a last desperate stand against the English. But what were elephants and old-fashioned muskets against guns and cannon? Defeated, he had been ousted from his kingdom, stripped of power, and left to live on a niggardly pension of 80,000 pounds a year!

That was twelve years ago. Still he nursed his grievance there in the small town of Bithoor beside the sacred Ganges. And Nana watched him. Nana, who was seven. Nana, who as his son would one day set the torch to his funeral pyre and inherit his riches. Nana Sahib, with the hard little heart and the strangely set uneasy eyes.

India. Oh, India belonged to England—if holding Delhi was all there was to holding India!

146

LI HUNG CHANG, A BOY OF CHINA

IT WAS a fresh new morning in an old, old village in China. Small Li Hung Chang, his round face washed and shining as the day itself, was starting out for school. Starting out was he, to fill his fresh young mind with the old, old lessons taught in the same old way that they had always been taught in ancient China. Li Hung Chang was seven and to him this was an autumn morning in the ninth year of the reign of the Emperor Tao Kwang. To the western world it was the year 1830. But Li Hung Chang, who was to become China's great Minister of Foreign Affairs, knew nothing of the western world, on this bright morning— except that the barbarians lived there.

He was thinking, as he caught a branch of the peach tree by the door and shook some shining drops of water on his tongue—he was thinking that he would go to school by way of the splendid Water Lake to see the goslings, but his mild mother was wise beyond compare.

"Lessons run away from loitering boys," said she. "Go to school the straight road by the fruit wall."

147

Li Hung Chang heard. So he jumped a shining puddle and hurried along the straight road to call for his friend Ho Kai. Ho Kai was a sleepy boy. He hadn't quite finished his rice and when they were on their way he confessed that he had forgotten how to draw the characters for his name! Li Hung Chang remembered.

He drew them with a sharp stick in the smooth damp earth beneath a crooked pine tree. Then he drew his own name too, while Ho Kai laughed and was proud to see how much his friend had learned. Li Hung Chang, pleased with the praise, drew the word for sun 日 and the word for rain 雨 and the word for man 人 and the word for woman 女 and kept on until he had filled up all the space. Then he remembered! School does not wait for loitering boys. So they ran fast —so fast that their two black pigtails stuck out straight behind them. Li Hung Chang could run faster than Ho Kai, just as he could think faster and memorize faster—faster and better than almost any boy in school. It was not long before he could recite many verses of Confucius both forward and backward.

It was not long either before he learned more about the western world. That was because of Ho Kai's father who had promised one day to make the boys a kite. But he was not there when they came home. They waited for him beneath the crooked pine tree until the sun was low and still he did not come. Ho Kai's mother said he had gone to the high village and turned her head away. There was something strange about it.

Next morning Li Hung Chang's father said he would go to the high village to look for his neighbor. Soon the boys at school were whispering that Ho Kai's father had learned to smoke the foreign drug.

FOREIGN DRUG? What was that? Li Hung Chang asked his father. And his wise parent told him that it was opium brought to China by the barbarians. As they grew older, he warned his sons again and again not to touch the ruinous drug which he said was being brought into the country against the command of the Honorable Emperor, Tao Kwang.

"Why then does not the all-powerful Emperor put an end to it?"

asked Li Hung Chang, but to that question the noble and severe parent could give that keen inquiring son of his no satisfactory answer.

Every day for many years Li Hung Chang and Ho Kai went to school together. Then Li Hung Chang had grown tall, and gone far along the straight road towards his Budding Genius Examinations, while easy-going Ho Kai had followed the footsteps of his father.

It was on an evening many years later that Li Hung Chang was supposed to have made this sad entry in his diary:

"This day though my Father has warned me strictly to avoid his Company, I went into the high Village in search of my good Friend Ho Kai. It was no trouble to find him, for the vile Place where he spends most of his Time is now known to all the Neighborhood, since it is said that more than two hundred in this District are users of the Foreign Drug." Later. "Ho Kai's Father is dead; it is the Foreign Drug that killed him. Ho Kai, himself, is no longer at his Home, but one of the miserable Beggars of the Highway. His Eyes are nearly blind. When I went along the Road yesterday he did not know me. . . ."

Spring had come again, and Li Hung Chang had won his Ready-for-Office degree when he is said to have recorded his next milestone:

"There is bounding Happiness in my inmost Heart today for I have been given a regular Place in the Office of Chin Fu and my start on the way to Political Progress has been made! My noble and severe Parent rejoices and my mild Mother is happy beyond compare. My Father has gone in his chair to tell My Uncle and to Invite him to a Feast we will enjoy tomorrow." That night he was too happy to sleep. "It is impossible for me to close an Eye and keep it closed so good do my Spirits feel over the Fortunate Tidings. Even my Uncle in his Home on the Hong Road heard the News before my Father arrived and had started for our House with two fat Geese and a Fish.

"Tomorrow I shall fast well and read some of my Poetry to the Guests. Someday I hope to be the 狀元 (foremost scholar) of China!

"People would laugh at me perhaps, but if a man has the education and the love and the desire and the purpose, he can do work I know, that will make his name live gloriously among his countrymen."

149

SLAVERY—WHAT TO DO ABOUT IT?

IZZY, as his friends called young Disraeli, returned to London from his visit to the Near East full of stories about Turkey and Egypt, which he embroidered with his sparkling wit. Extremely entertaining, he was much sought after in society, but in politics, thus far, a failure. By 1833 he had tried three times to be elected to Parliament and had been defeated.

On January 29, 1833, the first Parliament elected according to the new reform law, held its opening meeting. A few nights later, Disraeli, in a canary-colored waistcoat and white kid gloves, sauntered in to the House of Commons to hear the speech of a more fortunate friend who had just become a member. Not far away might have been seen a young newspaper reporter by the name of Charles Dickens, scribbling notes in shorthand. And down on the main floor, among the Tories, was a handsome young Oxford graduate newly elected, who was to become the fascinating Dizzy's greatest rival, William Ewart Gladstone.

Not that night, but six months later on the third of June, William Gladstone rose to make his "maiden speech." His subject was SLAVERY, Negro Slavery, and it was very timely. There was a resolution before the House to abolish slavery in all of England's colonies, so it was the most hotly debated topic of the day.

Young Gladstone believed that slavery should be abolished gradually and entirely, but it was not to express his views on it that he had chosen the subject. He spoke primarily in defense of his father, who had been publicly, and he felt, unjustly, accused of overworking his slaves, for Mr. Gladstone, senior, was a slave owner.

About the time that William had entered Eton his father had acquired a sugar plantation in the West Indies, and with it, of course, slaves. There was even then a movement on foot in England to abolish slavery. So a few years later when he heard that an uprising of the slaves had occurred on his far-off island, Mr. Gladstone attributed it to the meddling of the Abolitionists and their leader Mr. Wilberforce.

The Abolitionists claimed that the slaves had rebelled because of the cruelty of the overseer. Whatever may have been the immediate cause of it, the report of that uprising led slowly but surely to the resolution now proposed for freeing all the slaves in all of England's colonies.

In August 1833, two months after William Gladstone made his first speech in Parliament, and ten years after the uprising on his father's estate, the bill freeing the slaves was passed. The government bought them from their owners for $100,000,000 and gradually set them free.

The resolution had been hotly debated, however, before it was finally passed. Many other speeches on slavery were made on that same night in June when William Gladstone defended his father.

Seated in the gallery that night, peering down upon each speaker with unblinking interest through his steel-rimmed spectacles, was a youngish man from Boston, William Lloyd Garrison, by name. He had come to England for the very purpose of investigating the slavery problem.

Mr. Garrison was head of the movement for the abolition of slavery in the United States, and he was in deadly earnest. He was determined to free the American Negro, he said, even if he had to destroy the

Union to do so. With words of fire and brimstone he had condemned the Southern planters as sinners of the deepest dye, and the Constitution of the United States in dealing with them as "a covenant with death and an agreement with Hell!"

Those were the words he had printed in his newspaper the *Liberator,* which had first appeared on New Year's Day, 1831, and had since stirred up the greatest agitation wherever it was read.

"The man must have lost his senses," said the Southern planters. "What does he want to do, incite the negroes to murder us?"

Many Northerners, also, though opposed to slavery, were shocked at Mr. Garrison's violent words. One Boston paper called him a lunatic, and another urged people to "arm themselves with tar and feathers and when he returned from England give the man what he deserved."

Even the Reverend Mr. Beecher, strongly opposed as he was to the evil of slavery, did not see eye to eye with William Garrison. For a number of years past Mr. Beecher had been pastor of the church in Boston which William Lloyd Garrison attended. Just before the latter visited England, however, Mr. Beecher had accepted a call to be President of a Theological Seminary in Cincinnati, Ohio, and nine of the active Beecher family, including wiry little Harriet, had packed their bags and boxes and left by stage for the new home in the "West."

That move of the Beecher family was to be of consequence to the United States, for the town of Cincinnati was on the Ohio River, just over the border line from the slave state of Kentucky.

What Harriet Beecher saw there and later recorded in her famous story was to hasten the emancipation of the slaves.

Harriet was then twenty, and still not much bigger than a wren. She had been teaching school for the past six years, and it was not long after her arrival in Cincinnati, before she had tied on again her tidy black silk teacher's apron and was conducting classes, correcting papers, writing geography, composing a story about New England, and taking an active part in the Literary Society.

There she met a Professor Calvin Ellis Stowe, and a few years later after the death of his wife, was joined to him in the holy bonds of matrimony and so became Harriet Beecher Stowe.

It was during the first year after they were married, while Professor Stowe was on a trip abroad, and before the twins were born, that a riot over slavery occurred in Cincinnati.

"For a day or two," Harriet wrote her husband, "we did not know but there would actually be war to the knife."

The trouble had started this way: One summer a student at the Seminary, in order to earn his tuition, had lectured in the South, and seeing the evils of slavery had become an abolitionist. He in turn had converted a slave owner, who had freed his slaves and gone to Cincinnati to start an anti-slavery newspaper like the *Liberator*.

Kentucky slave owners immediately got wind of it. Wasn't one abolition paper enough? they exclaimed. Why let another get started? In an angry mob they came across the Ohio, marched to the newspaper office, broke in, smashed the presses and threw the type in the river. There was great commotion. Townspeople took sides at once.

"For my part," Harriet wrote, "I can easily see how such proceedings may make converts to abolitionism. No one can have the system of slavery brought before him without an irrepressible desire to *do* something; and what *is* there to be done?"

What *is* there to be done? That was the question everyone was asking all over the country.

Some years before, even before England set the example of purchasing the slaves, it had been proposed that the United States use the money from the sale of western lands to buy the slaves and set them free. The United States, however, deaf to suggestion, and blind to example, was to go on for years asking the question but avoiding the answer, until there would be but one tragic answer left.

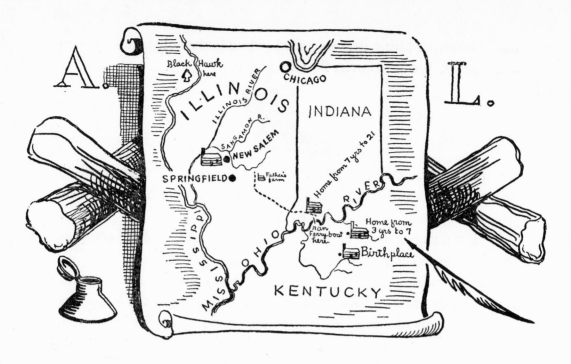

ABE LINCOLN OF NEW SALEM

THE SPRING of the year that the young Oxford graduate William Gladstone was elected to Parliament, and the little schoolma'am Harriet Beecher unpacked her black silk apron in Cincinnati, Abe Lincoln, who had never been to school a whole year in his life, announced that he would run for the State Legislature of Illinois. His friends in the log-cabin village of New Salem urged him to. He had been there less than a year, but everybody had taken a liking to the long, gaunt fellow, and, on the first day he arrived, he had had a hand, as you might say, in politics.

It had happened to be Election Day. Offut, his employer, had not yet arrived to start the new store, so Abe went loafing along the street past the Rutledge Tavern towards the voting place where the crowd was gathered. The election clerk, needing someone to help him, spied the newcomer and asked him if he knew how to write.

"I reckon I can make a few rabbit tracks on paper," drawled Abe. Folding his long legs under the table he took up the goose quill pen, and spent the rest of the day recording the names of the voters and sizing up their characters. James Rutledge was the man who owned the grist mill and the tavern and it seemed had a daughter by the name of Ann. The fattest, jolliest man in town was Squire Bowling Green, who was Justice of the Peace, and who chuckled till he wheezed over the comical stories Abe told that afternoon. He never did get over enjoying the one about the green lizard that ran up the preacher's pants.

After Election Day, still waiting for Offut to turn up, Abe got better acquainted. He saw Ann Rutledge, and though he didn't go in much for girls, she struck him as the sweetest thing he'd ever seen, with her blue eyes and hair between the color of gold and copper.

Finally the little man he was waiting for blew into town, full of big words and big ideas, ready to start his store. While Abe split logs and built the cabin for it, Offut patted himself on the back over the smart fellow he had hired. The last bolt of calico was hardly laid on the shelf, and the barrels of molasses and whiskey rolled into place before the storekeeper was promoting his clerk in extravagant terms.

"Abe Lincoln knows more," he boasted, "than any man in the United States. And strong! I bet you he can beat anyone in this country in a wrestling match."

"Not Jack Armstrong, I bet you," retorted Bill Clary, one of a rough rowdy gang known as the Clary Grove Boys who lived four miles away. "He can't beat Jack, I bet you ten."

A match was arranged to prove it. Abe said he didn't care much for that kind of "wooling and pulling," but he rolled up his sleeves and went at it, laid Jack Armstrong flat on his back in the dust, and won the lasting respect of the Clary gang. He was "the best feller," they swore, "that ever broke into the settlement."

"And the most honest one too," customers of the store were ready to add. One woman told how he had walked three miles to her place with six cents he'd overcharged her. Another said he was at her house before breakfast one day with a fourth pound of tea he'd measured short.

Honest, funny, shrewd, strong—Abe Lincoln had easily become the most popular man in New Salem, and so, by March, 1832, he had been persuaded to run for the legislature for which the elections were to be held in August. He was wondering what he could say to Ann Rutledge if he won, when suddenly his political affairs were interrupted.

It was on a wet morning early in April. Abe stood leaning in the doorway with an English grammar in his hand, when a man on a muddy horse came splashing down the street, calling for volunteers to fight the Indians! Black Hawk, he said, was back in Illinois!

No one needed to be told who Black Hawk was. Old Black Hawk, as everyone knew, was chief of the Sacs who had supposedly sold his northwest corner of Illinois to the United States and gone across the Mississippi River to live. Now he and his braves were back! Come to plant corn, they said, because the United States government hadn't kept its promise—but who cared what Indians said! The idea was to drive them out before they began to scalp and kill. So the governor was calling for volunteers . . . volunteers for the Black Hawk War.

Abe enlisted; so did the Clary Grove Boys. They elected him Captain. Didn't do any fighting, he said later, except against mosquitoes. But he tramped through fields of wild onions, saved the life of one old bewildered Indian who had wandered into camp, helped bury five men who had been scalped, told stories with the men around the campfire, and rolled in his blanket to dream more nights than one of a girl with blue eyes and coppery gold hair. Middle of July, when the war was over, he was mustered out at Whitewater, Wisconsin, and returned to New Salem to go on with his campaign.

It was at a county auction sale of bulls and hogs that he made his first election speech.

"Gentlemen and fellow citizens," he began. Then he stopped, stepped down from the platform, made his way through the men, picked up a trouble maker by the seat of the breeches and the scruff of the neck, pitched him out of the crowd, returned to the platform, and continued:

"Gentlemen and fellow citizens: I presume you all know who I am. I am humble Abraham Lincoln. I have been solicited by my friends to become a candidate for the legislature. My politics are short and sweet like the old woman's dance. I am in favor of a national bank. I am in favor of the internal-improvements system, and a high protective tariff. These are my sentiments and political principles. If elected, I shall be thankful; if not, it will be all the same."

He was not elected. There weren't enough people who knew him outside of New Salem. It didn't matter much. He was used to disappointments. Only he would like to have been elected an account of Ann. And by this time the store had failed. He was out of a job.

Didn't know what else to do, so he tried keeping store again, in partnership with a man named Berry. They paid for the store by giving notes, expecting to get out of debt when the store began to pay. But it didn't pay. Berry spent too much time sampling the whiskey. Lincoln spent too much time reading newspapers and the law. So the store "winked out." Abe was left with $1,100 worth of debts and no job again. And a young man who was a good businessman was engaged to Ann.

Things looked black. Abe was doing odd jobs to pay for meals and lodging when his friends got him the job of Postmaster in May, 1833.

After that the unexpected chance came to be a surveyor. He didn't know anything about surveying, but he got a book and studied day and night till, with the help of the school teacher, he had mastered the mathematics and was ready to start out with his chain and instrument. It was not long before the lanky surveyor, with his short trousers and comical stories, had made friends all over the county. When he ran for the legislature the next time, in 1834, Abe Lincoln was elected.

Ann looked pale and forlorn when he left for the state capital. The young man she was to marry had been gone for months. She was convinced that he had deserted her. There was not much then that Abe could say, but when he came back to New Salem in the spring, Ann turned to him and said that she would marry him. He had never been so happy. In August she was dead. Abe sat for days, his head in his hands, his clenched fingers in his coarse black hair, so deaf to all words, so plunged in a dry tearless grief, that friends despaired of his reason.

"REMEMBER THE ALAMO"

SOUTHWEST from the Cherokee village on the Arkansas, in November, 1832, went a lonely rider. Southwest from the wigwam of his Indian father old chief Oo-loo-te-ka, the man was riding, southwest through the dry grass of the windy prairies towards the Red River and the border of Texas. On his legs he wore fringed buckskin trousers, on his head a broad-brimmed white hat of beaver. Brass spurs jingled on his boots, and the rhythm of an old verse was in his heart:

"Fellow in arms whose deeds are known to fame . . ."

Sam Houston's heart was light with hope again. Ahead lay Texas, a new life for him—a new part to act. Behind him he was leaving the Sam Houston whose good name as Governor of Tennessee had been tarnished by slander. He was facing a new life. A new Sam Houston, he would redeem himself in the eyes of his great friend Andrew Jackson. He would capture Texas from Mexico, and lay a new empire at his hero's feet!

Confidently he rode the muddy trail of "el Camino Real" west to San Antonio and back east to the border. Then he wrote this letter:

"Gen. Jackson: Dear Sir:—Having been far in the province of Texas I am in possession of some information touching the acquisition of Texas by the United States. That such a measure is desired by nineteen-twentieths of the population I cannot doubt. Mexico is involved in civil war . . . powerless and penniless. Unless Mexico is soon restored to order my opinion is that Texas will, by 1st of April, declare all that country (north of the Rio Grande) as Texas proper and form a State Constitution. I expect to be present at the Convention and will apprise you of the course adopted.

"Your friend and obedient servant."

In this letter Sam Houston had gone ahead of the story. There were some at that time, but certainly not 19,000 Texans who wished to separate from Mexico.

Stephen Austin, Texas' foremost citizen, did not. Granted land in Texas when Mexico was first free from Spain, Austin had been for ten years a loyal Mexican citizen. The troubles that had recently arisen he was confident could be straightened out. After the Convention of April first he left for Mexico City, with the request that Texas be given a separate state government as granted by Mexican laws and the Mexican Constitution. Laws and Constitution? What cared Santa Anna for laws and Constitutions? Not a snap of his finger. And it was Santa Anna with whom Stephen Austin had to deal, for on April 1, 1833, Santa Anna had pronounced himself President of Mexico. Stephen Austin was thrown into prison. Instead of two months it was two years before he was free to return to Texas. Then said he, "War is our only recourse."

Texas went wild. There was a cry for independence—a call for volunteers. Santa Anna heard it. He sent hundreds of Mexican troops to Texas to put down the rebellion. A large garrison of soldiers under his brother-in-law fortified themselves in San Antonio. After some delay, the

159

volunteers attacked, and after four days' fighting, forced the Mexican general to surrender and drove out the Mexican troops. Texas people went wild again. "The war is over!" they cried. "War is over!"

"Over! The war has just begun," said Sam Houston, trying to organize and train a larger army, and also get Cherokee recruits enlisted before spring when he was sure Santa Anna would send his soldiers back again.

But Santa Anna did not wait for spring. In January, 1836, the infuriated little man himself was marching at the head of his soldiers over the winter desert to avenge the defeat of his brother-in-law. Towards San Antonio they were headed, and the mission fort in San Antonio known as the ALAMO. THE ALAMO!—It was held then by only a few ragged Texans. By February 22 the Mexicans were outside its walls, and had demanded its surrender. February 23 they laid siege to it. On February 24 the officer in command of the pitiful little band who were trying to defend it sent out this desperate but heroic message:

"To the People of Texas & All Americans in the world: . . .

"Am beseiged by a thousand or more of the Mexicans under Santa Anna. The enemy has demanded a surrender, otherwise the garrison are to be put to the sword if the fort is taken—I have answered the demand with a cannon shot & our flag still waves proudly from the wall. I SHALL NEVER SURRENDER OR RETREAT. THEN I call on you in the name of Liberty, of patriotism & everything dear to the American character, to come to our aid with all dispatch. I am determined to sustain myself as long as possible. . . . VICTORY OR DEATH.

"W. Barret Travis, Lt. Col. Com't."

Four days later, in the hands of a dusty rider, the note had reached Washington on the Brazos where delegates were then holding a convention to declare Texas independent.

The delegates were aghast but helpless. They had no troops at hand. Austin was not there. Houston had gone to the Indian country. The next day, however, he was back, dashing in on horseback in a Cherokee jacket, silver spurs and with a feather flying from his broad-brimmed hat. Then as large as that of John Hancock's, he scrawled his signature on the Texas Declaration of Independence, March 2, 1836.

Two days later with three volunteers he was off, to gather troops on the way, for the rescue of the Alamo, but that very day in the Alamo all was over. Halfway there, Sam Houston heard the ghastly story. It had been death for all the defenders of the mission fort. Only three survivors lived to tell the story, a wife, her baby, and a Negro servant.

Before the end of March another American force had been defeated. Settlers, volunteers—everyone was terrified. A scrambling retreat towards the east began. Men, women, children, carts, wagons, cattle, horses all in the most disorderly confusion, with Sam Houston trying to organize the panicky mob and also cheer up his fighting men.

On the San Jacinto River they halted, and there the Mexicans caught up with them. Until April 21 not much happened. Then during the siesta hour of early afternoon, when he knew the Mexicans would be sleeping, Sam Houston gave the order to attack their camp.

"Remember the Alamo!" was the cry. "Remember the Alamo! Remember the Alamo!" cried the Texans as they went pouring into Santa Anna's camp down upon his sleeping soldiers. Only twenty minutes and the Mexicans were overpowered and the battle ended, but in those twenty minutes Santa Anna had managed to escape. That night he was not among the prisoners. The next day, however, he was picked up, disguised in a blue cotton smock, and brought into camp.

Sam Houston was lying under an oak tree having his splintered ankle dressed and writing a note to President Jackson, when the little man in the blue smock and red felt slippers was brought up to him.

"I am General Antonio Lopez de Santa Anna," said the man bowing deeply. "President of Mexico, Commander in Chief of the Army. I place myself at the disposal of the brave General Houston. Born to no common destiny is he who has conquered the Napoleon of the West. It now remains for him to be generous to the conquered."

Some of the officers wanted Santa Anna killed at once. Sam Houston saved his life, and within the year he was sent back to Mexico.

"Restored to his own country Santa Anna will keep Mexico in commotion for years," said Houston, shrewdly, "and Texas will be safe."

So Texas became the Lone Star Republic, and, on October 22, 1836, Sam Houston took his oath as its first President. Almost the first act of the new republic was to ask to become part of the United States. In March, 1837, the last act of Andrew Jackson as President was to recognize the independence of Texas, and though he also wanted to see it admitted to the Union, that was not to be so easily accomplished.

Texas was a SLAVE state, that was reason enough to make the free states of the North shout a positive NO to the question of adding it to the Union, and slave states of the South reply with an equally positive YES. So for eight years, until just before Andrew Jackson died, the Texas question was to be argued back and forth and remain unanswered.

ON TO OREGON

WHILE TEXAS was fighting for independence from Mexico, far to the northwest wagon-wheels were rumbling for the first time over the long trail to Oregon. Five missionaries were going to work among the Indians. Two were brides,

162

the first white women ever to cross the Rocky Mountains. One was bright Narcissa Whitman, the brave-eyed young wife of Dr. Marcus Whitman, who had organized the party in response to the Indians' request.

It seems strange that four years before while poor old Black Hawk was making his last stand against the white man's greed, four Nez Perces Indians from Oregon had been traveling eastward seeking the White Man's Book of Heaven. From it they had been told they might learn a better way to worship the Great Spirit.

The end of a two-thousand-mile trail brought them to St. Louis, where General Clark at the barracks recognized them at once. Thirty years before on the expedition with Lewis he had passed through the home of these Indians in the Columbia River valley. They were most cordially received. All winter they were feasted and entertained, but they were disappointed. At the farewell dinner in the spring one of the two who were still living rose and addressed the company.

"I came to you over the trail of many moons from the setting sun. My people sent me to get the white man's Book of Heaven. You took me to where you allow your women to dance, as we do not ours: and the Book was not there! You took me to where they worship the Great Spirit with candles and images, and the Book was not there. You make my feet heavy with gifts, and yet the Book is not among them! I came with an eye partly open for my people who sit in darkness. How can I go back blind to my blind people? I have no more words."

The story of their visit published in a New York City religious journal was accompanied by a cry for missionaries to "respond to the call from beyond the Rocky Mountains." Two Canadians went first.

In the spring of 1835, Marcus Whitman was on his way, going with the annual caravan of fur traders from Independence, Missouri, when they set out for the northwest. Halfway to Oregon, seeing the need, Dr. Whitman returned to New York State to get more volunteers who would be ready to accompany the fur traders on their next spring's trip.

Marcus found Narcissa was willing to marry him and go, but he felt she might be lonely without another woman, and was glad when Eliza

Spaulding, in spite of delicate health, assured her husband that she also "had made up her mind for Oregon." Full of courage they started for Pittsburgh and down the Ohio River. At St. Louis the fur traders looked askance at the little party, at the women in their long skirts and the four-wheeled wagon that was to go, and refused to take them. Even after finally promising to, they slipped off without them.

Undaunted, the Whitman party set out alone, and after two weeks' chase finally overtook the fur traders and their caravan of two hundred persons and six hundred animals. Well—the fur traders had to admit that the women had spunk, 'n if they could live on buffalo meat, and not hold up the procession, they could come along—but NOT the wagon!

"Can't git a wagon over the mountings," they said, "tain't possible."

Marcus Whitman just smiled in his big quiet way, and took his wagon. On they went, through sagebrush, over rocks, down the river banks, up the canyons, and on went the wagon, through sagebrush, over rocks, down the river banks and up the canyons.

"Chick-chick-shan-i-le-kai-kash," cried the Indians when they saw it, trying to imitate the sound it made rustling through the grass and bumping over the rocks. They had never seen a wagon before. Nor had they seen white women. Their excitement was tremendous.

By July 4, 1836, the travelers had reached the Continental Divide in Western Wyoming. At twelve noon they had gone through the Pass and were able to celebrate Independence Day on the sunset slope where the rivers were flowing west. Women and a wagon had crossed the Rocky Mountains, and would soon enter Oregon.

At the rendezvous of the traders and Indians, agents of the Hudson Bay Trading Company of Canada met the Whitman party and guided them down the Columbia River in their bateaus to Fort Van Couver. There they were made welcome by snowy-haired, big-hearted Dr. Mc-Loughlin, who was in charge of the English fort. Oregon territory was then still held jointly by the United States and England.

At Walla Walla on the Columbia River, the Whitmans founded their first mission and opened to the Indians the white man's Book of Heaven.

INTO DARKEST AFRICA

DARKEST AFRICA" it was called when David Livingstone was moved to go to the great continent as a medical missionary. The young Scotsman, who was to become Africa's famous explorer, sent in his application to the London Missionary Society, the year that Dr. Marcus Whitman, also a medical missionary, took the Bible to Oregon.

David Livingstone was twenty-three years old that winter. Big, broad-shouldered, quiet-spoken, he was attending medical and divinity classes in Glasgow. In the summer he would return to his home in Blantyre to work in the cotton mill, as he had done since he was ten years old.

As a small boy he had begun as a "piecer," knotting the broken threads on the weaving machine, keeping at it from six in the morning until eight at night. After factory hours he had gone to night school until ten o'clock and then would go home to study, until his mother snatched the book away, sent him to bed and blew out the candle.

By the time he was nineteen he was promoted to work at the spinning jenny, and by frugal living had been able to save enough to study winters in Glasgow. He had studied hard, and was hoping that he might be sent to China, when he wrote out his application, but when he appeared before the examining board, he was told that he was not clever enough for a post in China or India either. His sermons were not eloquent, it seemed, and his prayers were not drawn out long enough. They were about to reject the poor disappointed fellow entirely, when someone suggested that there might be a niche for him in Africa.

One of their men who had founded a post seven hundred miles north of Capetown in the jungle called at Livingstone's boarding house one evening. He told of the vastness of Africa, of the thousands of villages where no white man had ever been, talked of the great work to be done, talked till the light shone in David Livingstone's eyes and he made his plans to go. Late in November, 1840, he went home to his village in Scotland to spend the last night with his family. There was so much to talk about with his father that he proposed staying up all night, but his mother would not hear of it, and blew out the candle.

"In the morning," said his sister later, "I remember we got up at five o'clock. Mother made coffee. David read the 121st and 135th Psalms and prayed. Then my father and he walked to Glasgow to catch the Liverpool steamer."

The little bent figure standing on the misty shore was the last sight David Livingstone ever had of his father, for now his face was set towards Africa, and for many years he would be lost to civilization. Very quiet, very patient, very sure, David Livingstone, a man who lived what he believed, was starting out to make "religion the every-day business of his life." Arriving at Capetown, he traveled north the seven hundred miles to the mission post, and from there on into the unknown interior.

And the leaves of the jungle closed behind him.

YOUNG LION VS. ANCIENT DRAGON

EVEN if he had been considered clever enough, David Livingstone could not have gone to China at that time. Traders, guns and opium, not missionaries, were then introducing China to the civilization of the west. The "abominable opium war" was on— the first war between any modern nation and the old Empire of China.

It began in the summer of 1839, about the time that Li Hung Chang, far back in his little village, saw many men ruined by the foreign drug. That summer down at Canton, the only port where the barbarians were allowed to trade, 2,500,000 pounds of the black sticky sweet opium was seized by order of the Chinese Emperor, deliberately ruined with lime and sea water and destroyed.

To the British traders who had brought it there from India against the Chinese law, that much opium was worth $11,000,000 even after the greedy, dishonest Chinese mandarins who allowed it to be smuggled in had received their bribe. When the first orders came from the Emperor to surrender the opium, the British refused.

But the Emperor Tao Kwang was in earnest. He had seen three of his own sons killed by opium, and was determined to do away with it.

Food and water supply were shut off from the British traders and their families at Canton, until they were obliged to surrender the opium and take refuge on the barren rocky island of Hong Kong.

As there was no telegraph, no cable, no Suez Canal to shorten the sailing distance, it was months before the news of their plight reached England and British warships returned. Returned, you understand, to protect the rights and lives of the citizens, not to protect those merchants engaged in the unlawful trade. Though they did nothing to stop it the English government would not protect it. The opium business, however, they chose to regard as a minor point.

The important thing was that the time had come to force China to treat the English as equals, not as barbarians. The old wall of pride and prejudice against all who were not Chinese had to be broken down.

It was not a difficult war to win. Compared to the English battleships the Chinese junks were like minnows to a whale. August 28, 1842, the treaty of Nanking was signed and China humiliated.

Five ports, instead of one at Canton, were opened to foreign trade.

Hong Kong was ceded to the British.

All the opium destroyed was to be paid for by the Chinese. Also the cost of the war (nothing else was said about opium).

Nothing was said about "equality" between the two nations either, but those who understood the Chinese custom of showing honor in documents saw that that point too had been surrendered.

The characters for England as well as those for Great China were

raised one space above the top row of the text.

Those for the Emperor Tao Kwang were raised two spaces, as usual, and for the first time the same honor was paid the ruler of another nation, in this case a Queen, for Victoria was now Queen of England.

"R" STANDS FOR REGINA

V ICTORIA WROTE in her diary faithfully every night before she went to bed, underlining all the words that she thought were especially important. And she often wrote to her Dearest, most Beloved Uncle Leopold in Belgium. She did both on the memorable day when she became Queen of England. The diary reads:

"Tuesday, 20th June 1837

"I was awoke at 6 o'clock by Mamma, who told me that the Archbishop of Canterbury and Lord Conyngham were here, and wished to see me. I got out of bed and went into my sitting-room (only in my dressing gown) and ALONE, and saw them. Lord C. then acquainted me that my poor Uncle the King was no more and had expired 12 minutes past 2 this morning, and consequently that I am QUEEN. . . . Since it has pleased Providence to place me in this station, I shall do my utmost to fulfill my duty towards my country . . . I am very young, but I am sure that very few have more real desire to do what is fit and right than I have.

"Breakfasted . . . Wrote a letter to dear Uncle Leopold and a few words to dear good Feodore. At 9 came Lord Melbourne, whom I saw in my room and OF COURSE QUITE ALONE. He was in full dress. I like him very much and feel confidence in him . . . At about half past 11 I went downstairs and held a Council in the red saloon . . . I was not at all nervous and had the satisfaction of hearing that people were satisfied with what I had done and how I had done it. . . . Wrote my journal. Took my dinner upstairs alone. Went downstairs. At about twenty minutes to 9 came Lord Melbourne and remained till near 10. I had a very important and a very *comfortable* conversation with him. Went down and said good-night to Mamma, etc. My DEAR Lehzen will ALWAYS remain with me as my friend. . . .

The letter written to Uncle Leopold told in a few words what had happened in the early morning. Many letters were exchanged between them before this one written a year later after the Coronation Ceremony:

"Buckingham Palace, 2nd July 1838

"MY DEAREST UNCLE:

"MANY thanks for TWO kind letters, one which I got last Monday. The kind interest you take in me and my country makes me certain that you will be glad to hear how BEAUTIFULLY every thing went off. It was a memorable and glorious day for me. The millions assembled to witness the progress to and from the Abbey was BEYOND belief, and ALL in the highest good-humour. It is a fine ceremony and a scene I shall EVER remember, and with pleasure. I likewise venture to add that people thought I did my part very well.

"Pray tell dearest Aunt Louise that I thank her much for her very kind letter. Ever and ever your most devoted niece,

Victoria R.

CORN AND POTATOES

POOR LITTLE QUEEN," sighed a certain English author, "she is at an age when she would hardly be trusted with the choosing of a bonnet, and she is called for a task, from which an archangel might shrink." Britain, he knew, had many unhappy people, both at home and in the colonies, clamoring for their rights. Working people of England wanted the vote; Ireland wanted a separate Parliament; Canada wanted a better government, and the free settlers in Australia wanted no more convicts. And no more were sent there after 1837. That demand was granted; the others were questions for debate.

It was the Irish Question that young Disraeli, now a newly elected member, chose for his first speech in the House of Commons. Well prepared, he rose with confidence, expecting the courteous attention usually accorded a new member's first attempt. Instead he was greeted with such an outburst of hoots, hisses, catcalls and laughter that though he tried to continue, he was obliged to sit down, humiliated.

The followers of O'Connell, the Irish leader, had started the commotion because they wanted to hear no reply to the speech which O'Connell himself had just made concerning the grievances of Ireland.

They were indeed many, those griefs of Ireland, and too long endured. Nine-tenths of the people were Catholics. Though long excluded, Catholics had recently been allowed to become members of Parliament, but they still had to support the Church of England. This was especially hard for the Irish people, because they were very poor. Three-fourths of the land of Ireland was owned by English landlords who charged their poor tenants such high rent for their small farms that, after they had sold their crops to pay it, they had almost nothing left to eat except potatoes. Irish leaders thought that there was little hope to better conditions unless Ireland had a separate parliament.

For the same reason the working people of England wanted to get the vote. Their employers still paid the factory workers starvation wages, and the cost of food was kept high by a tax.

This tax was called the Corn Law. (The word "Corn" was used in England to mean all kinds of cereal and grain.) Since England had too little land on her small island to raise food enough for her population, most of it had to be brought in from other countries. Yet in order to protect those few English landlords who raised what little grain was grown there was a high tax on all imported food. That made the price so high that the poor could scarcely buy enough to keep from starving.

For years, Liberal leaders in Parliament had tried to get the Corn Laws repealed, but in vain. The landlords opposed it and the working people were told conditions would never change until they got the vote.

In 1839 they were determined to try for it and drew up a petition to Parliament known as "The People's Charter," asking for the vote. It was signed by over a million names, but was rejected. Later another petition was drawn up, signed this time by *three* million names. It made such a huge roll that, after the "Chartists" had carried it proudly through the London streets to the House of Commons, they found it wouldn't go through the door. It had to be cut in pieces before it could be presented. It was voted down again by a huge majority.

The working people of England, therefore, were in a helpless, miserable condition, the common people of Ireland were desperately poor, while the pioneers and common people of America were more prosperous in 1837 than they had ever been before.

Opening the vast prairies of the West had brought abounding prosperity to the United States. There was land enough for every man to own his own farm and raise more food than he could possibly eat.

"I leave this great country prosperous and happy," said Andrew Jackson, whose term as President ended the year Victoria became Queen.

And then a strange thing happened. In the midst of this great prosperity, in spite of the fact that by the sale of western lands, the United States was completely out of debt and had $40,000,000 surplus, there came a financial panic. Andrew Jackson was hardly out of office when banks began to fail, factories closed, business houses crashed and people were frantic for money.

What had caused it? Nobody knew. But this is what had happened: First, Andrew Jackson had destroyed the "National" Bank. Believing that it was dangerous for a few bankers to control all the government money as they did at that time, he removed it from their "National" Bank. So far so good. But the government funds, taken from the bank, he then deposited in "pet" banks in the different states, and that was not so good. With all that easy money to spend, state politicians went to building roads, canals and railroads at a terrific rate. People borrowed large sums to gamble on western land, and fell for all kinds of crazy schemes to get rich quick, even investing in land that didn't exist. New and unreliable state banks issued worthless paper money to spend, and spending whirled on faster and crazier until Jackson had to jam on the brakes and stop it. He demanded that all further purchases of government land must be paid for NOT with paper money, but in COIN.

COIN? Where was it? Who had it? Nobody. No one could get hold of enough money to pay his debts. So came the crash. Fortunately it lasted only a year and good came out of it.

The United States established its Independent Treasury system by which government funds were to be managed in a businessiike way, and not by private bankers or politicians. Credit for this excellent system goes to Martin Van Buren, who followed Andrew Jackson as President.

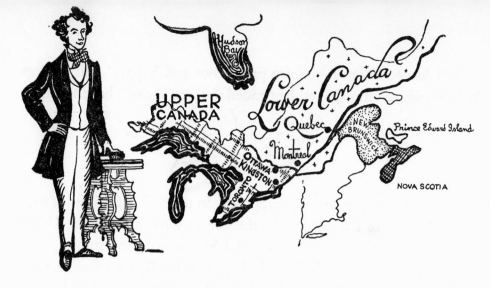

REBELLION IN CANADA

CANADA WAS SEETHING with discontent, the year that Victoria became Queen. And that year, while the United States was having a financial panic, rebellion against the government broke out in both Upper and Lower Canada. Those were the only provinces in British North America that used the name "Canada" in 1837. And none of them were united, all distinct in character and government as the thirteen colonies of the United States had been originally.

LOWER Canada, down the St. Lawrence, was the old French province of Quebec. Though some English were living there, most of Quebec's people were French, holding to their language, their customs and their church. UPPER Canada (now Ontario) had then only about one-sixth of the population of Quebec, but they were English-speaking. Many were descendants of loyalist refugees from the United States during the War for Independence. Many others had come from Scotland, as had the family of John Alexander Macdonald, a young man who was later to play the leading part in making a loyal and united Canada.

John A., a lean lanky lad, with a long nubby nose, was easily the homeliest fellow in Kingston. But he had a friendly manner, and always a good story to tell. Though only twenty-two the year of the rebellion he had already opened his own office as Barrister-at-Law. That spoke well for him, since at fifteen he had had to stop school and go to work.

Mr. Macdonald had not prospered so heartily in the New World as he had hoped to do when he set out with his little family from Glasgow. John A. was only five then, but he could remember the big boat that brought them to Quebec, and the long bumpy ride over the rough forest roads of Upper Canada to the town of Kingston. There John A. first went to school, and then was put to work in the office of a lawyer.

Later in life, he said he never would forget the first case he was allowed to try in court. He was eighteen, and it seems that both he and the opposing lawyer lost their tempers and took to their fists. "Order in court! Order!" shouted the old crier, circling about the flying fists. But each time he came around he whispered to his favorite, "Hit 'im again, John. Hit 'im again!" All his life John A. said that whenever he was in a tight pinch, he would hear the encouraging voice of the old crier.

At the time of the rebellion in 1837, John A. carried his musket and marched to Toronto, the capital—not to join MacKenzie and the rebels, but to help disperse them. That was soon accomplished, for they were few in number. Though all of the people of Upper Canada, except a few families who made up the governor's council, were dissatisfied, because they had no voice in the government, the majority were lawabiding, and did not approve of using violence to gain reform.

It was much the same in Lower Canada. There, too, a group of the more excitable people, inspired by the orator Papineau, and carrying liberty caps and French flags, marched against the government at Montreal. There, too the rebellion was easily put down. But it brought results.

It made the British government realize that something was very wrong in Canada, and take steps to correct it before it was too late.

Lord Durham was sent in 1838 to investigate the situation. His very wise report led in 1840 to an Act to Unite Upper and Lower Canada, under a single governor, who was "to oppose the wishes of the assembly only when the interests of the Empire were concerned." This was not to work well at first, but it was a step towards government by the people, and towards the final founding of the loyal Dominion.

The Sirius

The Savannah

The Great Western

STEAM ACROSS THE ATLANTIC

CROSS THE Atlantic Ocean by Steam Navigation? Bah! sniffed a learned Doctor of Liverpool, throwing aside his newspaper in which he had just read of the proposed attempt. "Men might as well project a voyage to the moon!" Already the *Royal William* from Canada and the *Savannah* out of New York City had made the attempt, but what proof was that? They had come only part way by steam; when the fuel gave out they had had to resort to sails. That was the trouble. No boat would ever be able to carry enough fuel to make the trip. Such was the Doctor's opinion in 1835.

Three years later, opening his paper filled with accounts of the coming Coronation Ceremony of his Queen Victoria, the skeptical Doctor was to discover that the impossible had been accomplished. Not one, but two ships propelled by steam had crossed the Atlantic Ocean.

It had marked the finish of an exciting race between two rival steamship companies, each eager to win the honor of crossing first. One, headed by an American living in London, had been building the *British Queen*, while an English Railway Company had been working at top speed on their first ship which was to be christened the *Great Western*.

On April 7, 1838, with the *British Queen* still unfinished, the *Great*

Western left Liverpool, and steaming along at eight and a half knots per hour reached New York City on the fifteenth day. The proud captain, sure that their arrival would be the signal for a great celebration, found to his amazement the celebration already in progress. What ship could possibly have beaten him, and how and why?

It was the *Sirius*, just a little coasting steamer, which the owners of the *British Queen* had chartered in a last desperate moment. Filling every inch of available space with coal, they had sent it out from Cork, four days after the *Great Western* left Liverpool. Chugging steadily along, the little craft had steamed into New York harbor on April 22, just six hours ahead of the *Great Western*.

So technically the *Sirius* had won, but not actually. The coal had given out and, in order to complete the stunt, mast, spars, furniture from the cabins, everything that would burn, had to be thrown into the boiler. The *Great Western*, however, had five days' supply of coal left, and besides had carried a real cargo. So she was the ship that actually opened the era of transatlantic steamship service.

FIFTEEN days from Europe to America! The average speed by sail was a few days over a month. Measured by traveling hours, the width, then, of the Atlantic Ocean had been divided by two, and the people of the Old World and the New brought that much closer together.

177

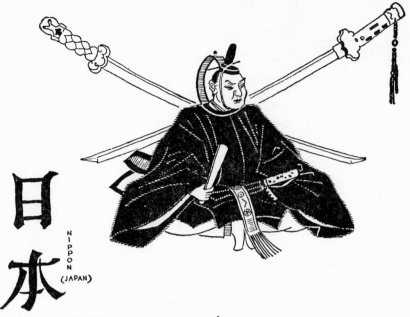

日本

BEHIND JAPAN'S CLOSED DOOR

JUST A LITTLE less than a year before these first steamships crossed the Atlantic, out on the Pacific an American sailing ship, the *Morrison*, attempted to enter a harbor of Japan. At sight of it, a hundred samurai, or warriors, rushed to the water's edge, scowling furiously, raised their old-fashioned muskets and began firing at it. The crew tried to get word to them that the ship was unarmed and that they were only bringing home seven shipwrecked Japanese sailors picked up on the Aleutian Islands and the Philippines. No matter. The ship was not allowed to land.

Japan's door to the outside world was still closed and bolted in 1837, as it had been for over two hundred years. Japanese knew nothing of the outside world and did not care to. Nor did they intend barbarians to enter and pollute the sacred land of the gods. The samurai, guarding the harbor, were but discharging their duty to the Emperor, or rather to the Shogun, military overlord and real ruler of Japan.

These particular samurai were members of the Hikone clan. So, too, was NAOSUKE II who, sixteen years later, when another American ship

178

should enter that same harbor, would dare to defy his narrow-minded countrymen and unbolt the closed door of Japan.

Naosuke would then be Baron Ii, fourteenth Lord of Hikone Castle, head of the clan, and Prime Minister of Japan, holding power second only to the Shogun. But now Naosuke, poor fellow, had slim hope for the future. A younger son, he was living alone in the country. Often at night, when he unrolled his sleeping pad and gave a last look at the moon shining on his lonely house, he felt that he was being "buried alive" and, like a piece of buried wood, might turn to stone.

His only consolation was that he was obeying the will of his honorable ancestor, the first Lord Ii, who had decreed that any descendant of his not first-born or adopted should be brought up in a most humble manner, believing as he did that hardships make a man grow strong. So it was with Naosuke.

Though the future looked dark, he determined to prepare himself so thoroughly that if the opportunity ever came to him, he might serve his country in a manner worthy of his honorable ancestor.

Constantly he studied literature and swordsmanship, and especially the art of dealing with an enemy in sitting position. He allowed himself only four hours' sleep a day, in order that by untiring practice he might enter the "serene state of perfect mastery."

"Nothing is more abominable to me," he said, "than to give up what I have set my hand to before it is fully accomplished." So for nine years he kept at his studies and with no change in his fortune.

Then in the spring came a sudden and unexpected summons to Yedo, the capital. His elder brother had died, and he, Naosuke, was heir to the title. He was to become the Baron Ii, Lord of Hikone!

Almost overwhelmed at the remarkable change in his fortune, he set out for Yedo, attended now by a large following of retainers. Seated in his palanquin, he drew the curtains, and "secretly," he said, "shed tears of gratitude." His chance to serve had come at last.

In Yedo Naosuke began at once to school himself in government affairs. The most agitating problem of the day, he found, was in regard to foreigners who became each year more annoying and persistent.

"How this foreign question will terminate no one knows," wrote Naosuke in his journal. "Though it is commonly believed that foreign vessels will not come to our shores during the winter season, we cannot be sure of this; because there is a rumor that a newly invented fire boat is shortly coming to pay us a visit. Heaven only knows what mighty calamity may befall our Empire. I can but heave great sighs!"

(An old Card)

" A New and much admired Pear to be introduced at the Royal Table "

WEDDING BELLS

VICTORIA WAS having such a glorious time being Queen, doing as she pleased, seeing people *alone*, and even sleeping alone in a room without her mother, that she had almost forgotten about Albert. At least, in 1839, she wanted to put off marrying him for a while, even though it was dear Uncle Leopold's wish. Albert and Ernest were coming to London on a second visit, and she wasn't sure that her *feelings* towards Albert might be "any more than that of a *cousin.*"

Three years had passed since the German cousins had made their first visit to London. Then Victoria had found them all that Grossmutter had pictured them—especially Albert!

"Albert is extremely handsome," she had written Uncle Leopold, "and possesses every quality that could be desired to render me perfectly happy!" And so she felt again when she saw him that autumn of 1839.

On his third day there, with a little flutter in her heart, she proposed to him and he accepted. It was her place as Queen to speak first and his duty to accept. He had long prepared himself to do so, though the thought of leaving home for a strange land where, as a foreign prince, he would not be too welcome, filled him with melancholy.

"My future lot is high and brilliant," he wrote a friend, "but also plentifully strewn with thorns."

They were married on the tenth of February, 1840, and left London after the ceremony for a three-day honeymoon at Windsor Castle. From there the bride wrote her uncle a letter bubbling with joy.

"Windsor Castle, 11th February 1840

"My Dearest Uncle—

"I write you from here, the happiest, happiest Being that ever existed. Really I do not think it *possible* for any one in the world to be *happier*, or AS happy as I am. Albert is an *angel*, and his kindness and affection for me is really touching. To look in those dear eyes, and that dear sunny face, is enough to make me adore him. What I can do to make him happy will be my greatest delight. . . .

"My love to dear Louise.

"Ever your affectionate,

Victoria R

181

Mary Todd became engaged to Abraham Lincoln the year Victoria was married. Mary Todd had always told the girls at school back home in Lexington, Kentucky, that the man she was going to marry would become President of the United States. Mary was the smartest, wittiest, most high-spirited girl in school, the daughter of Robert Todd, President of the First National Bank. She was a fiery little trick, with a saucy tongue and a violent temper.

One day in 1840 after a tiff with her stepmother, she flounced upstairs, packed her trunk, and announced that she was going to visit her sister, Mrs. Ninian Edwards, in Springfield, Illinois.

One of the first men she saw there was Abraham Lincoln, the young law partner of her cousin, Major Stuart. It was at a cotillion. She was dancing with Stephen A. Douglas, who, by the way, was not much taller than she was herself, when she spied with her bright eyes a tall fellow with his necktie just a shade askew, standing near the refreshment table, evidently telling a group of men some highly amusing story.

Mary Todd and Abe Lincoln danced the next waltz together. They talked about French and Geometry, or rather she did the talking, while he admired her cleverness, and tried to keep his big feet out of the way of her little slippers. She made fun of him afterward.

"When Mr. Lincoln asked me to dance with him," she told her sister, "he said, 'Miss Todd, I'd like to dance with you the worst way,' and—" she added, "he did!"

Six months later, Miss Mary Todd, giving no heed to her brother-in-law's opinion that he was not socially eligible as a husband, became engaged to marry Abraham Lincoln. She wrote the girls in Lexington about her engagement to the awkward fellow, but she said,

"I mean to make him President of the United States. You will see that as I always told you, I will yet be the President's wife."

Springfield was expecting to hear of the wedding, when rumor had it that Lincoln had taken out no license. Then it was learned in January that the engagement was broken off. Many conflicting reasons were circulated by neighbors who, of course, could only guess at the facts.

Whatever the cause, Lincoln was plunged by it into the blackest despondency, despair, regret and self-reproach. All New Year's night he wandered about like a man bereft of his reason, while his friends searched for him, fearing that he might kill himself. Too upset to even take his seat at the sessions of the legislature, he finally sought rest and peace at the home of a friend in Kentucky.

Early the next autumn he was back in Springfield working feverishly —working to forget his trouble, people said. As the months wore on through winter, spring and the following summer, they wondered, as people will, if he ever saw Mary Todd. In November, 1842, they learned the answer. The *Springfield Journal* carried this announcement:

"MARRIED. In this city on the 4th instant, at the residence of N. W. Edwards Esq., ABRAHAM LINCOLN Esq.; to Miss MARY TODD, daughter of Robert Todd Esq., of Lexington, Ky."

It had not been a happy wedding. There was just a handful of guests. The night was stormy. The rain came streaming down the windows as Mary Todd looked up at the future President of the United States and he slipped on her small plump finger a ring in which were engraved the words: *Love is eternal.*

AUTHORS & VISITORS

JANUARY 22, 1842, the year that Abraham Lincoln was married, Charles Dickens, Esq., the famous young English author "and his lady" arrived in Boston on the steamship *Britannia,* for a six months' visit in America. It was Dickens' first visit, and his first trip on a steamship. Neither ended as happily as it had begun. He had gone aboard in Liverpool in the highest of spirits, but the third morning out he was awakened, he said, "out of my sleep by a dismal shriek from my wife. Then I began to comprehend that the stateroom is standing on its head . . . the ship rights . . . before one can say 'Thank Heaven!' she wrongs again . . . she takes a high leap into the air . . . she throws a somerset. And so she goes on staggering, heaving, wrestling, leaping, diving, jumping, pitching, throbbing, rolling and rocking." It was appalling and horrible. Words could not express it.

Words almost failed to express also the wildly enthusiastic reception that America gave the author of the popular *Pickwick Papers* when to his infinite relief he was able to set foot on land again.

184

"There never was a King or Emperor upon earth so cheered and followed by crowds," he wrote to a friend at home, "and entertained at splendid balls and dinners. If I go out in a carriage, the crowd surrounds it and escorts me home; if I go to the theatre, the whole house (crowded to the roof) rises as one man and the timbers ring again. I have five public dinners on hand at this very moment, and invitations from every town and village and city in the United States."

Perhaps if he had stayed in Boston or New York where he seemed to enjoy himself the visitor might have kept his happy outlook on America. But after he had visited all the prisons and asylums, taken a trip on a crowded river steamer, and bumped over rough corduroy roads to the frontier city of St. Louis, he was so peevish and nervous, so sick and tired and "fed up" with America, that all he could see were men chewing and spitting great "gobs" of tobacco. All he could think of was getting "home,—home,—home,—Home,—HOME!!!"

At home again, he dashed off a book called *American Notes* which made such distasteful reading to his former hosts, that "All Yankee-doodle-dum," to quote Thomas Carlyle, "blazed up like one universal soda bottle." But the book sold well, and so perhaps achieved the purpose of its author. Before leaving England, in writing *Pickwick Papers*, he had had old Mr. Weller suggest sending Mr. Pickwick to "Merriker" and then having him "come back and write a book about the 'Merrikins as'll pay all his expenses and more, if he blows 'em up enough."

Emerson was one American too wise to take it seriously. On November 25, that wisest and most gentle of men was writing in his Journal of having read Dickens' book the day before. "It answers its end very well," he wrote, "which was plainly to make a readable book, nothing more. Truth is not Dickens' object for a single instant."

Mr. Emerson was seated that morning as usual among his books in the quiet village of Concord, Massachusetts. On his desk, beyond the open notebook stood a bowl of russet apples. Outside the snow was falling. He watched the soft flakes filling in the fresh footprints made by young Thoreau, who had just tramped off towards the river. He was wondering also how his friend Mr. Alcott was succeeding in England.

Mr. Emerson was fond of Mr. Alcott. He had given six lectures in New York that spring to make his friend's trip possible. He was also to help with the purchase of a home for the Alcott family, about a third of a mile away down the Boston Post Road. It was the one which Louisa May was later to describe as the home of *Little Women.*

Louisa May, or Jo, a wild high-spirited little tomboy, was ten years old in 1842. She adored Mr. Emerson. By the time she had reached the romantic age of fifteen she had taken him for her hero.

"I wrote him letters," she said, "but never sent them, left wild flowers on his doorstep, sat in a tall cherry tree at midnight singing to the moon till the owls scared me to bed."

It was in 1847 that Mr. Emerson was invited to lecture in England, and sailed for Liverpool on the *Washington Irving.* He enjoyed his visit, understood and liked the people, and won all he met by his gentle charm, despite what he called his "porcupine manners." Thomas Carlyle, then the most celebrated writer in England, showed him about London, where he met Dickens, Thackeray and Disraeli. George Stephenson, inventor of the locomotive, invited him to dinner, and Emerson thought the old Scotsman the most remarkable man he had seen in England. He went to visit Wordsworth, and found the poet, who was then eighty years old, just waking up from a nap, and not very hospitable at first. Tennyson, who was soon to succeed Wordsworth as Poet Laureate, reminded Emerson of his friend in Concord, Nathaniel Hawthorne.

"Take away Hawthorne's bashfulness," he said, "and let him talk easily and fast and you would have a pretty good Tennyson."

All in all it was a most interesting, successful and friendly visit. Nevertheless "I shall bring home," he wrote Mrs. Emerson, "a contentedness with home, I think for the rest of my days."

Returning to America in July, 1848, he began a series of lectures on his experiences in England, and wrote a most interesting and understanding book about the English people entitled *English Traits.*

TELEGRAPH AND PHOTOGRAPH

W HAT HATH GOD WROUGHT

That is the first message ever sent by the electric telegraph. It went in dots and dashes over the first telegraph wires in the world, from Washington to Baltimore, on the morning of May 24, 1844. Four years before, the first photograph of a human face had been made. Almost simultaneously they were perfected, those two inventions upon which the world today depends so much for news and information—the TELE- and the PHOTO- graph, Greek words, meaning "far-off writing" and "writing by light."

Samuel Finley Breese Morse is known as the inventor of the telegraph and the credit for the invention of the photograph, or daguerreotype as it was then called, is given to the Frenchman DAGUERRE.

Samuel Morse visited M. Daguerre in Paris in 1839, and so saw the Frenchman's invention the year it was perfected. In turn, Morse showed Daguerre his newly completed telegraph, for which he had come to Europe to try to secure foreign patents.

A portrait painter by profession, Samuel Morse was thrilled by the exquisite detail shown in the daguerreotypes, and was delighted to take one home with him to America. It was the first photograph ever seen in the United States.

Every scientific invention is the result of many that have gone before. Daguerre carried on from where Niepce, another Frenchman, left off. They had agreed to share any profits if successful, and though Niepce had died, Daguerre arranged that his widow should share the pension which the French government under Louis Philippe were to pay him for his secret process. As soon as these arrangements were complete, he was charmed to send his formulas to Professor Samuel Morse, at New York University, and did so.

Mr. Morse at once fixed up a "palace for the sun" and began experimenting with the fascinating new art. A professor, Draper, also tried his hand and while Daguerre himself had taken only landscapes, Draper succeeded in making the first successful portrait.

"Though," remarked Samuel Morse, "whether he or myself took the first portrait successfully, I cannot say."

It is hard for some people to share credit. For almost anyone it is difficult to tell just how an idea originates. It was on shipboard coming back from Europe in 1832 that the idea of the electric telegraph occurred to Morse. He had been talking with a certain Dr. J. from Boston about the recent investigations in electricity, and the possibilities for its use.

Thrilled with his telegraph idea, Samuel Morse had gone to work at once to make it practicable, working on it for years, scratching along to get money to buy the parts, and struggling to get Congress to pay for the telegraph line. Then with success in sight, he learned to his dismay that Dr. J. was claiming the credit for the invention, because he said it was he who had given Morse the idea. Possibly he had. Many people have ideas who do not or cannot work them out. The true scientist usually does not care to. His interest lies in discovering the great principles and laws that govern the universe—not in putting them to practical use. Such a man was Joseph Henry, whose improvements on the electromagnet had made the telegraph possible. This is his answer to a letter from Morse:

"Dear Mr. Morse:

"The idea of transmitting intelligence to a distance by means of electrical action has been suggested by various persons from the time of Benjamin Franklin to the present. The mere suggestion, however, is a matter for which little credit can be claimed, but the bringing it forward, and carrying it into operation are grounds of a just claim to scientific reputation. About the same time with yours Professor Wheatstone of London and Dr. Steinheil of Germany proposed plans of the electro-magnetic telegraph but I should prefer the one invented by yourself.

"With my best wishes for your success, I remain, with much esteem yours truly, —————.

JOSEPH HENRY."

On the day that Congress had finally passed the appropriation to construct that first telegraph line to Baltimore, the good news was brought to Morse by a young lady. It was her mother who suggested the first message to be sent. She opened her Bible and chose the twenty-third verse of the twenty-third chapter of *Numbers* and read the words:

What hath GOD wrought!

AND NOW what was spoken of elegantly as its "MANIFEST DESTINY" was about to be fulfilled by the United States. In other words, the nation was about to annex all the territory west to the Pacific Ocean, Texas, Oregon and California. Texas came first. In 1845, after eight years of argument, Texas, a territory five times the size of England, was made part of the United States.

1845

As a result, Mexico, which had never recognized even the independence of Texas, recalled her minister from Washington and war clouds began to gather. As another result, James K. Polk, a minor politician who had favored the annexation, was therefore elected President. Soon he was heard to say, confidentially, that he also wanted to see California acquired. And California belonged to Mexico! So it appeared very likely that war with Mexico might come.

1846

Oregon was acquired peaceably in 1846 by a treaty with England, although excitement over the settlement became so keen that for a time it looked like a clash instead of a compromise. Old John Jacob Astor, whose fort on the Columbia River had given the United States one early claim to the country, had barely lived to see his prophecy come true. After the War of 1812, when the peace commissioners claimed that nobody would be interested in far-off Oregon for at least two hundred years, he had shaken his head.

1848

"If ve lif," he had said, "ve should see drubble over it in less than forty years." And here it was!

Oregon, held jointly since that time, now had to be divided. All of the country might possibly have been annexed to Canada, had there not been so many settlers from the United States. And that they were there was due largely to the enthusiasm, energy and courage of our friend Dr. Marcus Whitman.

In the autumn of 1842, leaving Narcissa at the mission, energetic Dr. Whitman set out for the east on horseback and alone. After five months battling winter storms, starvation and all manner of hardships, he had completed the four thousand miles to Washington, D. C. On his return the following year, two hundred families in their covered wagons went rumbling after him over the Oregon trail. Other hundreds followed, and enthusiasm for the beautiful western country grew so great that soon the greedy were heard claiming all of Oregon as far north as the Russian territory, Alaska, or the parallel 54° 40'.

"Fifty-four forty or fight," became their foolish cry. England, on the other hand, wanted the Columbia River Valley. The 49th parallel was agreed upon as a sensible compromise, and became the dividing line.

Dispute over the northern boundary line of Maine had also been settled peaceably with England a few years before by Daniel Webster, acting for the United States. So the long northern boundary was complete from Maine to Oregon, from the Atlantic to the Pacific.

Added interest in Oregon and the Far West was aroused by the report of "AN EXPLORING EXPEDITION TO OREGON AND NORTH CALIFORNIA," undertaken by a young army engineer by the name of John Charles Frémont. The guide for the expedition had been Kit Carson, whom the young captain had happened to meet on a Missouri River steamboat. Two more dissimilar men could scarcely have been found than rash, impulsive Frémont with his sensitive French face, and sandy-haired Kit Carson, slow-going and cautious.

Though unable to write his name, Carson could speak Spanish and the Indian languages, so Frémont hired him at once.

The expedition took them not only to Oregon and California, but on the way back across what was then called the "Great American Desert," now the states of Kansas, Nebraska, Oklahoma, Utah and Colorado, but then supposed to be unfit for habitation. Frémont reported to the contrary, saying that east of Salt Lake he had seen "good soil and good grass adapted to civilization."

"Adapted to civilization"—Those words were responsible for the first settlement in that unknown American Desert, and for making the Valley at Salt Lake "blossom like the rose." For it happened that back in the Mormon tabernacle in Nauvoo, Illinois, those words written by Frémont were read by Brigham Young, leader of the Latter Day Saints of Jesus Christ, who were about to be driven out of Illinois.

"That's where we will go," he said to one of his twelve apostles, "to the desert in Utah near Salt Lake. That's in Mexico. We will be safe."

"But why choose a desert?" queried the other man.

"Because nobody else will want it," answered Brigham Young. "We will be left alone. We drained a swamp to make this city of Nauvoo; we can irrigate the desert." He sat with the palms of his strong hands planted on his widespread knees, already planning the great migration. Like Moses he would lead his people of Israel to the Promised Land and found a new Jerusalem, a more beautiful city of Zion!

The terrified Mormons had a strong leader in Brigham Young, who had taken command after their founder, Joseph Smith, was murdered.

Joseph Smith was a man who "saw visions" and could make other people believe in them. His first vision was of golden plates bearing strange inscriptions from which he made the Mormon gospel. Neighbors who didn't believe in visions chased him out of New York State, but Joseph Smith gained many followers. In Ohio he had a vision of a bank by which his Mormon colony there might grow rich enough to build a tabernacle. The bank failed and the saints were driven from Ohio. In far west Missouri they settled again, and spoke confidently of the time when all Missouri would be part of Zion. So the citizens of Missouri rose in wrath, attacked their village, burned their homes, and sent them fleeing east across the state . . . east across the Mississippi into Illinois. There they found sanctuary for a time.

The Illinois legislature, shocked at the persecution carried on by their sister state, gave the Mormons a site about one hundred miles north of Springfield, where they built the city of Nauvoo. All went well, until Joseph Smith had another vision. In this vision he saw himself like Solomon, a man intended to have many wives. That vision put into practice was just too much for the people of Illinois.

"Get out!" they told the Mormons. "Get out of this state at once!" and a mob of them killed Joseph Smith.

That was where matters stood when Brigham Young made up his mind to go to Utah and, having decided, sent word to the Mormons far and near to gather at Nauvoo and prepare to leave. Nights and days they worked, building wagons, filling barrels with food, making warm clothes, packing their belongings.

It was mid-winter when the first group started. After kneeling in the snow in prayer, they crossed the frozen Mississippi and, in a caravan two miles long, went creaking slowly westward into Iowa.

The plan was when spring came to plant crops that those who followed might have food, but the desperate, frightened people left behind in Nauvoo dared not wait for spring. They came trailing along by thousands, until the line of wagons, cattle, people and sheep stretched all the way across the state of Iowa. By the time he had reached the Missouri River Brigham Young had not 5000, but 20,000 people to look after. He set them all to work and they built a settlement that was the wonder of the countryside, but it was only a winter's stopping place.

In the spring, with about one hundred and fifty men, Brigham Young went on ahead to find the way to his promised land outside of the United States. In the foothills of the Rockies they met a scout.

"Crickets and sand and salt—ain't nothing else in that desert you're headed for," he told them, "less'n it's horned toads."

Discouraging words, those, to men who had come a thousand miles, but not discouraging to Brigham Young. He had faith in God and the courage of his convictions, and that is enough for any man.

He marched ahead and one day in July, 1847, looked down a sheet of silver lying in a valley encircled by a ring of snow-capped mountains— a perfect place! Perfect it was then, but within the year Utah, instead of belonging to Mexico, would be part of the United States!

War with Mexico was in the air, but had not yet been declared when Frémont, accompanied again by Kit Carson, started west on his next exploring trip, if exploring trip it could be called. Sixty-four men, all well armed, made it look more like a military expedition than a party bent on making maps. So it seemed, certainly to the Mexican general at Monterey, when that party of Americans marched into California.

Monterey, a sleepy Spanish village of two or three streets lined with low adobe houses, was California's principal town in 1845. Its only rival was Los Angeles, two hundred miles nearer Mexico and seat of the feeble Mexican government, whose control over California was very weak. San Francisco was merely a few wooden shacks and shanties belonging mostly to "Yanqui" traders, and huddled along the edge of the beautiful harbor, which Frémont at first sight named the "Golden Gate."

Some miles inland from San Francisco up the Sacramento River was a fort, owned by a Swiss, a former officer under Napoleon, Captain Johann August Sutter. Within the thick adobe walls of his fort, the sturdy captain lived with all the independent power of a pirate king.

Upon reaching California, Frémont went at once to Sutter's fort. He was welcomed hospitably by the genial host, but warned that the Mexican authorities were very doubtful about the purpose of the American expedition being purely scientific. Frémont, hastening to Monterey, assured the Mexican general that he was engaged in geographical survey purely and only wished permission to proceed to Oregon.

Permission was granted, but the Mexican raised a skeptical eyebrow as he did so, and when later he saw Frémont marching south instead of north, he sent sharp orders to him to leave the country, and at once! Frémont refused, built a log fort on a hill, and rashly ran an American flag to the top of a sapling. The Mexican general marshaled his men, marched halfway towards that flag, then faced about and marched away again. In three or four days Frémont also had a change of heart, and leisurely marched out of California—but not too far out, just across the border. Encamped there, he was waiting for months, waiting, of course, for news from Washington as to whether war with Mexico had been declared or not. Though he did little but wait, his presence seemed to encourage the energetic American settlers who, unlike the languorous Spanish, wanted to see California free from Mexico.

On June 14, 1846, a small force of these Americans attacked and captured a shabby little old military post called Sonoma, north of San Francisco. The next day they declared California independent, and ran up a flag improvised out of an old red-bordered petticoat. On it, painted in lampblack and pokeberry juice, was a grizzly bear eyeing a single star, and the words "Republic of California."

Frémont, fed up with waiting, which did not suit his rash, impulsive nature, threw caution to the winds, joined the revolution and, though Sutter protested at first, took command of Sutter's fort and organized the California Battalion of Mounted Riflemen. And still he did not know whether war had been declared or not.

A United States ship, meanwhile, had sailed into the harbor down at Monterey, under the command of a commodore so cautious that, even though he knew positively that war had been declared, hesitated to do more than gaze across the water at the adobe walls and red-tiled roofs of the village. Made more bold at word of the operations of Captain Frémont, he finally ventured ashore and, on July 7, 1846, raised the Stars and Stripes above the custom house and had the Proclamation of Occupation read aloud in Spanish and English. So there, beside the bay where Portola had planted the Spanish flag and Fra Junipero Serra had founded his mission, northern California, almost like a ripe fruit dropping from the stem, fell into the lap of the United States.

From Monterey, the Americans went south by sea to San Diego. The Mexican forces were rallying in the south, but Frémont and his men saw no sign of them as they marched northward to Los Angeles. When they entered the little town behind a small brass band, Frémont said it was more "like a parade of home guards than an enemy taking possession of a conquered town."

In September, Kit Carson set out to carry the good news of the capture of California overland to Washington, D. C. On the way he met General Kearny coming out to assume command in California, as his assignment in the war, for it was now four months since the politicians had trumped up sufficient reason to declare war on Mexico.

"TO THE HALLS OF MONTEZUMA"

THE STORY of the Mexican War must now be told. It is not a source of pride, but interesting because of the people who took part in it. There was General Zachary Taylor, sixty years old, known as "Old Rough and Ready," who was to become the next President of the United States. A warm-hearted, uneducated, hard-... old soldier, he was as unpolished as his muddy boots.

... opposite in every way, except that they were both good ... Winfield Scott, also sixty, known as "Old Fuss and ... the war to a close by prancing through Mexico ... endent in his best gold braid.

... a captain and engineer, served under ... given special mention by him for cour-... to Washington.

... of Ulysses Grant, lieutenant, but he ... charge of the dusty mules and supplies ... his duty, taking part in the battles ... especially this one.

... with a keen mind, cold and narrow ... Davis, and he was later to be elected ... whose flag would be the sixth one to

197

fly over Texas. Davis, who was thoroughly in favor of the war, was, like Lee, about the age of Abraham Lincoln.

Abraham Lincoln had been elected to Congress as Whig representative from Illinois just after the war had been declared. He kept his opinion on it to himself, as long as harm could be done by expressing it, but when the war was over he condemned it as one of aggression "commenced by the President, unconstitutionally and unnecessarily."

Unnecessarily, because, aside from recalling the minister, after the annexation of Texas, Mexico had made no further move towards declaring war, so it is very probable that there would have been no war if the President's party had wished to avoid it, and if Texas had been all they wanted. They had more in mind.

All that was spoken of aloud at this time, however, was a comparatively small strip of land lying between the Nueces River and the Rio Grande, which they claimed as part of Texas, but which had never at any time been considered by Mexico as belonging to that state.

Therefore, with the idea of irritating Mexico into making a hostile move that could be seized upon as an excuse for declaring war, General Zachary Taylor was sent to the Nueces River with orders to cross into the disputed territory. Mexico, busy at home with one of its frequent revolutions, still made no move. So Taylor was ordered to go further on to the Rio Grande. He did so and there, at last, the Mexicans came over and killed some of a scouting party.

"Ah!" said President Polk. "They have invaded our territory and shed American blood on American soil."

So, with that as a reason, war was declared on Mexico!

It started off brightly, with several victories won by General Zachary Taylor, there in the region of the Rio Grande. Then plans were changed in Washington. General Taylor received orders to send two-thirds of his men to Vera Cruz to join in a campaign against Mexico City under General Winfield Scott.

From an American messenger who was captured, Santa Anna learned of the new plans, and made plans of his own to block them.

He would defeat the small force left behind with General Taylor and then dash towards Vera Cruz in time to block General Scott's march to Mexico City. Taylor defeated him badly, but Santa Anna lost no time. He faced about, and gathering more soldiers as he went, reached a place called Cerro Gorde ahead of General Scott. That was where the road to Mexico City left the sweltering damp sea land of Vera Cruz and entered the foothills of the mountains. Posting guns halfway up the rocks on either side of the road, Santa Anna lay in wait for the enemy.

It was night when the Americans arrived. While most of them kept up a little firing to distract the Mexicans' attention, others under Captain Lee left the narrow road, clambered up the steep rocks by clinging to roots and branches. Then, with ropes, they dragged up a cannon to a ledge from which they could fire down upon the Mexican camp.

Santa Anna managed to escape and, with 7,000 men, hastened up the winding mountain road to Mexico City, and the Americans followed. Up the steep road they climbed, winding up into the mountains, until they reached a ridge 11,000 feet above the sea. From there they could look down upon the ancient city and its lake, lying in the green elliptical valley. Just so, from that ridge Cortez, conqueror of the ancient Aztecs, must have looked down upon the "Halls of Montezuma."

All roads leading on from there were heavily guarded. Major Lee reconnoitered, and with his engineers built a road across an almost impassable field of lava, over which the soldiers reached the city walls and forced their entrance. Santa Anna fled, saving his precious person, leaving the city to its fate. September 17, 1847, General Scott and his army entered Mexico City and the war was over.

Early in 1848 the peace treaty was signed. Mexico received $15,000,000. But the United States gained all territory north of the Rio Grande, Texas and all of California—more than half of the Mexican Republic. For that loss of territory, Mexico could thank Santa Anna. With more regard for law in dealing with Texas in the early days, he might have saved it all. And yet, who knows? Perhaps it *was* the "manifest destiny" of the United States thus to reach the Pacific!

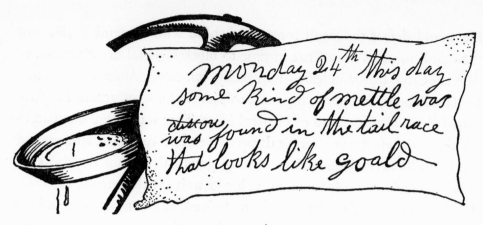

Monday 24th this day some kind of mettle was discou was found in the tail race that looks like goald

GOLD!

"G‑A‑L‑D," G‑O‑L‑D, no matter how you spell it, the "mettle" was Gold! Gold!! and it was discovered in January, 1848, behind the new sawmill being built by Captain Sutter some miles from his fort in California. It took a little time for the news to spread, but when it did, it started the craziest, wildest scrambling rush for the West that the United States had ever known.

This first mention of the discovery was written by one of the laborers at the mill. That afternoon the water was turned off in the tailrace, and one of the men walking in the loose gravel spied some bright bits, about as large as grains of wheat that looked to him like gold. Dropping a few in his slouch hat, he took them to the kitchen stove, found they wouldn't melt, but were soft enough to pound, and said he believed he had discovered gold! Some of the men laughed, but Marshall (that was his name) took his samples and rode off to Sutter's fort. Sutter looked up Gold in his encyclopedia, weighed the nuggets, tested them with sulphuric acid, and declared that they MUST be Gold!

"gold! Gold! GOLD!" read the headlines in the little San Francisco newspaper. Californians dropped their work, bought pickaxes and pans, and set out for the "diggin's." gold! Gold! GOLD! the magnetic words sped east across the continent. Farmers, carpenters, shopkeepers, clerks started for California—across the plains, around the Horn, over the isthmus, anyway to get there. The GOLD RUSH to California was on!

The "49'ers" were on their way! Then, only two years later another gold rush was on! GOLD was discovered in Australia.

Since 1788, England had been trying to establish a thriving colony on that continent but it was far from home, and after sixty years, not more than 50,000 Europeans were living there.

But then GOLD was discovered! And like a magnet, in a single year it drew over 200,000 people to Australia. After that, there was no need for England to worry over the future of her colony in the South Pacific.

CANADA

CANADA was still a troublesome offspring. In 1849, a mob of irate Canadians had set on fire and burned to the ground the government buildings in Montreal. That city was then the capital of United Canada, formed when the two provinces, Upper and Lower, had been united eight years before.

The first three governors sent out to United Canada had failed to be guided by the wishes of the assembly as they were supposed to be, so the people had been greatly disappointed.

Then in 1847, came Lord Elgin, who *did* uphold the vote of the assembly. And for that, a mob threw stones and rotten eggs at him and then burned the Houses of the Parliament.

That was not so much, however, because Lord Elgin had upheld the law, as because of the law itself, which was condemned by the furious people as one "to reward rebels for rebelling." For the Bill, put through by the Ultra-Liberal leaders, was one to reimburse those among them who who had suffered losses at the time of the rebellion in 1837. Those who now formed the jeering, hooting mob were some of the conservative people who had formerly condemned the rebels for resorting to violence.

At home, in the English Parliament, when the Canadian question was debated, Lord Elgin's stand was upheld. Thus government responsible for its actions to the vote of the people was established in Canada.

John A. Macdonald had by then become a member of the Canadian Parliament, and so was in Montreal at the time of the riot, but though he was a Conservative, he took no part in the rioting, whatever he may have thought of the bill passed by the Ultra-Liberals.

On the other hand, neither did he take his stand with those Ultra-Conservatives, who were so disgusted by the rioting and general disorder that they were ready and willing to have Canada annexed to the United States. While the ashes were still smoking, they brought him their Annexation Manifesto, but he refused to sign it.

"I firmly believe," he said, "that the prosperity of Canada depends upon its permanent connection with the mother country and I shall resist to the utmost any attempt which may tend to weaken that Union!"

Instead, he took steps to make the connection stronger, and also to promote a feeling of unity in Canada. This was not easy, for the Canadians were divided in so many different ways. The French against the English, the Protestants against the Catholics, the Ultra-Liberals from the Ultra-Conservatives, and each party in Upper Canada from the same party in Lower Canada.

But between the two extremes stood the moderates of each party, and these, with infinite tact and resourcefulness, J. A. Macdonald managed in 1854 to unite into the Liberal-Conservative party, of which he was to be the head during the rest of his life, and which for those forty more years would form the history of Canada.

CORN AND POTATOES (*Continued*)

SHORTLY BEFORE the Gold Rush to California began, and Lord Elgin went to Canada, thousands of Irish people came to find new homes in America, because of a grievous disaster that befell poor Ireland. A Potato Famine! The previous summer the entire crop failed. Ireland's main food. Winter came. Starvation set in. All who had or could borrow passage money sailed for America. Those left behind died by tens of thousands in their small thatched huts.

The United States and other countries shipped in gifts of food, but they were a mere fraction of what was needed.

The only way to save the people was to let in a great quantity of food from the food-producing countries. And the only way to do that was to get rid of the import tax. The English government finally realized it. Faced with the absolute necessity of doing so, Parliament repealed at last the long-cherished CORN LAWS, and Ireland was saved.

Not only that. By reducing the price of food, England was spared an uprising of her own hungry working people which, the government learned with alarm, was being stirred up by their leaders in 1848.

"The Chartists" were drawing up another petition, it was said, to ask for the vote. There was to be a great mass meeting held in Kensington Commons, which it was feared might give rise to riots and bloodshed. To quell any such possible disturbance, 70,000 special police were called out, and the old Duke of Wellington put in charge of the city of London. But no disturbance arose. The movement for reform died quietly away, largely because the most-needed reform had been already made and the working people were no longer hungry.

England, therefore, had no violent revolution in that year 1848, when revolution spread all over Europe.

THE YEAR 1848

THAT YEAR 1848 was to go down in history as the great year of revolution. Never before had Europe seen such a wholesale uprising in the cause of liberty. It brought about the most astounding event since the defeat of Napoleon—the downfall of Metternich. Downfall of that Austrian who, more than thirty years before, had united the Kings of Europe into a Holy Alliance to crush the liberty of the people. All those thirty years, people had dreamed of, but almost despaired of seeing, the day when his power would be broken. Now the day came.

In 1848 revolution broke out, not in Austria alone but all over Europe, everywhere from east to west, from the Baltic Sea to the Mediterranean. It had needed but a spark to set it off, and that spark was supplied as before by France.

There in France it was a Working Men's revolution. Its aim was to overthrow the rule of the middle class and their King, Louis Philippe, as the middle class had overthrown the aristocrats and Charles X in the famous three-day revolution eighteen years before.

What hope La Fayette had had after that revolution that Louis Philippe would then "make the best of kings"!

Instead, he had pleased nobody. Not the Aristocrats, of course, who had lost their power, and not even the Bourgeoisie who had gained the vote. He was too much like a shopkeeper—they thought—like they were themselves. There was no glamour about such a solid man—none of the glory of the "great" Napoleon! And certainly he had not satisfied the Republicans, nor the students nor the working men, nor any of those people who had hoped that under him there would be reform.

There had been no reform. Not a reform in the eighteen years that Louis Philippe had been king. And there was need for reform, cry for reform, demand for reform. To all these cries and demands, Louis Philippe had been deaf, but now the voices had grown so loud that the word reform echoed from every wall—reform—Reform—REFORM. On February 22 a "reform banquet" was held by a group of students.

"Vive la Réforme!" they cried with excited voices. Excitement spread to the working men's quarters. Barricades were raised. Working men and students marched to the home of the chief minister. Some unknown person fired on the guards; the guards returned the fire. Fifty men were killed. Their dead bodies were laid in carts by their comrades and drawn through the streets, while bells tolled a funeral dirge.

"Vive la Réforme! Long live reform!" they cried as they filed past the Tuileries. Inside Louis Philippe, deaf no longer, was ready to grant reform, but it was too late. The next cry he heard was:

"Long live the Republic! Down with the King!"

So the king abdicated, the last King that France would ever have. Disguised as "Mr. Smith" he fled to England, where he was received graciously by Queen Victoria, whose Uncle Leopold was his son-in-law.

In Paris, the crazy mob dragged the throne out of the Tuileries and made a bonfire of it. Then on the site of the old Bastille, still a symbol of tyranny, they proclaimed the REPUBLIC OF FRANCE.

Louis Blanc, one of the leaders of the new republic, and a socialist, promised every French working man a permanent job, in government workshops. Until these could be established, he distributed 1,000,000 francs among the laboring men!

Österreich=

La Réforme! Only a few days after the banquet held in France, the word was taken up in Hungary, by the eloquent orator Kossuth. Hungary belonged to Austria, and had long been crying for independence. Now mingled with Kossuth's cry for independence went a condemnation of the whole despotic system under which all of Austria's subjects were oppressed. The flaming Hungarian words were soon translated into German, and published in Vienna. There, in Austria's capital, students read them to the working men. Crowds surged to the palace crying, "Down with Metternich! 'Raus mit Metternich!''

The Emperor shivered and Metternich knew that his day was done, that he must leave if he would live. March 14th he left, his power gone. The Emperor shivered again and abdicated. The people shouted their joy. There was even talk among them of a Constitution!

What nonsense in Austria! Did they not know, these people, that old ways in Austria were not so easily jarred from their deep ruts? Before the year was over the old order had been well restored by the Austrian troops and a young new Hapsburg emperor sat upon the throne.

Austrian troops were also sent to Italy, for now again the people of Italy rose to fight for independence from their foreign rulers.

Italia!

All Italy was ablaze. The King of Sardinia or Piedmont, once lacking courage, now marshaled his forces against Austria. Grand Dukes of the northern states sent troops to join with his, and granted their people constitutions. There was much singing and great joy.

The Robert Brownings, newly married, were in the center of the excitement in Florence. Elizabeth Barrett describes in a poem what they saw from the "Casa Guidi Windows."

Italians long exiled returned. Mazzini hastened from London to Rome, whence the Pope had fled, leaving the city without a government. There Mazzini's ideal, a Roman Republic, was soon proclaimed.

Far off in South America, in Uruguay, Garibaldi heard of the good news and, with fifty followers, set sail for home. Fifty men in red shirts, borrowed from the gauchos, sailed the gray-blue ocean under their undaunted leader, their hearts with his in their beloved Italy. Fifteen hundred volunteers joined these "Red Shirts," when they landed in Piedmont, and marched with Garibaldi on to Rome.

Alas! The Austrians were also marching—marching into Italy. By them the King of Piedmont was defeated. Against them the Republic of Rome could not be defended. By them for thirty days Garibaldi was chased through the mountains; his army dwindled away. Hunted from one place to another he finally reached the seacoast and escaped to North America. Mazzini returned to England. The King of Piedmont abdicated in favor of his son. Austria was again supreme.

Preußen

From Prussia, also, citizens who loved liberty were to be expelled, for in Prussia, as in Austria, there was no room for non-conforming Germans who had ideas of freedom, and such foolishness.

There had been uprisings in Berlin, uprisings in western Prussia, uprisings in all of the thirty-five or more small German states, but of what use? The Prussian King did, it is true, grant a constitution of a sort. Other rulers made promises, but then changed their minds and answered further requests with bullets, stamped out the revolution and sent the rebellious subjects fleeing from the country.

Richard Wagner, the great composer who stood for freedom in government, as well as music, took refuge in Switzerland. His new opera *Lohengrin* was to have been produced for the first time, the day the revolution broke out in Köln, and he was obliged to flee the country.

Carl Schurz, the editor of a liberal newspaper, went to the United States, and became one of its most loyal citizens, the first man of German birth to be elected to Congress. There were many other such Germans who also came to find liberty in America and whose descendants in years to come would not forget why their ancestors left Germany.

So, within one short year, all over Europe revolution had blazed up and been stamped out, and, except in France, kings sat again upon their thrones. And things were as they had been? No—not quite.

SOCIALISM had been born.

Karl Marx, an exile from Prussia, a brilliant student of law and history, whose radical beliefs so pained the heart of his good mother, had written the birth cry of the party, the COMMUNIST MANIFESTO.

It was published in London, on the very day that the Working Men's revolution had broken out in Paris. That day the first copies came off the press, and these words were seen for the first time in print, words freighted heavily with both good and evil:—

WORKERS OF THE WORLD—UNITE!

It was a call to workers not of one nation but of every nation. Thus with the downfall of Metternich, who had once united the Kings of Europe against the people, came Karl Marx to unite the Workers of the World in the first political party designed to be International.

PART FOUR: WHEN

Abraham Lincoln

WAS A **LAWYER** FROM

Illinois

What other People were doing

FRANZ JOSEF who was to rule 68 years, until 1916, became Emperor of Austria,

1851 The **FIRST WORLD'S FAIR** was held in London in "The Crystal Palace"

NAPOLEON III became Emperor of France and **EUGENIE**, the Empress

NANA SAHIB took part in an uprising against England started by the sepoys in INDIA, 1857 (a Sepoy)

RICHARD WAGNER wrote his opera Lohengrin 1847

"**MARK TWAIN**" was a steamboat pilot on the Mississippi

1854 **FLORENCE NIGHTINGALE** was a nurse in the Crimean War

1859 The World's first **OIL** Well was drilled in Pennsylvania.

JENNY LIND made a concert tour in the United States.

and some Events that took place

when A. Lincoln was a Lawyer

STEPHEN FOSTER was writing his songs

Oh Susanna · *Massa's in de Cold* · *Old Folks at Home* · *My Old Kentucky Home*

In 1854

JAPAN was opened by Perry, and Japanese first visited the United States in 1860

1852 **HARRIET BEECHER STOWE** wrote "Uncle Tom's Cabin"

VICTOR EMMANUEL II became the first King of a united Italy.

WOODROW WILSON, c.1856 · **WILHELM** the Kaiser, 1859 · and **THEODORE ROOSEVELT**, 1858 were very small boys.

"The Ugly Duckling"

HANS CHRISTIAN ANDERSEN was writing his wonder tales

As the "Rail Splitter" and Republican Candidate, **LINCOLN** was elected President.

STEPHEN A. DOUGLAS ran against Lincoln, proved himself a good loser (Died 1861)

1860-1

SEVEN STATES SECEDED before Lincoln's inauguration

JEFFERSON DAVIS became President of the **CONFEDERACY**

WILLIE and **TAD LINCOLN** went with their father and mother to Washington **ROBERT, 17,** was at school in Harvard.

between the Years 1848 and 1861

German States

GERMAN CONFEDERATION: *inside heavy black outline*
HUNGARY, *Lombardy, Venetia, part of Austrian Empire, but not German Confederation*
HANOVER: *ancestral home of George I, King of England.*
x COBURG: *home of Victoria and Albert's grandmother.*

A BEAUTIFUL UNIFORM OR A SPIKED HELMET?

THIS IS YOUNG FRANZ JOSEF of Austria, as he looked in his dress uniform on his coronation day in 1848, and also from that day on. For from then on "Franzi," as his favorite brother Maximilian called him, was never seen in anything but a splendid uniform. He was shy and reserved; perhaps it gave him confidence. Certainly, in the stiff high collar and the tight trousers, smoothly fitting as a glove, he looked extremely handsome.

Shy and handsome, young Franz Joseph was also very proud, for he was a Hapsburg and the Hapsburgs were Europe's oldest royal family. Appointed, they believed, by the divine will of God, they had ruled Europe's most powerful nation for almost six hundred years.

Since the families of the Hapsburg rulers were always numerous as well as proud, every young Hapsburg had a host of uncles, aunts and cousins on or near the other thrones—(and also many less fortunate ones who were quite mad and shut up in gloomy castles).

Next to the drawing of Franz Josef is a partial list of his relatives beginning with his great-great-grandmother Maria Theresa, who had sixteen children. From the list you see that Napoleon's son was a first cousin of Franz Josef, as was also Pedro II of Brazil. Only five years old when he became Emperor of Brazil, Pedro had been ruling eighteen years when Franz Josef became Emperor.

That year 1848 was of course the year of revolution, which had over-thrown the old counselor Metternich. Franz Josef's uncle, who was then ruling, had gladly handed over the uneasy throne, and his father had been equally glad to sign away his right to it. So after seeing the crown placed on "Franzi's" smooth young brow, the two old unambitious brothers had gone off to eat dumplings and take life easy in one of the family castles. The inexperienced boy of eighteen was left (with the help of his mother and new councilors) to manage his rebellious and unwieldy old Empire as best he could.

Franz Josef, though he was ill-fitted for the task, began conscien-tiously to do his best, for he loved the Empire, and wished above all things to do his duty. Though he had no imagination, nor desire to learn anything new, he had an excellent memory and clung to the things he had been taught.

When he was only six years old, Prince Metternich had found a tutor for him, selected, Metternich said, "because he thought as I thought, saw as I saw." So it is plain to see what little "Franzi" had been taught. Naturally he came to the throne believing that the people had no rights, a king could do no wrong, and the way to rule Austria was for the Emperor to command and the people to obey.

He had also been taught to speak Hungarian (but very poorly), because Hungary was part of Austria, though a rebellious part, and, like northern Italy, always struggling to be free.

Hungary was in the midst of rebellion, started by Kossuth, when Franz Josef came to the throne. The Czar of Russia hastened to the rescue and helped stamp it out. Franz Josef then coolly ordered the Hungarian leaders killed in order to secure the safety of his Empire. Right or wrong, Franz Josef lived only for his Empire—that and nothing else—until he saw his "angel Sisi."

"Sisi" was his cousin Elizabeth, and from the day he had first seen her, he adored her. Exquisite, charming, she had come lightheartedly down the Danube from her home in Bavaria to marry her handsome lover, when she was sixteen and he was twenty-three. But once there in the old castle in Vienna, she was like an unhappy wild bird, beating her wings against a cage, until she died. Poor lovely Sisi, Franz Josef would adore her memory to the end of his long life.

Sixty-eight years he was to rule in Austria. Two years before the end, in trying to avenge the death of his nephew, the heir to his throne, Franz Josef, then an old man of eighty-four, would unintentionally start the first World War. In 1918, when that war was over, the last of the Hapsburgs would cease to rule, and of the once proud Empire of Austria there would be only a fragment left—like a broken hearthstone lying among the ruins of an ancient castle.

Soon after he came to the throne, young Franz Josef would see that Empire begin to crumble away, the Empire that he loved so much and wished to rule so honorably and well. First he would lose a province in Italy. Then he would suffer at the hands of Prussia.

Prussia was the German nation second in size to Austria. There was not and never had been a united Germany, only, in 1848, these two large nations, Prussia and Austria, and thirty-five or so smaller ones, some no larger than a good-sized farm. All were hung together loosely in a Confederation, which met at Frankfort-on-the-Main, and of which Austria was head . . . but Prussia WISHED to be.

215

Wilhelm—der Soldat

This man in the helmet is Prince Wilhelm, known as the Prince of Prussia. Though his brother was now king, he was soon to act as regent, and in 1861 was to be crowned King himself. Wilhelm was fifty years old in 1848, a great giant of a man, bluff and rugged and blond like some old hero from a German saga. And he was first and foremost a soldier. If he didn't actually sleep in that helmet of his, he certainly must have kept it hanging on the bed-post.

Frederick the Great, who ruled Prussia in the days of George Washington, was Wilhelm's great-uncle, and the king who actually put Prussia on the map. Before Frederick began his conquests, Prussia had been small and insignificant. His grandfather had been its first independent king. Plainly, then, the Hohenzollern family to which the Prussian kings belonged were mere upstarts compared to Franz Josef's family which could be traced back six hundred years.

Prussia, compared to the old empire of Austria, was decidedly a raw and upstart nation. But it was up and coming, and had the ambition of crowding Austria out of first place in Germany. What's more, Prussia was a nation of soldiers, with a standing army steadily increasing and a warlike Prince who was soon to be its King.

Soon also, a clever counselor for that King was to step onto the stage of European politics, a clever young man by the name of Otto von Bismarck. He was going to push the interests of Prussia to the limit—unite the German states by a cement of "Blood and Iron" into an Empire . . . and make this man in the helmet its first Kaiser.

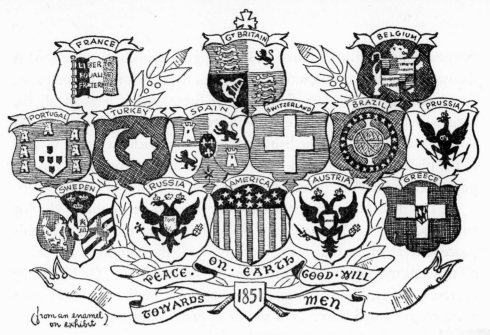

(from an enamel
on exhibit)

THE PEACE FESTIVAL

VICTORIA AND ALBERT, especially, took great interest in European affairs. Naturally with so many friends and relatives among the rulers they were particularly interested in the German states. The summer of 1851 they were glad to welcome as their guest Prince Wilhelm of Prussia, accompanied by his son, a nondescript young fellow of twenty. They had come to London to visit the great Exhibition, the First World's Fair, which had been planned by Albert, and opened on the morning of May the first.

What a beautiful morning it was, that first of May, 1851, a perfect day for the opening of what Albert thought of as a great Peace Festival of the Nations.

Victoria was so proud of him, and so happy as they sat at breakfast that morning, surrounded by their children, seven of them, now. The two oldest, Vicky, the Princess Royal, who was ten, and the nine-year-old Prince of Wales, were to ride with their father and mother in the state carriage to the "Great Exhibition." How excited they were when the cavalry rode out of the palace gates and the procession started! How the children exclaimed when they turned into Hyde Park and saw the

217

"Crystal Palace," a huge house of shining glass sparkling in the sun! A thousand feet long it was, and high enough to enclose two of the park's largest elm trees. On top, flying in the breeze, were flags of all the nations, while inside the great dome were palms, and fountains, and flowers and statues. And the bands were playing! Victoria, as she walked to the platform with her hand on Albert's arm, felt sure that it was the proudest, happiest day of her entire life.

"The tremendous cheers," she wrote later in her journal, "the joy expressed in every face, and my beloved husband the author of this peace-festival which united the industry of all the nations of the earth, all this was moving indeed. God bless my dearest Albert. God bless my dearest Country. To see the great conception of my beloved husband's mind crowned with success is a source of pride and thankfulness which none but a wife's heart can comprehend."

Albert, too, in his quiet way, was very happy. He was hoping, as he had said from the beginning, that this exhibition bringing together the products and arts and inventions of all the different countries of the world would lead to a better understanding between nations and people, and be a step towards the "unity of mankind."

But what a storm of objections had been raised against the scheme when he had first proposed it, most of them now too ridiculous to recall. It was fortunate that he possessed the patience and good temper to work steadily along until the objections had been overcome, for when the invitations had gone out to the various countries, there had been a most enthusiastic and gratifying response.

Fifteen thousand exhibitors sent displays. Visitors from all over the globe came pouring into London, thronging through the aisles and in and out of booths and balconies, admiring the beautiful products of the East and marveling at the inventions of the West.

They saw the Koh-i-noor Diamond from India shining in its case, elephant trappings and carved ivory tusks—jades and porcelains from China, painted silk, edible birds' nests, Persian rugs and Turkish water pipes—nuggets of gold from California, the sewing machine of Elias

Howe, and the Colt repeating rifle—false teeth and camel bags as well as all manner of ill-conceived and useless things supposed to be ornamental.

All were listed alphabetically in a large blue catalogue. Under the A's today's common metal aluminum was not mentioned. It was then almost unobtainable and so practically unknown, but there was a "submarine boat in the shape of a broad-backed carp," and demonstrations throughout the day of a grain reaper invented by Cyrus McCormick of Chicago, said to be "the most important addition to farm machinery since the invention of the threshing machine."

Charles Goodyear of New Haven, Connecticut, Inventor and Manufacturer, had a display of India-rubber goods, life boats and pontoons, as well as boots and overshoes. For now at last rubber was usable. Goodyear's invention had made it so. It would no longer get soft and sticky in summer, and hard enough to break in winter. It stretched and would go right back in shape. One of the marvels of the age!

And so there in the "Crystal Palace," gathered together for the first time, were the products of the world and the people of the world assembled to see them. Crowding the streets of London, filling the omnibuses and railway trains, they went streaming through the Great Exhibition from May until October. And from first to last nothing unpleasant happened. Only words of delight and praise were heard. Truly it had been, as Albert had hoped it would be, a "Peace Festival of the Nations." To Tennyson it even seemed a fleeting vision of that far-off day when the

War drum throbbed no longer, and the battle flags were furled,
In the Parliament of Man, the Federation of the World.

Albert was very weary when the Exhibition was over, but he kept up his long hours of work each day. As far as possible he relieved Victoria of all work and responsibility that went with her title. Every morning he was up at seven, and spent two hours in the sitting room working at his desk, lighted on dark winter mornings by a German lamp with a green shade. At nine o'clock he joined the Queen at breakfast and read the newspapers of the day, greatly concerned in the affairs of Europe as well as England, but grieved over Germany.

"I don't like to read of Germany any more," he would say, "the behavior of the governments is such that I feel ashamed. . . ."

One morning, the fourth of December, 1851, a little over a month after the great Exhibition closed, the papers were filled with the most startling news from France. Albert read it aloud.

"What!" Victoria gasped. Why only day before yesterday, the very day it had happened, she had written Uncle Leopold in Belgium that she did not think there would be any outburst "yet awhile in France." And here it was. She must write to him again. . . .

"Dearest Uncle," she wrote. "I must write a line to ask what you say to the *wonderful* proceedings at Paris, which really seem like a *story* in a book or a play! What is to be the result of it all?"

And what *was* that exciting news from Paris?

Louis Napoleon had seized the power on December 2, 1851, and was on the way to becoming the Emperor Napoleon III.

NAPOLEON III

DECEMBER 2, 1851. The night before had been an anxious one for Louis Napoleon in Paris. All night, while his conspirators went about their work, he had only to wait and listen to a gilt clock on the mantel tick off those endless hours that would make him either Emperor of France or again an outlaw. Down in the dark courtyard below horses were saddled, ready for his instant escape in case of failure. Failure?

He could not fail, he told himself, not on such an auspicious date as the second of December. For was it not on December 2, 1804, that his famous uncle had crowned himself Napoleon I? On that same date in 1805, had he not won his most famous battle? No, surely, on a December second, he, Louis Napoleon, could not fail!

Yet as the clock struck the hour, the small man turned nervously from the window where he had stood twisting the ends of his waxed moustache. He walked to the end of the room and back. He lit a cigarette, and then stood gazing blankly at the wall with those half-closed eyes of his that never gave any hint of what he might be thinking. He had many hours to think that night. And of what?

Of the future, perhaps, of the improvements he was to make in the life of the poor, in industry and commerce, plans for the prosperity of France and the peace of Europe. The Empire and Peace!

Perhaps he thought of the past, and saw himself as a small boy again, kissing his grandmamma Josephine. He was now forty-three years old, but of all the women he had since loved (and they were many) she still seemed most glamorous to him. He could still feel the softness of her skin and hear her seductive voice telling him never to forget that his uncle was the great Napoleon. He had never forgotten. Twenty years ago his cousin had died, Napoleon's son who might have been Napoleon II. Since then, considering himself heir to the throne of France, Louis Napoleon had made two attempts to seize the power. Both attempts had been so dismally unsuccessful as to make of him a laughingstock.

The first plan had been that he should enter the border town of Strasbourg, rouse the soldiers with his ringing words, and make a triumphal march to Paris. But when the time came he failed to think up those ringing words, and appearing to the King Louis Philippe less dangerous than ridiculous, he had not been imprisoned but was shipped out of France. . . . He went to the United States.

After two months in New York, receiving word that his beloved mother, Hortense, was dying, he hastened back to Switzerland. Then, obliged to leave Switzerland, he went to London, where he enjoyed himself in society, and also plotted for another return to France.

In 1840, it seemed to Louis Napoleon and his fellow exiles in England that the time had come. They chartered a small steamer, crossed the English Channel, and carrying supplies, proclamations and a somewhat mangy eagle, landed on a dark night at Boulogne, with much the same plan as before. Three hours later, however, instead of marching triumphantly on to Paris they were scurrying back to the seashore, chased and shot at by the National Guard. Plunging into the water the men swam out to a yawl, hoping to reach their steamer, but the boat capsized. Louis Napoleon was seized, taken to trial, and condemned to life imprisonment in the castle of Ham.

Ham was an old chateau that stood on marshy ground, about seventy miles north of Paris. Louis Napoleon was there six years, valuable years spent in study and research, that made him one of the best informed men of his day. He was well treated. His sitting room was lined with books, and he had a small laboratory. And his doctor, an old and faithful friend, was with him.

It was the doctor who watched over a dummy in the bed of the prisoner, supposed to be very ill, on the day that he made his astonishing escape. It was a cleverly simple plan. The rooms had been in need of repair, so for many days carpenters and plasterers had been coming and going. One day Louis Napoleon, dressed in laborer's clothes, with his moustache shaved off and a plank on his shoulder, simply walked through the courtyard, out of the gate, and next day was back in London! That was 1846.

Two years later came the revolution which made France a Republic and sent Louis Philippe, the Citizen King, hurrying out of Paris across the Channel to London. Immediately out of London across the Channel back to Paris hurried Louis Napoleon, without stopping to pack his bags. Too soon to be welcome, he went back to wait in London. In September he was elected and returned to Paris to take a seat in the Assembly. In December, by an overwhelming majority who rallied around him for various reasons, he was elected President.

Republicans believed him to be a friend of law and order, and hearing him take the oath of office, did not suspect that he intended to break it. But as the term passed and his popularity increased, a plot was hatched to overthrow the Republic and re-establish the Empire. Louis Napoleon, after much changing of his mind, had finally set the date of December second for the *coup d'etat*.

So came this night of waiting. The tray was filled with half-burnt cigarettes, as the gilt clock struck two. He sat forward in his chair to listen. According to plan, the troops would now be starting to move silently through the Paris streets.

At three he felt sure the seventy-eight political leaders who might cause trouble must have been arrested.

Four o'clock came. The proclamations, he thought, were to have been plastered throughout Paris before dawn. Five came and went, another hour passed and with six o'clock and daylight came the word that all, so far, had gone off to perfection!

Four hours later, at ten o'clock in the morning of that December 2, 1851, Louis Napoleon, accompanied by a cavalcade of officers in brilliant uniforms, rode through the streets of Paris.

"Vive l'Empereur! Vive Napoleon!" cried the people.

And Louis Napoleon, generous as ever, gave all that was left of his private fortune to be distributed among the poor.

There was some rioting in the streets; during the next two days a number of citizens were killed, but it was soon over. Within the year the Assembly had decreed the Republic dead, the Empire established. On December 2, 1852, Louis Napoleon became Napoleon III, Emperor of France, a title that the little man with the waxed moustache and the changeable mind was to hold for eighteen years.

And the Empire, he assured the people of Europe, stood for PEACE!

So once again France had an Emperor, and in the following year was asked to welcome another Empress.

This is EUGENIE, who became the Empress of France, and bride of Napoleon III in 1853. Eugenie was the daughter of a Spanish count, but her red-gold hair and deep blue eyes she had inherited from her mother's family, the Kirkpatricks, who were of Scottish origin. Her beauty had caught the roving eye of Napoleon III at once. Since all of his charm, however, advanced him no closer to her lovely neck and shoulders, he finally proposed marriage, she accepted, and the Countess de Montijo, her mother, sighed with satisfaction that the husband hunt for her spirited daughter had ended so successfully.

Napoleon III had aspired, if possible, to marry a princess from one of Europe's royal houses, but he had soon found that those royal families offered him a snub instead of a princess. So he cleverly made a virtue out of a necessity.

"The union I am about to make," he announced to the Councilors, "is not in accordance with ancient policy. Therein lies its advantage. I have preferred a woman whom I love to a woman unknown to me. In placing qualities of heart and family happiness before dynastic prejudices, I shall be more strong, in that I shall be more free!"

A marriage for love! The French people were charmed. And to so beautiful a bride . . . and so generous, giving her wedding gift of 250,000 francs to the sick, and her diamond necklace to be sold for the poor. What a pity that the gilt crown fell from the roof of the imperial coach on the way to the cathedral! A bad omen, *n'est ce pas?*

DER TOLLE BISMARCK

MAD BISMARCK they called him, those other German delegates to the Confederation at Frankfort in 1851. Frantically they wrote home asking for instructions as to what attitude to take regarding the incident for which the new Prussian delegate was responsible. A most extraordinary incident it was: Bismarck, the new delegate from Prussia, had dared to light a cigar and smoke in the presence of the ambassador from Austria. Mein Gott! Such boldness! The man, said they, must certainly be mad!

Mad? Far from it. Otto von Bismarck was anything but mad. He was an extremely clever man. This little smoke was just a puff to show which way the wind was blowing—just a hint that Herr Bismarck intended to uphold the honor of Prussia—that in time he might make Prussia instead of Austria head of that German confederation.

Bismarck was a Junker—that is, he was a country gentleman, one of Prussia's aristocracy. As such, he believed in upholding not only the honor of Prussia, but also the privileges of the upper class and the absolute and divine right of the King. One night in a beer garden in Berlin, he had overheard some stranger at the next table make a slighting remark about the royal family. He jumped to his feet at once.

"Out of the house!" he thundered. "If you are not off when I have drunk this beer, I will break this glass mug on your head."

That set off a great commotion, with all kinds of outcries, to which Bismarck gave no heed. He finished his beer, then brought the mug down on the skull of the offender with a crash that sent him howling to the floor, and smashed the glass in pieces. Then a dead silence, in which Bismarck asked calmly, as if nothing had happened:

"Waiter, what is the cost of this broken glass?"

In 1848, the year of revolution in Europe, Bismarck was acting as a member of the Prussian Diet or Assembly, at the request of the King, who had given the people a Constitution. The young Junker, then thirty-three years old, had taken his seat most reluctantly, because he did not approve of Constitutions, or of Assemblies or of any other such ridiculous democratic institutions.

Any person who believed in turning over government to the vote of the people, he said, must be either a knave or a lunatic. How could the will of the majority be always right, when nine out of ten people knew nothing about the law, and were not even educated? Why, most people, he contended, if they were asked about it, would vote that the sun revolved around the earth. But did that make it true?

Other members of the Assembly, on the contrary, were grateful to the King for the Constitution, and made speeches expressing their hope for the future of liberal ideas in Prussia. Bismarck jumped to his feet and spoke on the opposite side.

"I consider," he said, "that Prussia's honor lies in avoiding every shameful union with democracy."

The members hissed and shouted, but that young giant would not be shouted down. Taking a newspaper out of his pocket, he calmly read until order was restored and then completed his remarks.

Otto von Bismarck came from northeast Prussia, from Brandenburg, Pomerania, to be exact. He was born on his father's country estate on April 1, 1815. At six years of age he was sent to a very strict boarding school in Berlin and was there until, at seventeen, he had finished the gymnasium or high school. Off he went then to the University, where he distinguished himself highly for the amount of beer he could drink and the number of duels he fought. Once he had four on his hands at one time, and fought twenty-eight in his first three semesters. Oh, he was a lusty fellow, but keen, too, for he finished his course in the law and passed the state examinations.

Not long after, at a ball, he met for the first time his future sovereign, Prince Wilhelm, eighteen years his senior.

"Why aren't you a soldier?" asked the Prince, astonished to find that a young man six feet and over was not in the best of all professions.

"I had no prospect of advancement in the army, Your Highness," replied Bismarck tactfully. Truth was, he hated drill and discipline.

"You'll have no better prospects in the law," replied the Prince.

It seemed so for a time. After being misfitted in a few government positions, the young lawyer went home to Pomerania, upon his father's death, to manage the estate. Then to keep from being bored and despondent he gave parties so wild and hilarious as to become the scandal of the countryside. Pomeranian girls eyed him as dangerously exciting, while their mammas warned them against the "mad young Bismarck." Otherwise he had not distinguished himself particularly, before he was called to the Prussian Assembly by the King.

Now at Frankfort, as ambassador to the German Confederation, he had startled the old diplomats by impudently smoking a cigar.

"Mad Bismarck," they called him, those diplomats, little realizing then just how much method there was in that so-called madness. Neither did they know how much they amused him with their pompous manners, nor how he was sizing them up, and what a working knowledge of the ins and outs of diplomacy he was acquiring and storing up for future use. But Bismarck knew, and chuckled to himself.

"I am making enormous progress," he wrote home, "in the art of saying nothing in a great many words. I write reports of many sheets, which read as tersely as leading articles, and if any one can say what there is in them after he has read them, he can do more than I can." He chuckled as he wrote, and drew deep on his cigar.

"Mad Bismarck," was he? About as mad, that Bismarck, as a fox!

AT HOME IN SPRINGFIELD

L ATE IN THE SPRING of 1849, a tall man wearing a faded high hat, and carrying a shabby carpetbag descended from the stagecoach in Springfield, Illinois. Abe Lincoln was home again. His term in Congress was over . . . and, also, he believed, his political career. Doomed to failure, he was. Others succeeded. Stephen A. Douglas, who had entered the State Legislature the same year he had, was forging ahead, now a United States Senator with a brilliant future. Only he, Abraham Lincoln, failed.

Mary might have married Douglas, he thought, as he turned down Jackson Street and approached the frame house on the corner. Been better for her if she had than tied up to a failure. His wife didn't act as if she felt that way, though, when he opened the door and set down his carpetbag. He felt stimulated by her pride and spunk.

Mary Lincoln, whatever doubts she may have had about her husband's future during his absence, at seeing him again felt confidence in her first judgment of him. She was glad to have him home, and for once, at least, said nothing when he unwound his necktie and dropped it on the floor. She even held her tongue when he pulled off his boots and sat in his stocking feet playing with the little boys.

There were two of them. Bobby was five, Eddie was two years younger. They climbed all over their papa, while he hugged and kissed them, laughing as hard as they did when they tickled his ears, and tried to poke their fingers up his nose. He put first one and then the other astride his shoulders and gave them a ride around the room. They showed him the new kittens and it was time for supper.

Mary, who had had to help the new "hired girl" make gravy, came to the table irritated at her stupidity, and when the boiled potatoes weren't done in the center, she snapped at her so sharply that the poor thing stumbled out weeping into the kitchen, and next morning she was gone. The girl that followed cooked no better. Meals were never much good at the Lincoln house, but the head of the house didn't complain. Friends said Lincoln never seemed to know what he was eating. His wife thought sometimes he didn't even know that a meal was on the table. She'd see him sit staring into space—lost in thought. Suddenly he would laugh or speak.

"What would you say, Mrs. Lincoln," he asked one day, "to going out to Oregon territory, if the party gave me the job of Governor?"

"No!" said Mrs. Lincoln. "Absolutely not!" She had her reasons. Aside from the fact that living in Oregon would be duller than Springfield, which, heaven knows, was dull enough, it seemed to her that to bury himself in that far-off corner would certainly spell the end of any man's political career. So Lincoln turned back to the practice of the law in Springfield with his partner Herndon.

LINCOLN & HERNDON. So read the gilt letters on their sign that hung opposite the Court House. It creaked in the warm prairie wind, that first morning as the tall disconsolate man passed under it and up the wooden stairs, down the narrow hall to the dingy office.

Didn't seem hardly fair to share the proceeds from the business Herndon had worked to keep up while he was gone. He offered to withdraw but the younger man wouldn't hear of it, so the firm continued.

Lincoln took up life where he had left off, riding the circuit of the county courts all over the state three months each spring and autumn and trying cases there in Springfield in the winter.

Mornings when he went to the office about nine o'clock, the first thing he did was to lie down on the haircloth sofa, fling one leg on a chair and read the newspaper out loud. Then he might go over to the desk near one of the two grimy windows, jot down a few notes about some case, and drop them in his hat. Very few, however.

"Notes are a bother," he told a young law student. "Take time to make and more to hunt up afterwards." He relied on his memory, for though his desk was a mess, his mind was in perfect order.

"Talk to the jury," he also added, "as though your client's fate depended on every word you uttered."

"Lincoln himself did that very thing," said the youngster after watching him. "He steered the jury by skillful questions and by a joke or a quick retort as the trial progressed."

One day in court a man had brought suit against another for beating him up when he himself had provoked the fight.

"Reminds me," said Lincoln to the jury, "of the man who killed a farmer's dog with a pitchfork after the dog had bitten him. 'What'd you kill my dog for?' yelled the farmer. 'Why didn't you go at him with the other end?' 'Why,' replied the man, 'why didn't the dog come at me with his other end?'" The jury saw the point and laughed. Lincoln laughed too, and the argument over, sat down, giving a jerk to the single suspender that held up his pants.

The all-important button holding that single suspender was gone one day and he was whittling a plug of wood to take its place when a young attorney came up to him in the court room asking for some help.

"Just wait," said he, "till I fix this plug of my gallis' and I'll pitch into it like a dog at a root."

By "pitching in" Lincoln was always also turning up unexpected bits of evidence as in the case of his old friend Jack Armstrong's boy who had been accused of killing a man.

"I seen him do it," swore one witness. "The moon was shining just as bright as daylight."

"You're sure about that?" asked Lincoln, and then produced an almanac that proved that on that particular night there was no moon.

Then by an appeal that moved the jury to tears, while the boy's widowed mother sobbed beneath her bonnet, he won the freedom of his client. Few days of tears, there were, however. On many more the court room roared with laughter, when Lincoln had a case on trial.

Judge Davis, who was judge of the circuit court, enjoyed the stories Lincoln told as much as did the jury. The four or five lawyers who rode the circuit with him from one little county seat to another would gather at the end of the day in the judge's bedroom, and laugh and swap stories half the night. Lincoln's were the funniest by far, and he had great fun telling them. Judge Davis, who also knew his fits of melancholy, was always glad to see him when he was happy.

Saturdays, when they were near enough to do so, all the other lawyers would go home. Lincoln never seemed to want to. He stayed on wherever they happened to be, until the season was over. Then jogging over the countryside behind "Old Buck" he would go home to Springfield, to the house on the corner, to Mary's sharp tongue, to his little boys and to the dusty law office with its creaking sign.

Often at the office he would tip back in his chair, with his head against the wall, and sit as he did at home, staring into space with unseeing eyes, lost in thought. One day he suddenly dropped his feet to the floor and turned to Herndon.

"Billy," he said with a strange tone in his voice, "I fear I am going to meet with some terrible end . . . but that," he added, "accords with my philosophy." There was law and order, cause and effect, in all things. Why, then, should not a man's character with its strength and weaknesses lead his life inevitably to a foregone conclusion?

He went out of the office, then, and down the stairs, and soon Herndon heard him in the street below chatting with a group of friends and laughing as if he never had a serious thought in his mind.

231

FREE SOIL AND SLAVE

AMERICA was now coming to be looked upon more and more as the land of opportunity. In 1853, the *London Daily News* printed this article: "An American merchant has just arrived in Europe on a pleasure trip. His private yacht is a monster steamer, said to surpass in splendor the Queen's yacht. Mr. Cornelius Vanderbilt is a sign of the times. America was not known four centuries ago, yet she turns out her Vanderbilts small and large every year. America is the arena in which men have free play. All its citizens have full permission to run the race in which he, Vanderbilt, has gained such immense prizes."

It is no wonder, then, with such advertisement, that thousands of immigrants from Europe were coming to the United States each year. Landing in New York, they had almost doubled its population in ten years. Now a city of 600,000, it was known as "America's Front Door."

San Francisco, the door to the west, had grown even faster. In one year after the gold rush began, San Francisco had grown from a hamlet of four hundred people to a rough rowdy city of 20,000 and one of the five leading seaports in the world. California itself had 100,000 people, most of them swarming like bees around the lawless mining camps, and in 1849 California asked admission to the Union as a state.

Up came the old question of slavery again—not because there was any thought of making a slave state of California. There was no need for slaves in mining camps. California would be free. No, it was the same old trouble. There was then no territory also ready to come in as slave. So the balance between the slave and free states which now stood 15–15 threatened to be upset again, as it first had been thirty years before when Missouri asked to be admitted.

Young Henry Clay had then hushed the trouble with a compromise. Now in 1850 "the Great Peacemaker" proposed another one. He was an old man now, Henry Clay. This compromise of 1850 was to be his last.

"California will come in as a free state," he said. Very well. Then, in all other states made from the territory gained from Mexico let the people living there, and not Congress, decide whether they should be free or slave.

And, in addition, see that a strict FUGITIVE SLAVE LAW be enforced. That is, have officers in every state in the Union catch all runaway slaves and send them back to their owners.

That in the main was his proposal. It brought on an argument more intense and bitter than any argument over slavery had ever been before. While conservatives in both parties supported it, anxious to preserve the Union and keep peace at almost any price, both extreme pro- and anti-slavery men condemned it. Abolitionists damned the Fugitive Slave Law. Pro-slavery men cried that the division of territory was unfair to the South. What guarantee was there that the rest of the Mexican cession would be slave? What about Kansas, Nebraska and all the rest of that northern territory?

John C. Calhoun, great champion of slavery and states' rights, was determined to express the sentiments of the South for one last time, but he was old and too ill to speak. A friend read his speech.

"Senators," he began, "it can no longer be disguised that the Union is in danger. The southern States cannot remain as things are now with safety in the Union"—not unless, he said, there was equal division between the sections, and all anti-slavery talk by the Abolitionists was stopped. "If you who represent the stronger portion are not willing to settle on these principles, say so, and let us separate in peace."

"Separate in peace!" those words brought old Daniel Webster to his feet. Third of those young statesmen who had started out together, his hair was now white, but his eyes were as snapping black as ever. However much Daniel Webster hated slavery, he loved the Union more.

"Secession!" he cried, facing Calhoun. "PEACEFUL Secession! Sir! Your eyes and mine are never to see the division of this country without violent opposition. Why, sir, our ancestors—our fathers and grandfathers —would reproach us, and our children and grandchildren would cry out 'Shame!' No, sir! There will be no secession. . . . Let the compromise be accepted, by all means, if need be, to save the Union!"

Thus the three old statesmen spoke their final words in American politics. Younger men now stood ready to take their places.

JEFFERSON DAVIS   STEPHEN A. DOUGLAS   Wᴹ.H. SEWARD

William F. Seward, the new Senator from New York, spoke for the Abolitionists, who were shocked at what they called the "treachery" of Daniel Webster.

Jefferson Davis, Democrat Senator from Mississippi and a cotton planter, held out for the right of any man to go anywhere in the United States and take with him all property, including slaves.

Stephen Douglas, Democrat from Illinois, upheld the compromise, and after months of argument the compromise was finally passed.

Nobody was satisfied. The Abolitionists, and many other people, thought the Fugitive Slave Law was too unjust to be obeyed. Instead of returning them, a regular system arose for helping the slaves escape. Hidden by day, they would be taken at night from one place to the next northward from the Ohio River until they were safely over the border into Canada. These secret routes, traveled under cover of night, came to be spoken of as the "Underground Railway."

With this possibility of help, more and more slaves along the border attempted to escape. Southerners who saw people of the North actually breaking a law to rob them of what they honestly believed to be their property, became more and more convinced that union with the free states would only do them harm.

"Let them go in peace," then said the Abolitionists. Good riddance to bad rubbish. But those rabid Abolitionists were few.

Most Northern people felt that they must obey the law and in order to preserve the Union keep their mouths closed and say just as little about the dreadful question of slavery as possible.

That was how matters stood in the summer of 1850.

In the spring of 1850, little Mrs. Harriet Beecher Stowe, after almost twenty years in Cincinnati, was on her way back to New England with her family of small children. On her way to Maine, where Professor Stowe was to teach, she stopped off to see her brother, Henry Ward, in his church in Brooklyn, and her brother Edward and his wife in Boston. Everywhere she went she heard people discussing the new Fugitive Slave Law, and was shocked to find so many, even ministers of the gospel, upholding the compromise which included that sinful law.

"To me it is incredible," said Harriet, her small figure tense with feeling. "It cannot be that these people know what slavery is. They do not see what they are defending."

UNCLE TOM'S CABIN:

H B Stowe

1852

TRANSLATIONS

La Cabine de l'Oncle Tom (French)
La Capanna dello Zio Tommaso (Italian)
La Cabaña del Tio Tom (Spanish)
KHIZHINA DYADI TOMA (Russian)
Onkel Tom's hütte (German)
ONKEL TOM'S STUGA (Swedish)
Chatka Ojca Toma (Polish)
Setä Tumon Tupa (Finnish)
TAMÁS BÁTYA (Hungarian)
Καλυβη του Θωμα (Greek)

After she reached Maine, a letter came from brother Edward's wife. "Hattie," it said, "if I could use a pen as you can, I would write something to make the whole world see what an accursed thing slavery is!"

"I *will* write something," said Harriet in a low voice, crumpling the paper in her small thin hand. "I will write something."

Thinking over all that she had seen and heard of slavery out on the Ohio River, it occurred to her that the faithful slave husband of a free Negro woman whom she had known would be the perfect pattern for the main character in her story. She might call him Uncle Tom.

Sitting in church one Sunday morning, her mind sailed away from the little New England meeting house to a plantation in the Deep South. There she imagined Uncle Tom as an old man being beaten to death by a cruel master, and saw it all so vividly that she "shook with sobbing." She wrote that last chapter first. Then the rest of the book, characters and scenes, fell naturally into place.

She called it UNCLE TOM'S CABIN, or "Life Among the Lowly." And

236

it was a pitiful story, that tale of Uncle Tom, sold to pay the debts of his good Kentucky master—of Eliza who crossed the river on floating ice cakes—of the cruel slave driver Simon Legree with his cracking whip and his trusty bloodhounds . . . of Topsy, the black imp who "jes" growed," and angelic little white Eva who was too good to live.

Thrilled by it while she was writing, Harriet was so exhausted when it was finished that she was afraid nobody would read it, and that it would do no good for the anti-slavery cause.

Instead, it made the evils of slavery and the Fugitive Slave Law come to life to all who read it. And it was read by thousands, not only in America but all over the world, translated into many languages.

Published in book form on March 20, 1852, within the year eight presses running day and night could not keep up with the demand.

Letters of congratulation came pouring in to the author in Maine. An early one came from the "Swedish Nightingale," Jenny Lind, who was on her first American concert tour. She had "a feeling about *Uncle Tom's Cabin* that great changes would take place because of it."

Mrs. Stowe sent a copy to Charles Dickens, whom she addressed as "the first author of our day to turn the attention of the high to the joys and sorrows of the lowly." And he replied that he had read her book "with deepest interest and sympathy," but that if he "might suggest a fault in what had so charmed him, it would be that she went too far and sought to prove too much." "I think," he said, "this extreme championship likely to repel some useful sympathy and support . . ."

Harriet herself had been afraid, on the other hand, that she had been too moderate, and feared that by showing some slaveholders to be just and kind, she would antagonize the Abolitionists. Instead, the entire South rose up and attacked it, as a completely unfair picture, while the Abolitionists welcomed it, as a great help to their cause.

"What a glorious work Harriet Beecher Stowe hath wrought!" wrote John Greenleaf Whittier, the Quaker poet, to his great friend, William Lloyd Garrison. "THANKS for the Fugitive Slave Law, since it gave occasion for *Uncle Tom's Cabin*."

LAND OF NOBLES AND SERFS

RUSSIA'S GREAT author, Tolstoy, then but a young man in his twenties, was reading *Uncle Tom's Cabin* on an early September day in 1854, using his English dictionary occasionally, as he also had had to do in reading *David Copperfield*. Though he had a gnawing toothache, and was on his way to war, that story of "Life Among the Lowly" so excited his sympathy that he read on without interruption to the final page.

Tolstoy was a nobleman, but all the later years of his life, after giving away his fortune, he was to live and work among the lowly people of Russia, preaching the simple way of life. He had already started a school to teach the children of the serfs belonging to him.

Upon his father's death, Tolstoy had inherited Yasnaya Polyana, the country home near Moscow where he had been born, and with it 5400 acres of land and 350 serfs. In Russia, where a nobleman's wealth was rated by the number of "souls" or serfs he owned, a mere 350 did not make young Count Tolstoy a wealthy man.

No. Not in Russia. There, to be considered rich, a man must own at least 10,000 souls, for in Russia in 1854 twice as many peasants as there were people in the United States were held in bondage. There were roughly 23,000,000 serfs belonging to the Czar, and 23,000,000 more owned by the nobility. Bound to the land on which they lived, they were bought and sold with it like the other livestock and the buildings. Except that they could not be sold without the land, they were as slaves. A serf worked three days for his master each week, then three days for himself, in order to earn enough to pay taxes to the Czar, from which his master, being a nobleman, was exempt.

Yet these noblemen, of which there were only about 140,000 families, and the Czar owned nine-tenths of all the land of Russia, which meant that they owned nearly one-sixth of all the land on earth. That was the size of this largest of all nations. Largest in area, but most lacking in freedom of any empire in the world, it was ruled over by Europe's most despotic sovereign, Nicholas I.

Nicholas I, known as the "Iron Czar," had ruled for almost thirty years. He had come to the throne in the midst of rebellion, which he had stamped out by beheading the leaders and sending thousands to exile in Siberia. Then by a system of spies and censorship, he proceeded to shut off from the Russian people as far as possible all ideas of progress, science, liberty—everything that might disturb their blind obedience and worship. Then with his empire set to rights in frozen order, that most absolute of Czars looked outside of Russian boundaries and sought to extend his influence for good.

Like his grandmother, Catherine "the Great," and all Russian rulers before him, Nicholas I cast his eye on Turkey. With that empire growing weaker year by year, Turkey was looked upon by Russia and the other nations as the "Sick Man" of Europe. In 1853 Czar Nicholas I felt that Turkey's pulse had grown weak enough for him to relieve the Sultan of some responsibility. Therefore, he made it his "Christian" duty to interfere in Turkish affairs, and so started the useless slaughter known as the Crimean War.

Tolstoy was on his way to this war on that September day in 1854 when he was reading *Uncle Tom's Cabin.* He was waiting then to be transferred to Sevastopol, where the great siege of the war took place.

A LAMP IN THE CRIMEA

THE CRIMEAN WAR was the first great war in Europe since the fall of Napoleon in 1815, almost forty years before. Many claimed there would have been no great war in the Crimea, that England and France would not have joined in with Turkey, had it not been for another upstart emperor—Napoleon III.

Everyone knew, they said, that Napoleon III had a grudge against the Czar, because haughty Nicholas only, of all the European rulers, refused to call him "My dear Brother" as one king to another. Besides, Napoleon III was none too sure of his position at home. Feeling wobbly on the throne, he wanted a war to gain prestige and glory.

On the contrary, said others, Napoleon III did not want war. He had said on his coronation day that the "Empire meant Peace" and his ambition was to be the Peacemaker of Europe. He had gone to war only to make peace, they said. It sounded a bit confusing, but perhaps "Napoleon the Little," as Victor Hugo called him, *was* a bit confused!

It was a religious argument that the Czar had raised with the Sultan of Turkey. Many Christians were living in the Turkish Empire, often as cruelly treated by the Mohammedan officials as the Greeks had been when they rebelled. Jerusalem was also under Turkish rule. The Czar, therefore, as head of the Greek Orthodox Church, claimed the right to protect Christians in Turkey and also the shrines in the Holy Land. That did not please France. France was a Roman Catholic nation and held that, by a treaty with Turkey, she had the sole right to do whatever protecting was to be done. Roman Catholic and Greek Orthodox Christians of that day could not work together, so they went to war. Mohammedan subjects of the Sultan, if they thought of it, must have found it strange to see two so-called Christian nations squabbling over the holy shrines of their religion, which taught peace and good will on earth.

England was drawn into war for a practical reason. Far better for her that "the sick man of Europe" hold on to life, than that Russia gain so much power in Turkey as to possibly interfere with her main route to India. So France and England, and also little Piedmont (for reasons not yet disclosed), became allies of Turkey, and in 1854 declared war on Russia and sent off their boys to die in the Crimea.

The siege of Sevastopol, Russia's stronghold on that Black Sea peninsula, was one of the great events of the war. The other, made famous by Tennyson, occurred at Balaklava. There, in an effort to recover some guns captured by the Russians, an officer had blundered and sent the Light Brigade charging to certain death.

Half a league, half a league,   "Forward, the Light Brigade!
Half a league onward,   Charge for the guns!" he said.
All in the valley of Death   Into the valley of Death
   Rode the six hundred.   Rode the six hundred.

Tennyson, at home in England, could imagine only the glory of the charge. He was not on the battlefield. Young Tolstoy was there in the thick of it, at Sevastopol. And although he served bravely, he questioned why. He told how the French and Russian soldiers hobnobbed together like friends during the truce to allow the dead to be buried. "Then," said he, "the white flags are lowered again, the engines of war are sounding again, again the air is filled with moans and curses."

Florence Nightingale, too, heard those moans and curses. As a trained nurse, she could almost hear them in London when she read in the London TIMES that no sufficient preparations had been made for the care of the wounded. "Not only are there not sufficient surgeons," the article continued. "There are no nurses. There is not even linen to make bandages. Not only are the men kept in some cases for a week without the hand of a medical man coming near them, but many are brought down three days after the battle without their wounds having even been washed. Most of them have died from want of proper care."

Into this horror went Florence Nightingale, the first woman nurse to serve in war. With thirty-seven nurses she sailed from London for the Crimea, four days after the Charge of the Light Brigade. With her courageous spirit, her skill as a nurse, her executive ability, she set to work with furious energy to establish order and bring comfort to thousands of these stricken soldiers. To them she appeared like an angel of mercy. They even blessed her shadow thrown by the lamp she carried as she went her rounds during the long hours of the night.

The story of her heroic service spread. Far off in his quiet study in Massachusetts Longfellow wrote of her:

"Lo! in that house of misery
A lady with a lamp I see
Pass through the glimmering gloom
And flit from room to room."

The war ended with the siege of Sevastopol. Before that, Nicholas I had died, so it was with his son Alexander II that the treaty of peace was signed. What the war accomplished is difficult to see.

The Sultan was made to promise that he would treat his Christian subjects better, but later didn't keep his word. For making that promise, however, Turkey, hitherto looked upon as a barbarous nation, was admitted to the European family of states.

Napoleon III also came out in higher standing among the kings Host to the peace commissioners who met in Paris, victorious foe of powerful Russia, intimate and trusted ally of England, he was quite the man of the day in Europe . . . at least a man to be reckoned with. He and Eugenie were even on visiting terms with Victoria and Albert.

England's Royal Family

FAMILIES AND FRIENDS

"HOW STRANGE," thought Victoria, "that I, the granddaughter of George III, should be dancing with the Emperor Napoleon III, nephew of England's greatest enemy, and in the *Waterloo* Room! And to think that only six years ago he was living in this country an exile, poor and unthought of."

It was the evening of the court ball, which she and Prince Albert were giving in honor of Napoleon III and Eugenie on their first visit to England as Emperor and Empress. It had been Albert's idea to invite them. He had met Louis Napoleon at Boulogne a few months before and been rather well impressed by him, and also pleased to discover that he spoke German even better than English.

Eugenie had been thrilled, but distinctly awed at the prospect of the important visit. It had been a foggy day when they arrived in London. As they drove across town and Louis Napoleon pointed out to her the house where he had lived when there in exile, she felt even less sure of herself as an Empress. The Queen's natural, cordial greeting when they reached Windsor Castle that evening put her more at ease, but what despair was hers when, upon going to her room to dress for dinner, she discovered that her trunks had not arrived!

"I knew that fog was a bad sign," she moaned. "What *shall* I do?"

"You might pretend to have a sick headache and stay in bed," was her husband's not too helpful suggestion.

One of the ladies-in-waiting, however, saved the situation by offering a "little blue silk" of hers with the full crinoline skirt, which Eugenie wore and in which the Queen thought she looked very charming. In fact, Victoria was altogether pleased with Eugenie, who was "so gentle, graceful and kind," she said, "and so modest and retiring."

Napoleon III also pleased his hostess, who felt that there was "something so fascinating, melancholy and engaging about him."

The guests spent a week and, in August, Albert and Victoria went to Paris to return the visit, taking with them Vicky, the princess Royal, in a pretty bonnet, and the Prince of Wales dressed in a Scotch plaid suit. Cheering crowds, bands playing *God Save the Queen*, signs of welcome enthusiastically misspelled with two "l's," greeted England's royal lady. It was the first time a ruler of England had set foot in France for over four hundred years. The weather was extremely hot but Victoria, holding aloft a small green parasol, wanted to see everything that there was to see, both historical and gay.

It was a rainy day when they visited the tomb of Napoleon. Outside the thunder rolled, while inside the wavering torches of the guards lighted the gloom. Victoria was moved to tears, and made the Prince of Wales kneel by the tomb of that man who, when alive, had been England's greatest enemy!

"Strange and wonderful," she thought it was. "As if in this tribute to a dead foe, old enmities were wiped out forever between the two great nations."

The visit ended with a ball in the Hall of Mirrors at Versailles, a dazzling affair of diamonds and jewels, bare shoulders, gold-trimmed uniforms, wide tilting skirts, full beards and astonishing moustachios.

Dressed in a pure white uniform was a huge German with a smooth-shaven chin, but a bushy red moustache, who bowed deeply to England's Queen as he was presented. Herr von Bismarck, the Prussian minister at Frankfort. It was their first meeting.

"She is unsympathetic towards me," thought the shrewd man, and if he thought so, she was. Certainly she would have been more so had she known then how "unsympathetic," to put it lightly, he was to be towards her Vicky, who was so soon to go to Prussia as a bride.

Vicky was almost sixteen. As soon as the Paris visit was over and they were home again, the son of Prussia's warlike Prince Wilhelm, who had visited the Great Exhibition with his father, came to England to pay another visit. Vicky's engagement to him was then arranged. Both families were very happy, feeling that the marriage would be a strong bond between Prussia and England.

In January, 1858, the marriage took place, and a year later, in Berlin, Vicky's son was born. Victoria's first grandchild—"dear little William," she called him, little knowing that he was to become Kaiser Wilhelm II, as great an enemy of England as Napoleon I.

"Strange and wonderful" it is indeed how old enmities are wiped out and new ones arise.

Grandpa: Wilhelm

Papa: Frederick

Mama: "Vicky"

Grandma: Victoria

These first years following the visit to Paris seemed especially full of births, engagements and marriages of especial interest. The year before "Vicky" was married, her youngest sister was born, making Victoria and Albert's family of four sons and five daughters complete.

In 1856 a son, the Prince Imperial, had been born to the Empress Eugenie and Napoleon III.

That same spring Victoria learned of dear Charlotte's engagement to the charming Archduke Maximilian of Austria.

Charlotte was the daughter of Uncle Leopold. She was an attractive, very intelligent girl, whose face was made almost beautiful by her large dark eyes, which were not brown, but an unusual shade of green, and fringed with long black lashes. Seventeen, she had been dreaming of a romantic future, but at the same time fearful that, for the sake of politics, she might have to marry some one very ugly, when lo and behold! Prince Charming himself appeared upon the scene, the Archduke Maximilian!

Extremely blond, divinely tall, and almost handsome, Maximilian, who was then twenty-five, had always been the favorite brother of Franz Josef, although since Franzi had become Emperor he seemed to care for nothing outside of his empire and "Sisi."

In the spring of 1856, Maximilian had set out on a tour of the European capitals to find himself a wife, not that he wanted to. His mother insisted upon it, to get him away from a bewitching Hungarian Countess, with whom he had been so impractical as to fall in love.

Making it also a pleasure jaunt, Maximilian went first to Paris, where he spent twelve enchanting days, and wrote home with great enthusiasm of the improvements being made there by Napoleon III. Old tenements were being torn down, and an architect was transforming the narrow, crooked streets into broad, beautiful boulevards. The Emperor himself did not appeal to Maximilian.

"His stubby stature," he wrote Franz Josef, "his shuffling walk, ugly hands, sly inquisitive glance, make a most ungainly impression. His interest in every attractive female is also becoming notorious, and will greatly diminish his prestige as a sovereign."

Eugenie, he had to admit, was "undeniably beautiful"—Eugenie, who was to help bring about that fine young Maximilian's tragic death and the even worse fate of poor little Charlotte.

Charlotte had fallen in love with the young Austrian at first sight, and in spite of himself those wonderful eyes of hers cast their spell upon Maximilian. He could not forget them when he left. Upon his return to Vienna, therefore, the marriage was arranged.

As a wedding settlement, Franz Josef had decided to give Maximilian his two northern provinces of Italy—Lombardy and Venetia.

A month before their marriage in Belgium, the young Austrian bridegroom crossed to England to visit his new "Cousin Victoria," who promptly wrote to Uncle Leopold how much they liked him.

"He is so charming," she wrote, "so kind and amiable, so *English* in his feelings, and so anxious for the best understanding between Austria and England. I wish you really joy, dearest Uncle, at having got *such* a husband for dear Charlotte . . . He may and will do a great deal for Italy" . . .

For Italy? The Archduke Maximilian wanted sincerely to do a great deal for Italy and, when they went to live there, Charlotte so fell in love with the sunny land that she even changed her name to the Italian Carlotta. Both felt that they would be happy to stay on forever in the Palazzo at Milan. But it was to be only two years before Maximilian and Carlotta would have to pick up their things and flee!

For in two years the Italians, aided this time by France, were to be at war with Austria . . . fighting again for independence.

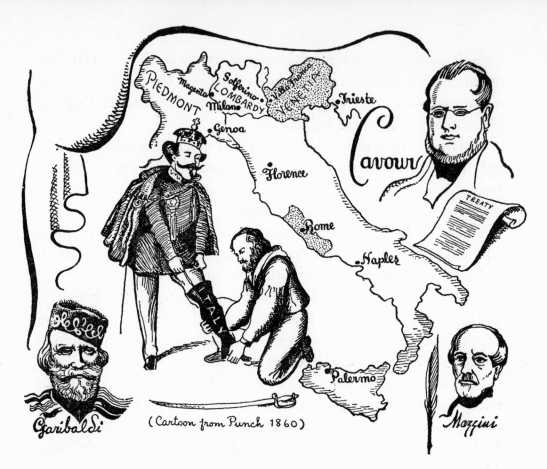

(Cartoon from Punch 1860)

"VIVA L'ITALIA!"

ONE FINE DAY in July, 1858, riding in a natty carriage along one of the airy mountain roads outside of a health resort in eastern France, two men had been planning that war of Italy and France against Austria. The one with the pointed, waxed moustache who held the reins and did the driving was our friend Napoleon III. Beside him sat a portly man, wearing small steel-rimmed spectacles on a large round face. He was Cavour, Count Emile Cavour, Prime Minister of Piedmont, one of the sanest men and cleverest diplomats in Europe. He had come incognito for this secret meeting with Napoleon III with the single purpose of gaining his help for Italy. He did not intend to return to Piedmont without news for his King, Victor Emmanuel, that the arrangements were complete.

Count Cavour was an upright man. He did not like dealing with Napoleon III, who had broken a solemn vow in order to become Emperor, but he had long felt that the help of France was necessary to Piedmont. So three years before he had laid the groundwork for this meeting, by sending Italian troops to help France in the Crimean War. That was a subtle way of reminding the French Emperor of his old promise to help Italy. Many years before Louis Napoleon had made this vow:

"When I shall preside over the destinies of France, I shall support with all my strength the claims of Italy to become a nation."

Then he was a French exile helping Italy fight for freedom, and then, no doubt, intended to keep that promise. As Emperor, however, it seemed that he had changed his mind, or else forgotten about it.

An excitable young Italian, in fact, had so brooded over this forgetfulness of Napoleon III that, only six months before, he had tried to assassinate him. Unsuccessful, the Italian had gone to his death warning the fickle Emperor with his last breath not to break his vow to Italy.

All things considered, then, it seemed to the little man who did the driving that afternoon that the time had come to fulfill his promise. But, as protector of the peace of Europe, he could do so only if it was plain to see that he was helping a weaker nation against an aggressor. Therefore he said he would help Piedmont, provided only that Austria could be made to take the first hostile step.

Count Cavour agreed to that proviso. It would not be very difficult to bring about, though it might take a little time. He bade Napoleon III adieu, went home to Piedmont and sent out a message.

It brought results. One day early in 1859 his servant reported that a blond man in a red blouse and an embroidered cap was at the door, asking to see him, but refusing to give his name.

"Let the poor devil in," said Cavour. "No doubt he has some petition to present," and when Garibaldi entered he closed the door behind them and explained his plan for provoking Austria.

Soon thereafter what appeared to be a spontaneous uprising of Italian soldiers occurred all over northern Italy, with the great adventurous Garibaldi at their head. Austria was on the alert immediately.

"Disarm those soldiers at once," came the cold positive order from Austria to Piedmont in the name of the Emperor Franz Josef.

Piedmont refused. Austria, seeing therefore that she would have to disarm the Italians herself, sent troops over the border into Piedmont, thus taking, as Cavour had planned, the first hostile step. It was then up to Victor Emmanuel to take the next one; he was ready.

Victor Emmanuel, King of Piedmont, was a rough, brusque, courageous man, and very level-headed. His feet were firmly planted on the ground, while his moustache swooped boldly across his face like the handlebars of a bicycle, and his voice had force behind it.

"People of Italy," he now proclaimed, "Austria assails Piedmont. I can with free conscience take up arms to defend my throne and the liberties of the whole nation. "Viva l'Italia!"

Victor Emmanuel then met Napoleon III at Genoa, and they went off to the front together. At the same time, Franz Josef left Vienna. The old Austrian commander who had put down the former Italian uprisings had died, and since there seemed no one to take his place, Franz Josef, inexperienced though he was, felt that the duty was his.

Emperors and King therefore were approaching each other. So too were their soldiers. The Italians and French were well-trained, seasoned troops from the Crimea, equipped with modern weapons.

The Austrians, who hadn't fought a war in forty years, came to this one decked out gorgeously in "brass helmets, white coats, green plumes and cockades, maroon capes and silver bayonets," and carrying weapons so antiquated that they belonged in a museum.

"Surprising," Napoleon wrote Eugenie, "that they aren't still wearing powdered wigs!"

Eugenie, the Empress, was in Paris, acting as Regent during her husband's absence and praying devoutly every day for the success of his expedition. In Vienna "Sisi" was also praying for the safety and success of her handsome Franz Josef, and writing him wild, tearful letters. In reply he would beg his "dear dear only angel Sisi" not to despair.

"That one must bear trials with resignation and do one's duty in all things." . . .

He wrote those words after the battle of MAGENTA, which was a smashing defeat for Austria, and such a complete victory for France and Italy that the Italians sang with joy, and in Paris the modistes began to feature a new shade of bluish red, calling it "Magenta"!

The battle of Solferino was another great victory for Italy and France, and another dreadful defeat for Austria. One of the worst battles of the century; 40,000 out of 260,000 men were killed. From opposing hills, in a blazing July sun, the two emperors watched the dreadful slaughter, Franz Josef stoically. Not so, Napoleon III. The sight of blood nauseated him. He had had enough. Also in his pocket was a note from Eugenie which made him worry about his own affairs.

So at once, after that great victory at Solferino, without a single word to his ally, Napoleon III asked Franz Josef to meet him across the river at Villa Franca and arrange for peace. There the French Emperor informed the Austrian that Lombardy must go to Piedmont, he might keep Venetia, after which, bidding him a jaunty *auf-wiedersehen* and giving a twist to his waxed moustachios, Napoleon III was off for Paris. His part in this war was over.

Cavour, Garibaldi, Victor Emmanuel, who were working for but one cause, the union and freedom of their country, were aghast at Napoleon's "treachery." Cavour, ill from overwork, Garibaldi frantic with anger, both rushed to Victor Emmanuel and threatened to resign. The King was enraged as they were, but his feet were more firmly planted on the ground.

"No!" said he. "We have gained much. Italians must neither lay down their arms nor be discouraged."

So the fight for freedom in Italy went on.

In the spring of 1860, Garibaldi set out with his legion of a thousand Red Shirts on what was to be his most famous expedition. Secretly, on the night of May fifth, they sailed from Genoa for Sicily to conquer that island, to set it free from its despotic ruler, and to make it part of a united

251

Italy. Sicily was guarded by an army of 50,000 men. Garibaldi had only 1000 and scantily equipped, but in less than a month they had accomplished their purpose. The King had fled, the island was free! It was a remarkable feat, a true adventure more daring and amazing than even those invented by Garibaldi's author friend for the "Three Musketeers"!

Strangely enough, that very author was there with Garibaldi in Sicily. It happened that three days after the Red Shirts left Genoa, Alexandre Dumas, the great rollicking French genius, with his warm heart and mop of kinky hair inherited from his Negro grandmother, had sailed into the harbor at Genoa aboard his new play boat the *Emma*.

He was bound for the Orient, but hearing the news, followed in the wake of more exciting adventure. So there he was standing in a balcony in Palermo, Sicily, waving a banner, as Garibaldi came marching in from a glorious expedition, followed by the victorious Red Shirts singing through the streets. It was a thrilling sight.

"Oh! if you could only have been with me on this balcony," wrote Dumas in a letter to his old friend, his "dear, dear Victor Hugo."

From Sicily, Garibaldi crossed to the mainland and captured Naples. On November first he welcomed Victor Emmanuel and gallantly, nobly, declining all honors, like a knight of old, laid liberated Sicily and Naples at his sovereign's feet. So with Garibaldi holding it, Victor Emmanuel, Italy's first King, shoved his foot firmly into the boot of the peninsula. Venice and the country immediately surrounding Rome still remained to be liberated, but otherwise Italy was at last a free and united nation.

It was a great victory, in which each of four men had played his part.

MAZZINI, the idealist, who had sounded the first cry (and now came home from a long exile in London);

CAVOUR, the practical statesman, who faced facts as they were;

GARIBALDI, the adventurer and soldier; and

VICTOR EMMANUEL, the level-headed King.

Well might they cry now, those four patriots, "Viva l'Italia!"

THE DEVIL'S WIND

IN ENGLAND the summer of 1857, a new medal, the Victoria Cross, was just being awarded to heroes from the Crimea who had fought to protect England's route to India, when suddenly from India came shocking news of a rebellion. A Sepoy Rebellion, a revolt of the native soldiers, or sepoys, that had been caused by a new type of rifles recently sent out from London. The Indians would not use them. The cartridges were greased with beef tallow and lard, so they refused to bite off the patches with their teeth. And who could blame them, when to taste the fat of the sacred cow or the foul pig would render them outcaste and damn their souls forever?

The British officers in India, knowing the belief of the Hindus, might very easily have seen to it in the first place, that another grease was used, and so avoided the trouble. They did not. Therefore, the "Devil's Wind," as the natives called it, had begun to blow. In the military report the officers spoke of it as a "mutiny."

Mr. Disraeli, however, in a speech to Parliament described it as a national revolt, citing causes which in his opinion justified it.

The rule of the East India Trading Company was generally known to be far from perfect. And it was by this trading company, never directly by the English government, that India had been ruled for the past hundred years. Just a hundred years it was since the English General Clive had defeated the French, driven them out and established England as supreme. According to an old prophecy, one hundred years after that victory, in 1757, the power of the English East India Trading Company would be overthrown. It was now 1857.

One hundred years had passed. Ten years more than the life of old Shah Mohammed Bahadour, who now, in his ninetieth year, was still living with his tremendous family in the rose-red palace beside the Jumna River in ancient Delhi. But when he was gone, his sons would no longer live there, so the British had decreed.

Therefore the old man was glad when one morning, from a balcony overlooking the river, he saw a regiment of mutinous sepoys coming up from Merrut, where the uprising had begun. He was glad to see them cross the river on a bridge of boats, circle the walls to the Rajghat Gate, and burst into the European quarters with "swords drawn and murder in their eyes." From there they rushed down the Street of Silver past the diamond merchants, with their scarlet teeth, on to the palace fortress. There they murdered five British officers and took possession of Delhi. All that pleased old Shah Mohammed Bahadour.

Two hundred miles away at Bithoor on the sacred Ganges, word of that mutiny also sounded sweet in the ears of a much younger man, one with strange uneasy eyes. For it was he, Nana Sahib, who now nursed a grievance there beside the sacred river, instead of his adopted father.

The Peshwa of Poona was dead. He, Nana Sahib, had applied the torch to his funeral pyre as a son should do, expecting also as a son to inherit his father's pension. But the British had refused to pay it. Therefore they, the British, had made him no longer a son of his father and, by so doing, damned his father's soul for all eternity! And also, do not forget, deprived him of a fortune!

"Ah!" said he with satisfaction at word of the mutiny in Merrut and the capture of Delhi. At once he went to Cawnpore and offered his help to the British commander to protect the English women and children there in case the mutiny should spread. Nana Sahib's eyes were shifty, but his face was round and jovial, and his cordial manner hid the murder that was in his heart. So the old British commander, who looked upon all the natives as "his children," supposed Nana Sahib was friendly and accepted his offer, gratefully.

Nana Sahib then brought three hundred of his soldiers into that city of Cawnpore and caused a massacre of all English men, women and children. The last few, huddled together in a little dark house known as the Bee-bee-ghar, were killed at twilight one June night by two Hindu butchers and dumped into an empty well.

It was all too hideous. So, too, was the revenge taken by the frantically furious British soldiers, as they came marching up the Ganges, hanging thousands of innocent people who had taken no part whatever in the mutiny. The siege of Lucknow was the last chapter in the Sepoy Rebellion. There kind and wise Sir Henry Lawrence died.

"Until we treat natives as having much the same feelings as we have ourselves," he had often said, "we shall never be safe in India."

That was the way, of course, all sensible people felt. Victoria was shocked to hear some saying that all natives of India were cruel, and was happy to hear of the many instances during the trouble when both Hindus and Mohammedans had shown great kindness and generosity. The Maharajah of Singh, whom she and Albert had known well for many years, was, she said, the kindest and most gentle of men.

A little over a year from the time trouble began, the siege of Lucknow had been raised, Nana Sahib had fled from Cawnpore, Delhi was again in English hands, and the Devil's Wind had ceased to blow. The rebellion which, if successful, might have been called the Indian War for Independence was over.

In 1858, a year late, the old prophecy was fulfilled. The government was transferred from the East India Trading Company to the English Government. The Proclamation issued by Queen Victoria to announce that change ended with these words: "It is our further will that our subjects of whatever race or creed be freely admitted to our service, the duties of which they may be qualified to discharge."

It would still be another nineteen years before Victoria would be given the title of Empress of India by Disraeli.

ABOUT "PEACE" AND FOREIGNERS

For China, the year 1858 was the seventh year in the reign of the Manchu Emperor Hien Feng. It was also the seventh year of a revolt to overthrow that Emperor and his Manchu Dynasty—a ruinous civil war known as the TAIPING REBELLION. Li Hung Chang was twenty-eight years old at the outbreak of this war and loyal to the Empire which had educated him. Now one of the foremost scholars in China, he had been graduated with high honor from Hanlin Academy, or "Forest of Pencils" at Peking, and the fame of his beautiful handwriting had spread throughout the provinces.

His noble and severe father and his mild mother were proud beyond compare that their son had brought such honor to his village. He, too, was well pleased with his accomplishment and praise. He had memorized all the Analects of Confucius, he could recite backward or forward whole volumes of the Classics, and write essays or verses on any subject. In other words, he had all knowledge ever considered necessary to equip a Statesman or Scholar in ancient China.

But Li Hung Chang soon realized that all ways of ancient China did not fit a modern world, and saw that there were other things to learn if a Chinese statesman was to hold his own among the aggressive foreigners from the west.

The first foreigners Li Hung Chang came to know well were two adventurers who took part in the Taiping Rebellion, helped put down the rebels and prevent the Manchu Dynasty from being overthrown. By that they actually rendered China a doubtful service.

The Manchu Dynasty had become corrupt, and the government was rotten to the core. Originally the Manchus were foreigners. The first emperor, a wild Tartar horseman, had come down from the north and conquered China about 1640, or the time that European traders had first come sailing into Chinese waters. To show that they were conquered, he had decreed that his Chinese subjects must shave their heads, leaving only a long queue like the tail of his wild horse.

The Manchus had otherwise adopted all of China's customs, soon were foreigners no longer, and most Chinese had almost forgotten in 1858 why they wore the pigtail. That is, the Chinese of the north and central part. The tribes in the mountains of the south had never worn it. They had never been subdued, always rebellious. And it was there in the south that the Taiping Rebellion started.

There a secret society had grown strong with the purpose of overthrowing the Manchu Dynasty. But their plans were weak and ill defined, until in 1851 a wild-eyed fanatic had become their leader. The son of a poor farmer near Canton, he had studied hard to become a schoolmaster, then tried for the Budding Genius Examinations and failed. One day the disappointed fellow was in Canton, and met a Protestant missionary who gave him some literature, which he read so feverishly that he began to have visions and hallucinations.

"I am the Heavenly Prince, the younger brother of Jesus Christ," he told the people of his village. "God the Father urges me to take up arms against the Manchu Emperor." And his voice was so strong and vibrant with emotion that he convinced those people.

A thousand followers started north with him, capturing villages as they went, and adding to their ranks. They were 100,000 strong when they reached the mouth of the Yangtse Kiang in 1853 and captured the city of Nanking.

There, in Nanking, the "Heavenly Prince," as he called himself, established his new dynasty, which he called "Taiping" or Great Peace dynasty. Then as Emperor he sat himself comfortably down in a luxurious palace, supplied with plenty of rice-wine and concubines, and enjoyed this "peace" of his while the war continued.

His rebel army of 100,000, plundering and looting as they went, now set forth in the direction of Peking, the Purple City, where the Manchu Emperor was still sitting on his Red Dragon Throne.

Then it was that Li Hung Chang entered the Taiping Rebellion as a soldier, to help put down the rebels and protect the Manchu Emperor. He was in the city when the rebels reached Shanghai. Shanghai was even then an international city. Many Europeans were living there, and when the rebels attacked, French and English sailors came to the rescue and drove them off.

Li Hung Chang was impressed with the skill with which they did it, and looking about for someone to teach Chinese soldiers those western methods, his eye lit upon an American by the name of Ward.

Ward had sailed the world for sixteen years on Clipper ships, fought with Garibaldi in Uruguay, and had drifted into Shanghai, spoiling for more adventure. He fell in with the idea, and organized what he called his Ever-Victorious-Army.

Carrying a crown in his knapsack, it was said, just in case he should be lucky, Ward began to fight the rebels. He was killed.

A British administrator, soon known as "Chinese Gordon," took his place, and from Gordon, Li Hung Chang, who had already gained a healthy respect for foreigners as soldiers, learned that foreigners could also be straightforward and trustworthy.

Gordon, to put it bluntly, could not say as much for Li on one occasion. But then Li, on that occasion, could not see how Gordon could be so impractical. They didn't get each other's point of view.

Gordon had promised pardon to seven rebel chiefs, if they would surrender. Li Hung Chang knew of that promise, but nevertheless allowed the rebels to be tortured and beheaded. Gordon was perfectly furious. Li was quite at a loss to understand why, with so many bandits in China, Gordon should make such a fuss about the merest handful.

"This handful of bandits," said Li, "would have only returned to the path of rebellion, and tens of thousands would have suffered in consequence." Li Hung Chang had great skill with words.

The Rebellion finally ended after thirteen years with the capture of Nanking, suicide of the "Heavenly Prince" and overthrow of his Taiping Dynasty. Gordon was honored with the Peacock Feather and a yellow jacket. Li Hung Chang was made Governor of a province and began his career as China's great diplomat.

And the corrupt Manchu Dynasty was to continue its evil rule over China for another fifty years.

So the Taiping Rebellion ended, but in the midst of it, in 1858 the same year that the Sepoy Rebellion ended in India, France and England pointed their big guns at China, torn by civil war, and forced her to sign humiliating treaties.

Treaties were also signed by China with the United States and Russia, but less reluctantly, as there were no rankling grievances against those nations. With France and England it was a different story.

France wanted a chunk of Indo-China, and so claimed that the Chinese had killed a French missionary and should be "taught a lesson."

England and China had had a sharp argument as to whether the crew of a ship called the *Arrow,* who the Chinese said were pirates, should be tried by the British at Hong Kong, or by the Chinese Viceroy at Canton. The latter, growing weary of the many words, had chopped off some heads, which ended the pirates but not the argument.

Thus matters stood when representatives of the United States and Russia joined with those from France and England to secure better trade agreements with China. The four met with the Chinese Viceroy at Chihli and drew up four similar treaties which were sent on to Peking.

The American and Russian treaties came back shortly, signed and approved by the Emperor.

England and France received no word. They asked why and received no answer. An envoy tried in vain to reach Peking. Forts at the mouth of the river fired on English ships. An American, offering to act as go-between, made his way to Peking, and asked to see the Emperor. If he did, he was told that he must perform the kowtow, that is bow down before the Emperor and beat his head nine times upon the floor, which the American naturally refused to do, and left.

China, therefore, having unceremoniously slammed the door in the face of Europe, was to have it smashed in by force.

The following summer of 1860 found British and French soldiers marching through the gates and into the Purple City of Peking, from which the Emperor had fled. Then to "teach the Chinese a lesson" they went north, and, behaving like the barbarians they were supposed to be, ruthlessly burned the Emperor's beautiful summer palace to the ground. Needless to say, the treaties were signed by which:

壹 Envoys of foreign nations were allowed to reside in Peking.

弍 Foreign merchants might travel anywhere in China, ships trade all along the coast and even inland up the rivers.

叁 The sale of opium was made legal.

260

Naturally many Chinese were furious and cried for revenge. They still believed that China was a powerful nation, as it had been in the ancient days. They still cherished the idea that outside barbarians should be glad to kowtow before the Dragon Throne.

Li Hung Chang, however, was not so deceived. Quick as ever to learn his lessons, he saw facts as they were. A few years later, when he held a more responsible position, he expressed his views in a recommendation to the Emperor.

"The truth is," he said, "that at present foreigners are powerful and China is weak. If we are to cherish a feeling of revenge, it will be necessary to wait until we have large armies and abundant supplies to cope with them. . . . It is often said that foreigners are crafty and malign and full of unexpected tricks. But is it not the fact that Chinese are the same, perhaps even more so?

"The humble opinion of this writer is that in conducting affairs with foreigners one should avoid exciting their contempt. If they feel respect for China, even difficult questions can be settled by compromise. Not foreigners alone, but *all* persons are influenced by this feeling. It moves the minds of the whole human race."

And so Li Hung Chang, China's great statesman of the nineteenth century, said what China's great teacher Confucius had told ancient China 2500 years before:

"By nature all men are much alike, by custom only they grow wide apart," or in other words—

"Men of the four seas are brothers. . . ."

Li Hung Chang's Visiting card (about ½ actual size)

261

SHRINKING THE WORLD

CHINA was now opened to the world. Europeans were living in Shanghai. Factories, railroads and telegraph lines were being built in India. European traders had greater need than ever for a shorter route to the Far East, but still, as thirty years before, there was no canal across the Isthmus of Suez. Though Ferdinand de Lesseps still cherished the dream of building that great international river, his plans were not yet realized.

Mohammed Said, the fat boy who so loved macaroni, was now Viceroy of Egypt. He had approved the plan of his good friend, and offered large sums from Egypt's treasury, but, alas, the necessary consent could not be gained from his overlord, the Sultan of Turkey.

Certain politicians who happened to be in control of England's foreign policy at the time were whispering in the Sultan's ear.

"Don't do it," they said. "You'll regret it. Egypt may grow strong enough to secede from your Empire, or be taken by France."

What they actually feared was that in some way or other that canal might endanger England's route to India. All English statesmen were not

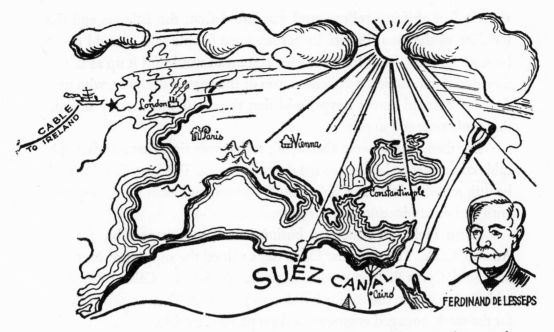

so narrow-minded. Gladstone for one, declared himself utterly disgusted.

"Nothing could be more deplorable than their attitude," said he in the House of Commons. "No one casting his eyes over the globe can deny that a canal through the Isthmus of Suez must be a great step towards the welfare of the whole world."

That didn't stop the opposition.

In France, too, de Lesseps struck a snag. Napoleon III couldn't make up his mind whether to support the plan wholeheartedly or not.

De Lesseps appealed to the Empress Eugenie, who was his cousin, to use her influence upon the Emperor. And for years he kept his carpet-bag packed, and traveled constantly back and forth from Cairo to London, to Constantinople, to Paris, to Cairo again and back to London, talking with everyone in authority who might help him in the great undertaking in which he had such faith.

Finally his persistence and faith were rewarded. The House of Commons voted its consent. The Emperor Napoleon III promised his support. The people of France bought bonds to supply the funds necessary in addition to those provided by Mohammed Said. And in 1859, the first shovelful of shifting yellow sand was lifted from the Isthmus and the building of the canal begun. Even then some people said it could never be accomplished. Mud from the Mediterranean would fill it up as fast as they dug it out. Robert Stephenson, son of the engine designer, who preferred a railroad across Egypt, said that the canal was a crazy scheme that could only end in ruin!

But then, people were also saying at that very time that no telegraph cable could ever be laid across the Atlantic Ocean. The Suez Canal would be dug and the Atlantic Cable would be laid, and each because of the faith and determination of a single man. . . .

Cyrus Field, an American business man, was responsible for the Atlantic Cable. The year that De Lesseps gained the support of Mohammed Said, Cyrus Field started to organize his Atlantic Cable Company, with Peter Cooper, the engine builder, as president. Then he raised funds for the work, engaged engineers and prepared the cable.

In 1857, two ships met in mid-ocean, one American, and one English, spliced the ends of their cables together, then gradually unwinding them, sailed back towards the opposite shores. The cable broke. Another attempt was made. Another failure.

Finally, the great wire rope was successfully unwound, and on August 16, 1858, the first message by telegraph went between England and America, to the great joy of those who had accomplished it. Their joy soon faded. The sounds grew weaker, and in October stopped entirely. The insulation, it seemed, had been burned off by using too strong an electric current. The work had to be done again.

"No use to try," most people said. "Plain to see it can't be done."

Cyrus Field thought it could. Undaunted he started in again, and for another eight years, while Ferdinand de Lesseps was digging away to shorten distance between Europe and Asia, Cyrus Field was working to shorten time and space between Europe and America. Also at that same time there was effort being made to shorten the distance across America from the Atlantic to the Pacific. Everywhere it seemed, men were trying to squeeze the world and make it smaller.

It took fifteen days to send a message by steamship from New York to London in 1859. It took twice as long, a month, for a letter from New York to reach San Francisco, sent the usual way by ship to Panama, overland across the isthmus, and by ship again up the western coast. Mail could go overland, across the continent, but the time was almost the same, and it was less sure to get there.

The railroad carried it as far west as Missouri. Telegraph wires had also reached Missouri. From there on, letters and messages were carried by the swaying, rattling stagecoaches of the Overland Mail Company, which went in the general direction of the old Santa Fe Trail to New Mexico, on to Los Angeles and up to San Francisco. A twenty-two days' trip. The letter might arrive and it might not, depending upon whether or not the coach was held up by bandits or attacked by Indians.

Californians, especially those lucky "Forty-Niners" who had about everything that gold could buy except fresh news from "home" were clamoring for speedier mail service. The same demand came from Colorado where gold had been discovered near Pike's Peak in 1859, and from Nevada where the great "Bonanza" silver mine had just been opened up. They also wanted news and better transportation.

Back in Congress it was being discussed. Jefferson Davis suggested using camels, and seventy-five were imported from Arabia. A stagecoach owner in Kansas had a more practical suggestion.

"Why not have horseback riders carry the mail in saddlebags?"

That suggestion caught on, ponies were rounded up, boys hired to ride them, and relay stations established every twenty-five miles or less, between Missouri and California. And in April, 1860, the first mail left Sacramento for the East and from St. Joseph, Missouri, for the West on the PONY EXPRESS.

With each rider making about seventy miles a day, at a speed of fifteen miles an hour, jumping from one to another of six ponies, and at the end of his run hurling his mail bags to the next, the mail was raced across the 2000 miles of Indian country from the Missouri River to the Pacific Ocean in nine days. Nine instead of twenty-two!

Meanwhile a thin line of telegraph poles, which would replace the Pony Express in two years, was creeping out from either end.

There was also much talk of building a transcontinental railroad. That would be a tremendous undertaking.

"They'll never get it over the Rocky Mountings," came the voice of the chronic can't-doers.

But that too, like the building of the Suez Canal, was to be accomplished, and only three years after the Atlantic cable was successfully laid. In the spring of 1869, the first locomotive would make the trip across the continent, and six months later the first ship would sail through the Suez Canal.

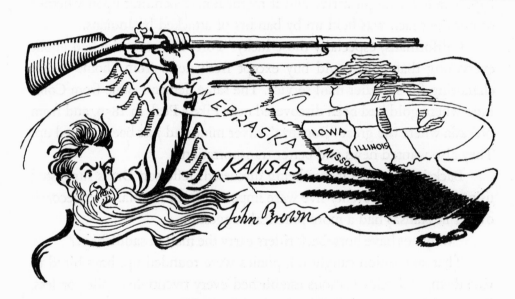

BLOODY KANSAS

A FOURTEEN-YEAR-OLD Kansas boy named Bill Cody, later known as "Buffalo Bill," held the record for the longest run ever made on the Pony Express. Three hundred twenty miles in twenty-one hours on twenty horses. Bill had been born in Iowa, but had been brought out to Kansas by his family when he was seven. Just over the Missouri River and a few miles out along the Salt Lake trail from

266

Leavenworth, Kansas, Bill's father, Isaac Cody, ran an Indian trading post. That is, he had, until he got stabbed in the back with a bowie knife by a border ruffian from Missouri. For he had dared to say, Isaac Cody had, that he was an Abolitionist and didn't want to see any slaves in Kansas. That was dangerous talk in 1854, for that year Congress had passed the Kansas-Nebraska Act.

Two years before when they left Iowa, the Codys had no idea that there would be any row in Kansas over slavery, or that Kansas would soon be made into a territory. There weren't enough white folks in that Indian country, no more than eight hundred in the entire region, and none of them had slaves. Besides, Kansas was free territory, because it was north of the slavery line set by the Missouri Compromise. So there'd been no talk about it—not until this new law was passed and then there was "hell to pay" in Kansas!

Politicians down in Washington, it seemed, had decided to make Kansas and Nebraska into territories and let the people who lived there decide themselves by vote whether they should be free or slave.

Soon the land was swarming with emigrants, both North and South making a frantic effort to fill up the country and control the vote. Out from Boston came bands of New Englanders with abolition books and rifles. The southern planters didn't move so easily, so border ruffians from the slave state of Missouri acted for them. As soon as free-soilers from Iowa, Illinois, Ohio, put up a cluster of tents or cabins, over the river from Missouri would come rough men in red shirts with bowie knives in the top of their boots, and stake out their claims to land with whiskey bottles stuck in upside-down.

One gang emptied too many of those whiskey bottles on a certain night and, swaggering forth, destroyed half of a new town built by northern settlers. That so raised the blood of "old John Brown," lately come from Iowa, that he and his sons killed five pro-slavery men on Pottawatomie Creek. Then with the fire of a crusader in his eye, "old John" headed east for ammunition to carry on his "holy" war.

Meanwhile down in Congress, Stephen A. Douglas, the Illinois

Senator who had proposed the Kansas-Nebraska Act, was bidding his countrymen rejoice. That act, turning over to the people of Kansas the right to vote whether it should be free or slave, had banished, he said, forever the dreadful question of slavery "from the Hall of Congress to the prairies of the west."

Far from banishing the question, however, the Kansas-Nebraska Act roused the entire country and so divided Congress, Democrats and Whigs, over the question of slavery as to make any further compromise between North and South impossible. It also brought before the nation the great country lawyer who was to lead in the final struggle.

Nine years Abraham Lincoln had been practicing law in Springfield and riding the circuit in Illinois, with no desire to return to politics until the Kansas-Nebraska Act gave him the incentive. The night that he and Judge Davis had been discussing it, he did not sleep. He sat on the edge of the bed, a tragic figure even in his clumsy yellow night-shirt.

"I tell you," he said, "this nation cannot exist half slave and half free. But the problem is too great for me. May God in his mercy superintend the solution of it."

Then while the Judge slept, Lincoln sat staring into the darkness reviewing all that he knew and had seen of slavery since his first trip to New Orleans. Sat until the cold gray river dawn came in through the window. Then he had decided, come what may, he must speak the truth on the problem as he understood it.

When Douglas returned to Illinois and tried to justify his Kansas-Nebraska Act to the people, Lincoln was ready to meet him, and denounced that Act which helped the spread of slavery.

Lincoln did not intend to do away with slavery in the southern States where it already existed. He did not think it was yet possible, but he firmly believed that it must not be allowed, even by vote of the people, to spread any farther.

As Whig candidate for the Senate, he went down in the election with the general ruin of that party. The new Republican party then rose to take its place, and two years later when Douglas ran for re-election,

Abraham Lincoln opposed him, as the candidate for the Republicans.

Now he spoke with ever greater firmness, for now the Dred Scott decision had been handed down. By it the Supreme Court so upheld the cause of slavery that Lincoln felt its advancing shadow fall on the entire nation. For now a man might take his slave, like any other property, into any territory! That had been the decision in the trial of the Negro slave Dred Scott. According to that, not in any territory, even by vote of the people, could the spread of slavery be stopped.

"But if it be not stopped," said Lincoln, "its advocates will push it forward till it shall become alike lawful in all the states, old as well as new, North as well as South; for this nation, I believe, cannot permanently endure half slave and half free. A house divided against itself cannot stand; it will become all one thing or all another. . . ." And which was it to be? That was the serious question which Lincoln challenged Douglas to answer in the summer of 1858 in a series of debates that were to become famous in American history. . . .

The Lincoln–Douglas Debates took place in seven little towns in Illinois. For each one, huge crowds came from the surrounding country-

side. On the night before, their campfires could be seen for miles across the prairies. Next day, as they gathered around the rude wooden platform, there was all the gayety and hubbub of a county fair, with bands playing and fakers peddling their wares.

But when the speakers appeared the hubbub subsided, while the people watched the two men take their seats, compact Stephen Douglas, only five feet three, and long, gawky Lincoln, six feet four. Silent and intent, they listened as first one and then the other spoke.

Senator Douglas would step forward, well groomed, graceful, sure of himself, a brilliant man with a success behind him and the possibility of being President ahead. And with his eye on that possibility, and in the hope of offending no one, he would speak. Adroitly he would lead his hearers around and about the unpleasant subject, "saying nothing in a great many words," but holding the crowd spellbound by the resonance of his voice and his liquid-flowing sentences.

Then Lincoln would rise. Tall, ungainly, awkward, he would step slowly forward, hesitate over the first few sentences in his high thin voice. Then the words would come, plain, honest forceful words that any man could understand, with homely anecdotes that struck straight and fairly at the truth, for to him the Truth was all that mattered.

In the last debate he took the broadest view. This struggle, he said, was but part of the eternal struggle in which "right and wrong had stood face to face since the beginning of time." "You work and toil and earn bread, and I'll eat it." Those, he said, were the words of slavery, no matter whether said by a king to his people or by one nation or race who sought to enslave another.

And so ended the famous debates between Douglas, the "little Giant," and Abe, "the Giant Killer." Most famous of them all was the debate at Freeport, where Douglas, in order to please Illinois and win the state election, was forced to answer a question put to him by Lincoln in a way that completely antagonized the South and split the Democratic party. Reported in newspapers all over the country, the debates, especially this one, put the name of Lincoln, the back country lawyer, before the nation. Invitations to speak came to him from many northern states, and Republicans of Illinois began to mention him as their candidate for President, in the 1860 election.

In the winter of 1859, after some hesitation about facing an eastern audience, Lincoln accepted an invitation to speak in Henry Ward

Beecher's church in Brooklyn. Then, on arriving, he found that he was to speak before an even larger audience at Cooper Union in New York. So he spent two more days going over his speech and perfecting it.

It was the most distinguished audience he had ever had to face, and when he stood before them that night he felt keenly, as always, his lack of education, and for the first time was conscious of his wrinkled and ill-fitting clothes. For in that gathering were such men as the publisher Horace Greeley and most of the city's leading citizens. Somewhere also, no doubt, was a staunch young Republican by the name of Roosevelt, then the father of a year-old baby boy called Theodore. Men of culture they were and education, waiting curiously to pass judgment on this country debater who had suddenly risen in the West. They heard his first hesitating sentence uttered in a high voice in which a slow Kentucky drawl mingled with the twang of the Middle West. Then his words came more easily. The audience became interested, stimulated, and then lost in admiration at the simple logic, the perfect phrasing, the honesty and fairness of his entire speech which ended with this challenge, in which lay his strength:

"Let us have faith that right makes might; and in that faith let us, to the end, dare to do our duty as we understand it."

Courage and understanding. Not all people can have both.

Only that fall, in Virginia, poor "old John Brown" from bleeding Kansas had dared to the end to do what seemed to him his duty, lacking not in courage, but in understanding. With a few bewildered followers he had attempted to seize the United States arsenal at Harper's Ferry in the confused idea that he might so liberate the slaves.

United States soldiers under Colonel Robert E. Lee put down the attempt. John Brown was tried and executed. . . . But "his soul went marching on," so sang the Abolitionists of New England, for to them he was a martyr. The people of the South called him a murderer. To Lincoln he was only a misguided and peculiar case. A fanatic, he had but driven deeper the wedge of bitter feeling that now had almost split the North and South apart. . . .

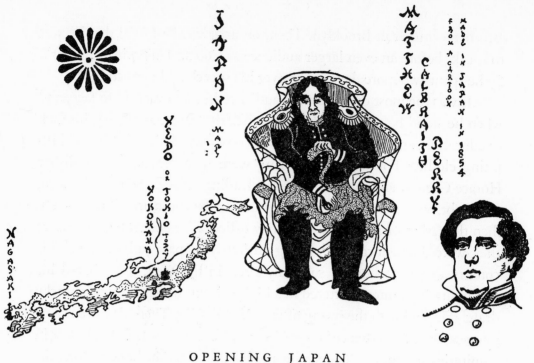

OPENING JAPAN

IN THE SPRING OF 1860, shortly after Lincoln spoke there, New York City welcomed the first delegation from Japan ever sent to the United States. There in New York the Japanese visited the former home of Commodore Matthew Calbraith Perry, who in 1853, five years before his death, had induced the Japanese to open the long closed door of their country to him.

"Great bloodshed and misery will probably precede the opening of Japan," an English journalist had written shortly before Commodore Perry's peaceful entrance. And it had been peaceful because he had approached the problem with a mixture of imagination and tolerance.

Long before he started Perry had tried to learn all he could about the mysterious land. He sent to Holland for all available books, pictures and maps of Japan. These he spread out and studied over all of one summer in the library of his country home, which, by the way, adjoined the estate of Washington Irving up the Hudson River.

Washington Irving was an old man then, looking backward instead

272

of forward, and marveling at the changes time can bring. To think, he often said, that the little four-year-old girl he had once "dandled on his knee" in Spain was now the Empress Eugenie! . . . Time does bring changes, but not in human nature, and something of the same tolerant spirit that made friends for Washington Irving in Europe brought results for Commodore Perry in Japan.

Holland, where he had sent for the Japanese books and maps, was the only European country allowed to trade with Japan, but only one ship a year were the Dutch allowed to send, and then only to one small island in the harbor of Nagasaki.

As he read, Perry saw the reason for it. Japan was a nation with a proud caste system. Tradespeople were considered low class, and foreigners were "scum." The Dutch, being both foreigners and traders, naturally had to deliver their bundles at Japan's back door.

If, on the contrary, someone of apparently high caste approached Japan with the proud but courteous formality which Japanese could understand, would he not at least receive consideration? It seemed worth trying, and in that manner Commodore Perry planned his entrance.

In November, 1852, he sailed out of Chesapeake Bay, on the uncertain mission, taking with him as secretary his son, Oliver Hazard, named for the uncle who had fought the battle on Lake Erie. A Dutch interpreter also went. And in an elaborate rosewood box inlaid with gold was carried a letter, inscribed on parchment bound in blue velvet, from the President of the United States to the Mikado of Japan.

On Friday, July 8, 1853, four American steamships entered Yedo Bay. To their left across the harbor at the blue water's edge lay the town of Uraga, with piney green hills rising behind it and against the distant sky the white peak of the sacred Fujiyama.

As soon as the excited natives on shore saw these strange smoking ships "carrying volcanoes," a gun was exploded in the hills, gongs rang and the bay became alive with small boats. Several government boats sped out immediately and surrounded the American ships. As they approached the flagship *Susquehanna,* they were motioned away. One Japanese, however, threw aboard a scroll of paper with a message in French ordering the ships to leave at once. Others threw ropes up and tried to clamber aboard, while the American crew warned them off with pikes. Then came a voice from one of the Japanese boats.

"I can speak Dutch," it said. "Are you Americans?"

"Ja," replied the Dutch interpreter, going forward.

"We wish to speak to your commander," said the Japanese.

"I'm sorry," replied the American, "but Commodore Perry is 'Lord of the Forbidden Interior.' Only people of equal rank may see him."

"But the Vice-Governor of Uraga is aboard this boat."

"The Lord of the Forbidden Interior," the American regretted to say, could not speak with the Vice-Governor. Would he then please appoint a lesser person to confer with their Vice-Governor, came the request. The request was granted. The Vice-Governor came aboard.

And why were the Americans here, he asked. To deliver a letter from their honorable ruler? So sorry, they must turn about and deliver it at Nagasaki. The Americans said they wished to deliver it in Uraga. The Vice-Governor said that was impossible, but finally agreed to take the matter up with the Governor, bowed, and returned to his own boat.

Next day the boat returned, bearing the Governor himself in a gold kimono embroidered in peacock feathers. He was escorted to the Captain's cabin, though the Lord of the Interior still remained hidden.

The American letter, the Governor said, must be delivered at Nagasaki. Very sorry, said the Americans, but they must obey their President's orders. The letter was to be delivered at Uraga, by Commodore Perry himself and to some high Japanese official of equal rank.

The Governor would like to see the letter. At sight of the beautiful rosewood box inlaid in gold, his manner changed at once. He would take the matter up with a high Councilor at Yedo, he said, bowed, returned to his boat and disappeared.

Three days later he returned and after many more words spent in a last attempt to send the Americans to Nagasaki with their letter, he said that a meeting had been arranged to take place two days later near

Yokohama. There the First Councilor of the Empire would receive the letter from the American Lord of the Forbidden Interior.

Two days later all was in readiness. A special pavilion had been constructed with a three-pointed roof and walls of painted screens. On top fluttered colored flags, and from nine tall standards, long scarlet pennants floated. Drawn up on either side of the path were soldiers of Japan with shining shields and polished lacquer headgear. The United States boats approached. One hundred marines landed and stood at attention on either side of the wharf, followed by two hundred sailors. Then a barge drew up and from it the Lord of the Forbidden Interior, Commodore Matthew Calbraith Perry, in blue uniform and huge gold epaulets, stepped silently and majestically ashore!

Preceded by two tall seamen carrying the Stars and Stripes, two ships' boys bearing the rosewood box, and, as a special bodyguard, the first two Negroes ever seen in Japan, Commodore Perry passed through the entrance of the pavilion, into a room hung in violet silk.

At the far end on a dais sat two elderly men in handsome kimonos. At a signal from them, Perry walked the length of red carpet and presented to the First Councilor of the Empire the President's letter. With the announcement that he would return in the spring for the answer, the ceremony ended. March, 1854, he had returned, a treaty of friendship was signed between Japan and the United States, and Commodore Perry's part in the opening of Japan was over.

This was a treaty of friendship only, that was signed in 1854, but the President's letter had been a request for more than that—for a trade agreement between the nations. That treaty was not to be signed for another four years, not until 1858, and then only because of the foresight and courage of Lord Ii Naosuke.

That year 1858, Ii Naosuke had been appointed Prime Minister of Japan, or Tairo, the highest office under the Shogun and one filled only in a time of national emergency such as this caused by the knocking of the Americans on their door.

Japan was torn into two factions, bitterly opposed. Many government officials wished to continue their old policy of isolation and drive off all foreigners by force. Ii Naosuke, and a smaller group of his countrymen, realizing how strong the foreigners were and how impossible resistance would be, favored signing the treaty of commerce, if necessary. His adversaries spoke against it.

"The proposal of constructing large ships to send abroad for tradal purposes sounds admirable," said one of them, "but this is the most risky thing conceivable. The Japanese nature is restless, facile and superficial; so if our countrymen should go to foreign lands and mingle with foreigners, they will only fall into the pernicious state of the crow trying to whiten its feathers in imitation of the stork."

"But if we persist in clinging to our antiquated system," said Lord Ii, "Heaven only knows what calamity may befall our Empire." He pointed to the disastrous fate of China now being forced by Europeans to sign humiliating treaties. Rather than allow similar humiliation to come upon his own country, Ii Naosuke determined to take the full responsibility upon his own shoulders and sign the treaty.

"Do not, we beg of you," implored his loyal retainers. "Some calamity will surely befall your honorable and historic family."

Ii Naosuke, however, felt that it could not be avoided. Therefore, in the face of tremendous opposition, he courageously signed the treaty on July 29, 1858, and so unbolted Japan's door from within.

For that he was called a traitor and a rebel. One day in March, 1860, before the cherry trees, which were late that year, had blossomed, Ii Naosuke was being carried in his palanquin to a meeting with the Shogun when he was beset by hostile samurai and murdered.

Gradually as the years passed, his countrymen came to see that Ii Naosuke was a man far ahead of his times, that he had performed a service to the Empire well worthy of his great and honorable ancestor. In 1908 a statue of him was unveiled in the port of Yokohama.

It was in February, just a month before Naosuke was killed, that the first envoys from Japan sailed for the United States, to bring back to the Shogun a report of what the outer world was like. They made many sketches and took many measurements. One kept an interesting diary. On April 28, they were in Washington, D. C., and he says:

"We are going to the home of the ruler in carriages this morning. We are putting on our finest kimono. The ruler of this country is called President. He is President Buchanan. There is no policeman in the President's house and no fortress in his yard. It is very beautiful but quite different from what we expected.

"The people of this country, both men and women, are white.

"Ladies are highly honored in America as parents are in Japan.

"The people of America are big-hearted, honest and faithful. The Americans do not scorn foreigners and are kind to strangers. The Americans are simple and honest like Japanese born in the mountains or on the farm who have never been spoiled by the big city. The Russians are like the Americans.

"May 21. In Washington and all other American cities, the mothers do not carry their babies on their backs, but in small carriages.

"There is a telegraph line between New York and Philadelphia over which messages are sent as fast as lightning. But I cannot describe it.

"June 9 [they were in New York]. At 1 o'clock in the afternoon we accompanied our chief commissioners to the home of Commodore Perry who went to Japan several years ago. Commodore Perry became sick and died some time ago but his son was at home. The home was very fine and decorated with many Japanese mementoes. We were entertained with wine and cake. Two Japanese spaniels in the house sniffed our clothes and realizing that we were Japanese, danced at our feet, leaped in our laps and would not leave us. They showed their affection so plainly by their voice that we were quite sad and shed a tear when we left.

"July 13. The anchor was raised at noon and we sailed East."

"GOOD OLD ABE, THE RAIL SPLITTER"

POUNDING AND HAMMERING was going on at a great rate in that spring of 1860 out on Lake Street near the Chicago River, where the old Sauganash Tavern used to stand. "Used to stand was right," any Chicago booster would have told you. "Been torn down now for a week. Once was the only tavern around, but that was back in the days of old Fort Dearborn, way before Chicago was born. Been a town now more'n twenty-five years, Chicago had. In 1833, when it got started, there weren't forty houses, and less'n two hundred folks. An' look at it now, twenty-seven years old, and a city of 112,172!" That's the way a good Chicago booster talked.

And it *was* amazing how the town had grown. A husky young giant of a city, born in an onion swamp, it was now actually pulling itself right out of the mud. Pieces of new sidewalk and pavement were seven or eight feet up above the old ones. Some of its buildings were down, others jacked up on piles, when Chicago spoke up and invited the Republican party to hold its National Convention there in 1860.

That was what all the pounding and hammering was about. There was no building big enough to use for a meeting hall, so Chicago had had to take a day or two off and build one. A big rough shed of clapboards, they christened it "The Wigwam."

On May 16, 1860, in that Wigwam, after three ballots for President, Abraham Lincoln was nominated and "pandemonium broke loose."

"Such a yell went up," it was said by someone, "that a thousand steam whistles, ten acres of hotel gongs, and a tribe of Comanche Indians might have mingled with the scene unnoticed."

One man yelled to a man on the roof, and he spread the news to the crowd below, and on it went. Cannons boomed, factory whistles shrieked, guns were fired, locomotives of all fifteen railroads now coming into Chicago blew their whistles and rang their bells.

Fence rails were bundled up to ship all over the country. Soon young "Wide-Awakes" in oilcloth capes and carrying torches were zigzagging down the streets, cheering for good old Abe the Rail Splitter!

Down in Springfield, Abraham Lincoln had waited in the newspaper office for the results. When they arrived he said that he "reckoned there was a short little woman down at his house that would like to hear the news," and went off with the telegram in his hand.

The next evening, the committee from Chicago, among them the former German, Carl Schurz, tendered the formal announcement. Lincoln received them in a grave but friendly manner, and then since he never kept wine in the house, served them what he had, a pitcher of water.

There were then six months to wait for the election, which there was little doubt that he would win, for the Democratic party had split. After the election came four more months of waiting in which Mrs. Lincoln was busy ordering bonnets and dresses and shawls, one of fashionable "Magenta," while Lincoln, unable to raise a hand, had to watch conditions grow steadily worse. Every mail brought him threatening letters.

"Come with me," he said one day to Mrs. Lincoln in an odd tone of voice, leading her into his room where a long mirror hung opposite a sofa. "Do you see anything strange about that glass?"

She said no. He peered into it intently for a moment, and then told her that twice, lying on the sofa, he had seen himself reflected in that mirror with TWO faces, one much paler than the other.

Mrs. Lincoln was worried . . . afraid that it was a bad sign. It might be, Mr. Lincoln said, and it might mean nothing. . . .

In January, when he still had over a month to wait, he went "down state" to bid goodbye to the one who had believed in him the longest, Sally Bush Lincoln. She was over seventy, and though Thomas Lincoln was dead, she was still living in the log house which Abe had helped them build. It was shadowy inside, so she took his hand and had him sit in the window where she could get a good light on his face. As she brushed back a lock of hair and looked into his eyes she saw her boy again . . . just her boy . . . except, she thought briskly, except for that beard. Why had he grown a beard, she wondered?

"I reckon because a little girl wrote me a letter saying she thought it would improve my face," he laughed.

His stepmother laughed too, but her eyes were blurred. And as she watched him go down the path she knew it was for the last time.

The relief at having the waiting over was so great that Lincoln seemed in high good spirits the day before his departure, when he came down to his office to pick up a few last things.

"Billy," he said, "we've been together over sixteen years. Let the old sign hang on undisturbed. Show clients that the election of a President makes no change in the firm of Lincoln & Herndon."

The morning of February 11, 1861, was cold and drizzly. The smoke from the funnel-shaped stack on the little engine hung low about the Springfield station and the crowd of people gathered there. Mrs. Lincoln and the boys had gone on into the train, as Lincoln himself in his high hat and shawl about his shoulders, stood on the back platform in the chilly air. He had not intended to speak, but as he looked down on all those familiar faces the words came from his heart:

"My friends, no one not in my situation, can appreciate my feeling of sadness at this parting. To this place and the kindness of these people I owe everything. Here I have lived a quarter of a century, and have passed from a young man to an old. Here my children have been born and one is buried. I now leave, not knowing when or whether ever I may return, with a task before me greater than that which rested upon Washington. Without the assistance of that Divine Being who ever attended him, I cannot succeed. With that assistance I cannot fail. Trusting in Him who can go with me and remain with you and be everywhere for good, let us confidently hope that all will yet be well. To His care commending you, as I hope in your prayers you will commend me, I bid you an affectionate farewell."

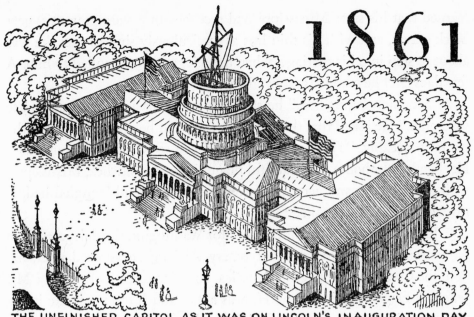

~1861

THE UNFINISHED CAPITOL AS IT WAS ON LINCOLN'S INAUGURATION DAY

THE MAN AND THE HOUR

THE ELECTION of Abraham Lincoln, a so-called Black Republican, gave the final blow to the wedge of ill-feeling over slavery, and split the United States in two. Before he took the oath of office, seven states in the Deep South had seceded. South Carolina took the lead. Then Alabama held a mass meeting under a banner reading "Resistance to Lincoln is obedience to God," and Yancey, a hot-headed radical, proclaimed that he would "fire the Southern heart and precipitate a revolution." At the same time a hasty orator of Georgia was urging the people "not to let the rising sun of March fifth find them in the Union." So Alabama and Georgia followed South Carolina—also Florida, Louisiana and Mississippi. Six, by February, were gone.

Meanwhile President Buchanan, old and timid, feebly wrung his hands and wondered what to do. Every day congressmen from the seceding states were packing their bags and leaving Washington for home. On the ninth of January Buchanan spoke a few futile words to the Senate.

That day Senator Jefferson Davis, on his way to hear that speech,

281

learned that his state Mississippi had seceded. In a slate gray suit, neat black cravat, and with his thin lips as meticulously shut as ever, he was about to step into his carriage, when the telegram was handed to him. A few days later he made his farewell speech.

"Secession is justified," he said, "upon the basis that the states are sovereign." He asked that those that had seceded be allowed to leave the Union peaceably. "There will be peace if you so will it," he concluded. He then left for home, his beautiful plantation near Natchez, Mississippi, with its four thousand acres of cotton, its gardens, and "tangled hedge-rows of brier and Cherokee roses."

Just one week before Lincoln left for Washington the delegates from the six seceded states met at Montgomery, Alabama, organized a new nation, the Confederate States of America, and elected as its President Mr. Jefferson Davis of Mississippi. He was a man much too moderate in his views to suit the fiery Yancey of Alabama, but the latter rose to the occasion, and praising him as statesman, soldier and patriot, proclaimed that "The man and the hour had met."

Jefferson Davis had been making rose cuttings in the garden with Mrs. Davis when the news of his election was delivered to him. Excited crowds met him at the little station in Montgomery. As the band played *Dixie,* his carriage was drawn by four white horses to the Capitol build-ing of the state. There at one o'clock, beneath the tall white columns of its portico, on February 18, 1861, Jefferson Davis took the oath of loyalty to a nation whose cornerstone was Slavery. He then declared his deter-mination to maintain "that proud position and make all who opposed it smell Southern powder and feel Southern steel.

"Our separation from the old Union," he said, "is now complete."

But *was* it? *Could* the states separate from the Union? Had they the right to do so? Abraham Lincoln said no. Andrew Jackson had said no. Down in Texas Governor Sam Houston said no, and opposed to the last day the secession of Texas, but to no avail. In late February Texas became the seventh state to follow South Carolina. An old man now, Sam Hous-ton thought back to the good days when his hero Andrew Jackson had made short work of South Carolina's first threat to secede. Abraham Lincoln also looked back to Andrew Jackson's proclamation of that day. A copy of it had lain on his desk in Springfield as he carefully wrote out what he was to say at his inauguration.

But would there *be* an inauguration? Would Lincoln ever *reach* Washington? Men in Washington, and everywhere else, were of the opinion that he wouldn't. Much better, said many, if he didn't. A back country lawyer, with no experience, he should never have been elected. Seward should have been. William H. Seward, Senator from New York.

William H. Seward had also been Governor of New York. He was undoubtedly a man of experience. Lincoln, believing him to possess "integrity, ability and learning," had already asked him to fill the position of Secretary of State. William Seward had accepted, thus proving that he also had the quality of good sportsmanship. As the acknowledged head of the Republican party, he had expected to win the nomination in Chicago. His defeat had been a great disappointment and his followers had begged him to bolt the party.

"No, gentlemen," he had said, "the Republican party was not made for William H. Seward, but Mr. Seward, if he be worth anything, for the Republican party, and I believe I still have work to do."

He had then returned to Washington. From there, hearing of plots to prevent the inauguration, he had written Lincoln suggesting that he arrive earlier in the capital. Lincoln, not easily alarmed, had preferred to go on with the initial plans. Accordingly on February 20th he reached New York City. There his trip was being ridiculed as that of a cheap clown, cracking rough jokes at every station. The New York *Herald,* not given to humor, printed these words:

"A grand opportunity now exists for Lincoln to avert impending ruin, by surrender of his claims. If he persists in his position, he will totter to a dishonoured grave, driven perhaps by an assassin."

Lincoln folded the newspaper, and went calmly on to Philadelphia. There he was met by a Chicago detective named Pinkerton.

"We have come to know, Mr. Lincoln," said this man Pinkerton, "beyond a shadow of a doubt that there exists a plot to assassinate you. A barber of Baltimore," he said, "was boasting that before Lincoln reached the Washington depot he would 'be a corpse.'"

Only a few hours later the son of William H. Seward arrived from Washington with a note from his father describing the identical plot, and urging Lincoln to take an earlier train through Baltimore.

The next morning, February 22, still according to plans and in celebration of Washington's birthday, Lincoln raised the flag over Independence Hall, in Philadelphia. Eighty-five years before the United States of America had been founded there upon the principle of liberty. Now that Union and the principle were threatened, but rather than see either fail, Lincoln said that he would be willing to lose his life, if need be.

That life his friends felt was now uselessly in danger, and so they persuaded him to change his plan. Therefore, with a single companion, detective and guards, he slipped secretly out of Philadelphia, caught the night train from New York, passed through Baltimore while the assassins still lay asleep, and was safe in Washington the following morning. There he was well guarded.

And on March 4, 1861, beneath the unfinished dome of the capitol building, Abraham Lincoln was inaugurated President of the United States. In his address he spoke particularly to "such of his fellow countrymen as were dissatisfied," urging them "not as enemies but as friends," to think calmly, not to act in haste.

"In *your* hands," he said, "and not in *mine* is the momentous issue of civil war. The government will not assail *you*. You can have no conflict without yourselves being the aggressors."

Then he took the solemn oath to "preserve, protect, and defend the Union of the States," which he saw as perpetual from its beginning and also strengthened through the years "by mystic chords of memory stretching from every battlefield and patriot grave to every living heart and hearthstone over this broad land."

Thus, contrary to all predictions, Abraham Lincoln had become the nation's President. The great man and the tragic hour had met.

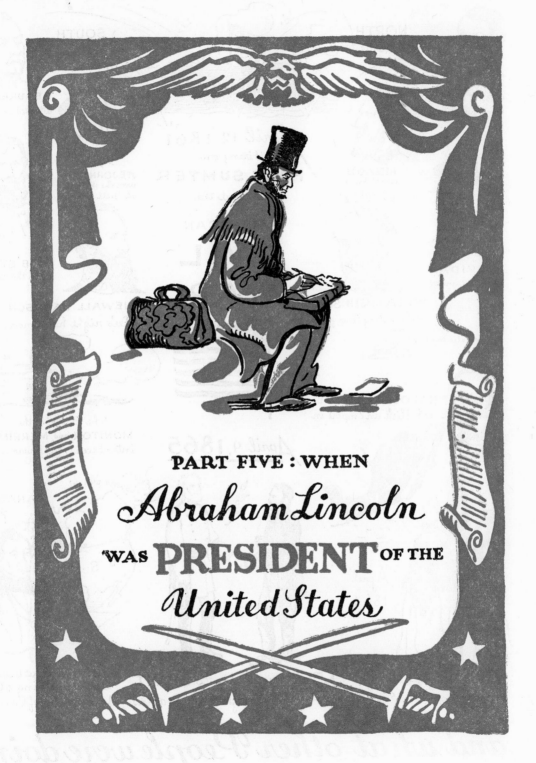

PART FIVE : WHEN

Abraham Lincoln

'WAS **PRESIDENT** OF THE

United States

Some Events that took place

NORTH
"the Blue"

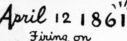

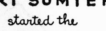

SOUTH
"the Grey"

G.B. McCLELLAN
ran against Lincoln
for President in 1864

MEADE
won the battle
of Gettysburg.

April 12 1861
Firing on
FORT SUMTER
started the

BEAUREGARD
attacked Ft. Sumter

Jᵒ E. JOHNSTON
won the 1st battle
at Bull Run,

"PHIL"
SHERIDAN
led the cavalry.

AMERICAN
CIVIL
WAR

"JEB" STUART
led the cavalry

Wᵐ TECUMSEH SHERMAN
went "marching through Georgia"

"STONEWALL" JACKSON
was Lee's right hand man.

(private's cap)

Flag flown
at Ft. Sumter

NAPOLEON III tried to
establish an Empire in

The Battle of the
MONITOR and MERRIMAC
introduced metal warships

April 9, 1865

April
1864

MAXIMILIAN & CARLOTA
were made Emperor and Empress;

LEE's surrender to GRANT
at Appomatox brought the war to an end.

JOHN A. MACDONALD
lead in making plans
for uniting of Canada.

and what other People were doing

while Lincoln was President

1864
The International Red Cross Society was founded in Switzerland

The great Russian author, **TOLSTOY** started schools for the peasant children,

ALEXANDER II was hailed as the "Czar Liberator"

RUSSIA FREED HER SERFS 1861

1862

Bismarck became the Prime Minister the "Iron Chancellor" of **PRUSSIA**

LINCOLN BEGAN FREEING THE SLAVES 1863

GEO. WASHINGTON **CARVER** scientist, was born 1864 ?

BOOKER T. WASHINGTON great educator was born 1859 ?

Queen **VICTORIA** became "the Widow of Windsor" Prince Albert died 1861

EDWARD, Prince of Wales married **ALEXANDRA** of Denmark

TENNESSEE

ANDREW JOHNSON who was made Vice President in 1864, became President 1865

1864 in U.S.A **THANKSGIVING** was made an annual holiday

JOHN WILKES BOOTH the Assassin

LINCOLN was shot in this box at Ford's theatre, and died next day

April 15, 1865

between the Years 1861 and 1865

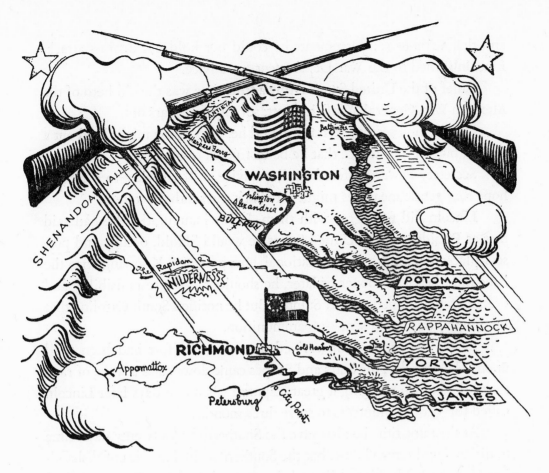

1861: THE TORN MAP

THE AMERICAN CIVIL WAR began on April 12, 1861. It was a war fought not to abolish slavery, but to restore the Union, to bring together again the nation which slavery had now torn apart. On April 12, 1861, the opening guns were fired on Fort Sumter, a fort belonging to the United States government, and guarding the harbor of Charleston, South Carolina.

Upon seceding, South Carolina had demanded that the fort be evacuated and turned over to the state. President Buchanan had refused, and so South Carolina had prevented food from reaching it.

On his first day in office Lincoln received word from Major Anderson at Fort Sumter that his provisions would last no longer than a week and that without reinforcements he could not hold out against attack. Lincoln turned to the War Department for advice.

Chief of the United States Army at this time was the old hero of the Mexican War, General Winfield Scott, seventy-five years old.

"Evacuation seems inevitable," said he. "Anderson might hold out a month, but it is my advice that he be instructed to evacuate."

Secretary Seward offered similar advice, still clinging to a foolish hope that gentle measures might lure back the southern states.

Lincoln did not agree with them. In his inauguration he had said that as President of the United States he would "Hold, occupy and possess places belonging to the national government." Knowing that the issue must be faced sooner or later, he shouldered the responsibility and ordered food shipped to Fort Sumter. But he notified South Carolina that food, only, was being sent—no ammunition.

Before the supply ship arrived, however, the fort had been fired upon. The next day, the Stars and Stripes came down, and a wave of rage swept the North, bringing a great response when two days later Lincoln called for 75,000 volunteers to serve three months.

At the same time he also gave the Southern forces twenty days' time to disband and return home, but the Southerners had no idea of disbanding. A great celebration followed the surrender of Fort Sumter. It had been fired upon for the very purpose of shaking the remaining eight slave states out of the Union and into the Confederacy. Four of them responded to those shots and seceded, Arkansas, Tennessee, North Carolina and Virginia, making eleven in all.

As soon as Virginia seceded, a rumor spread that Chief of the Army General Winfield Scott, had resigned and gone with his native state. It was false. The mere suggestion insulted him.

"Stop!" he said. "Go no further. I have served my country under the flag of the Union for more than fifty years, and so long as God permits me to live I will defend that flag."

General Scott was not only old, but tremendously fat, ill, and swollen with gout, but he worked seventeen hours a day during those first weeks of war, organizing and preparing for the new army.

"We are gathering a great army," said Seward to the old soldier one morning. "But what are we going to do for generals?"

"That is our great problem," replied General Scott. "Unfortunately for us, the South has taken most of the higher officers. But there is one who would make an excellent general, though I do not know whether we can rely on him. I am expecting him today."

The officer was, of course, Colonel Robert E. Lee, who had served under General Scott in Mexico. Recently recalled from Texas, Colonel Lee had spent the past month with his wife and family across the Potomac River at their home in Arlington. He called that day to pay his respects to General Scott, but had then practically decided that he must join the Confederate Army. Two days later he sent in his resignation, saying that "save in the defense of his native state he never desired again to draw his sword." So Robert E. Lee, who loved Virginia too well to do otherwise, resigned from the army of his country.

Meanwhile, out in the little town of Galena, Illinois, a poor seedy-looking man, who had also fought in Mexico, was trying to get back into that army to which he had once belonged, but with no luck.

"Luck" so far certainly hadn't followed the footsteps of Ulysses

Grant. He and Julia had had a hard time, ever since they married, and especially after he was ordered out to the Pacific Coast. Fred was a baby then, and not daring to take him across Panama, Julia had gone home to St. Louis. In a couple of years, Lys was also back in St. Louis, out of the army, out of work, and without a cent in his pocket.

He tried farming, selling real estate, but things went from bad to worse, till his brothers had had him come to Galena and clerk in their leather store. So there he was, discouraged, but trying hard to support a wife and four children when the war began.

He was asked to drill the Galena Volunteers, because there was nobody else to do it, but when the company left for the state capitol at Springfield, one of the men he had drilled went as captain, and he just tagged along behind. He had a letter to the Governor, but it didn't do much good. A friend encouraged him, and so he wrote a letter to the War Department, offering his services. He said that "having served fifteen years in the regular army, he felt competent to command a regiment if the President saw fit to entrust one to him. He added that a letter "addressed to him at Springfield, Ill.," would reach him. No answer ever came. His letter was lost in the shuffle. And no wonder!

Washington had been a scene of utter confusion for the past six weeks. Troops of volunteers were pouring into the capital, buildings turned into barracks overnight. Everywhere a frantic haste made to fortify the city against attack from the Confederate army, while impatient newspapers were already crying "On to Richmond!"

Richmond, Virginia, was the new capital of the Confederacy. There the Southern troops were also assembling, the young blades highly confident that five Yankees would go down before the gallant fighting spirit of one Southern gentleman. "On to Washington!" they cried.

By the end of May, the Union army had crossed the Potomac River into Virginia and was encamped just over the Long Bridge at Arlington. The Confederate army under General Beauregard had advanced to a little creek known as Bull Run and so was just twenty miles away. On July 21, though neither army was ready for it, they fought their first battle, the battle of Bull Run. It was Sunday, and from Washington, people drove out in carriages to view the battle as if going to a horse race or a picnic.

From noon on Lincoln was listening in the telegraph office of the War Department with General Scott. The first news was good, and by five o'clock he was so encouraged that he went for a short drive. At six Secretary Seward rushed to the White House.

"Find the President," he croaked hoarsely. "The battle is lost!"

Half an hour later the President returned. In a few hours crowds of panic-stricken people arrived who had witnessed the disorderly rout, in which soldiers, carriages, sightseers, had been tangled in a mad mix-up. The rebel army, they said, was now headed for Washington! They would be coming over Long Bridge at any moment!

Fortunately they did not come. In the Confederate camp there had been unbounded joy over this first victory, and bold proposals were made to go on and capture Washington. Jefferson Davis, their president, however, disapproved. So the chance was lost. Washington was saved!

Washington was safe, yes, but that was all, and that was due more to good luck than good management. There was no denying that the first battle in the war which was to "end in ninety days" had been a disaster. The ninety days were up, and volunteers, many of them, who had enlisted for that time, were ready to go home. Everywhere, newspapers and speakers were blaming the government for the catastrophe.

"An indignant people demand the immediate retirement of the present Cabinet from the high places of power," shouted the *New York Tribune*, whose editor was Horace Greeley.

Stanton, the man who was soon to become Secretary of War, called the defeat at Bull Run "an irretrievable misfortune and national disgrace." It was due, he declared, to "the weakness of the Administration and the painful imbecility of Lincoln."

On Friday, Lincoln, whose heart was with the common soldiers, asked Seward to take a "run over the Potomac with him to see the boys."

They were shown about camp by General William Tecumseh Sherman, a man who spoke his mind in a snappy fashion. He was glad that a call had now been issued for 300,000 volunteers to serve three years. Said, " 'Twas no use trying to put out a house on fire with a squirt gun!"

The North, shocked by the defeat at Bull Run, more than answered the new call for volunteers. Also very soon came a demand that the general who had met defeat at Bull Run be replaced by a popular young general who had been successful in West Virginia, and whom the newspapers were calling the young "Napoleon of the West!"

Into Washington therefore on July 26, came that dashing young man, Major-General George B. McClellan, ready and willing to "save the country." He began at once a thorough reorganization of the Army of the Potomac, but was soon complaining that he could do nothing so long as that "confounded old General Scott" was in the way.

The impudence of the young cock was more than the old general, sick and overworked, could swallow. On October 31, gallant old General Winfield Scott asked to be relieved. Next day G. B. McClellan took his place as Chief of the Army. And a far too busy and important personage he then became to be bothered by the President. If the President must come "browsing" around to have a word with him, let him wait his turn!

Friends of the President were indignant at the discourtesy. But Lincoln was no more ruffled by it than he had been by Stanton's remarks about him, or by the one brief attempt to run the government, made at first by Secretary Seward, to his later regret.

Personal resentment never entered into Lincoln's judgment of a man's ability, nor warped his sense of values. So now, instead of uttering any rebuke, he merely remarked that "he'd be willing even to hold McClellan's horse, if he'd only bring a victory!"

Months passed, however, and McClellan brought no victory. He did not even move. All was "quiet on the Potomac!" Far *too* quiet! But other excitement was stirring: By Christmas, the United States had barely escaped war with England!

(from Punch, Jan. 11, 1862)
ENGLISH CARTOON AT THIS TIME SHOWS JOHN BULL AS HUNTER, AND LINCOLN AS RACCOON "UP A TREE".

WHAT ABOUT ENGLAND?

PRINCE ALBERT was largely responsible for the fact that Christmas, 1861, found the United States and England still on peaceful terms. Prince Albert died just before Christmas. It was ten years since his Peace Festival of the Nations. And it is pleasant to think that this, his last act, was also one to further international friendship.

When the Civil War began in America, England had determined to remain neutral, though both the United States and the Confederacy hoped for England's active friendship.

The North counted on the strong anti-slavery feeling held by the majority of English people. But the South knew that the English aristocrats felt more akin to its gentlemen planters than to the Yankee tradesmen of the north, who were also looked upon as rivals by the English merchants. Cotton was also needed by English mills, and since the blockade of Southern harbors by the North cut off that supply, Jefferson Davis saw reason to hope for England's help.

The British government, however, declared a strict neutrality, and warned her Majesty's subjects to give no assistance to either side. But in November that neutrality was almost overturned. At the news that *The Trent*, a Royal Mail Ship, had been held up by a ship of the United States, "999 English people out of 1000," it was said, "were for declaring immediate war on the United States." Eight thousand troops were actually sent to Canada.

Washington got word of the embarrassing Trent Affair, two weeks before London did, for it took place at sea just one day's journey from Havana. The English ship was carrying to Europe two envoys from the Confederate States. The men were just congratulating themselves on their lucky escape through the blockade at Charleston, when suddenly *The Trent* was halted by a United States warship. Whereupon the impetuous Captain, acting on his own initiative, boarded *The Trent,* captured the Southerners and took them back to the United States as prisoners of war.

"Those prisoners will prove about as useless to us as White Elephants, I fear," was Lincoln's first remark. It was embarrassing and contrary to American principles to board a neutral ship. "We fought Great Britain in 1812," he said, "for insisting on the right to do that very thing. If Great Britain now protests, we must stick to our principles and give those prisoners up."

The country in general, however, went crazy with excitement. They praised Captain Wilkes, gave him banquets, and Congress even considered having a gold medal made for him. It was fortunate that they did not see the first angry message prepared by England's foreign ministers before its arrogant tone had been softened by Prince Albert. Otherwise Congress might have been swept away by that kind of passion often mistaken for patriotism, and have overruled the saner judgment of President Lincoln and Secretary Seward.

Prince Albert had just returned from a trying visit to the Prince of Wales who was then at Cambridge when that angry message arrived at Windsor for the Queen's approval. Albert was wretched and ill, but when he read it, he saw that something must be done. So he sat down by his green-shaded lamp and spent all night going over it, smoothing every phrase that might irritate the United States. Eight o'clock next morning he showed it to Victoria.

"*Ich bin so schwach,*" he said in German, "so weak . . . I could hardly hold the pen." His head was feverish, and he could barely reach his bed. The next day he was even weaker. Each day he grew worse. The doctors were worried, but "I do not cling to life," he had told Victoria one day. So he let go of it easily and a few hours later he was gone. He died four days before the message tempered by his peaceful spirit reached the United States.

A courteous request it was then from England's government, asking for the "liberation of the gentlemen and a suitable apology." Lincoln read it calmly. On December 19 Seward, whose duty as Secretary of State lay with foreign affairs, prepared the answer.

At ten o'clock on Christmas morning Seward read the reply that he had written to the Cabinet. The United States, he said, would surrender the prisoners to the British minister at Washington, but felt that no apology was necessary since the Captain had not been acting under government orders. Though it was like swallowing a bitter pill for some of the so-called patriotic congressmen, they agreed to acknowledge the mistake, and so as James Russell Lowell put it,

> "We give the critters back, John
> Cos Abram thought 'twas right."

Christmas, 1861, found Queen Victoria desolate and heartbroken, without Albert, but "I shall live on with him and for him," she told Uncle Leopold. And to her ministers she said firmly that from then on she would be guided only by what Albert would have wished.

The friendly reply from the United States, arriving early in the new year, gave her the comfort of knowing that Albert's last work had been successful. To the Prime Minister she wrote that she was sure "he could not but look on this peaceful issue of the American quarrel as greatly owing to her beloved prince." The observations on the draft she said "were the last things Prince Albert ever wrote."

AN "EMPIRE" FOR MEXICO

NAPOLEON III was well aware that one war at that time was quite enough for the United States to handle, and that they were no more eager to have war with France than with England. It appeared to him therefore to be an opportune time to defy that Monroe Doctrine of theirs and undertake a project of his own in Mexico, but one to be kept secret till the proper moment.

As for Mexico: On January 11, 1861, Mexico City had been gay with flying flags. There had been a great fiesta in celebration of the newly elected President, Benito Juarez. Nothing had been missing except the President himself, who did not approve of such extravagant display. Two weeks later, therefore, dressed in his usual somber black and wearing a high hat like that of Abraham Lincoln, the sober, brown-faced Indian lawyer came riding into the city quite unnoticed, his small black carriage

298

drawn by four white army mules. Crossing the quiet plaza, he went to work at once upon the problems that faced him.

Mexico had now been free from Spain for forty years and in that time had had many more than forty chief executives. Of them all Juarez was perhaps the only one who cared more for Mexico than for himself. He had served well as Governor of Oaxaca, and for fifteen years had been married to the lovely Dona Magarita de Maza. It was her father who had once paid tuition in the Seminary for a poor Indian boy, who had now become the President of his country.

The presidency of Mexico was no bed of roses in 1861. Many revolutions and unscrupulous leaders had almost ruined the country. Mexico's treasury was empty. Worse still, the nation was deep in debt. It owed England, France and Spain more than $80,000,000. With government expenses pared to the minimum, Juarez figured that it would take at least two years to get the farms and mines back into operation and the country on a paying basis. Therefore he asked for that much time before beginning to pay the foreign debts.

But how could France, Spain and England know that this president of Mexico was more responsible than the others? In October, 1861, representatives of these three nations met in London and decided to send ships to Mexico and act together in collecting their debts.

At word of their arrival Juarez sent his foreign minister down to Vera Cruz to confer with them. The English and Spanish, convinced of Juarez's good faith, easily came to an agreement. They were amazed to hear France refuse and name the outrageous sum of $12,000,000 to be paid at once! Instantly suspicious, Spain and England drew apart from France and returned home at once. Their suspicions were soon justified by the development of Napoleon's plot.

That plot of Napoleon III, now revealed, was to establish an Empire in Mexico. It was not original with him but had been suggested by the Empress Eugenie. She in turn had imbibed the fascinating idea from a Mexican exile, a suave Spaniard, whose acquaintance she renewed one summer afternoon in 1858. She was driving to a bull fight just across the

Spanish border from her summer home at Biarritz and, passing him, invited him to accompany her.

Barely seated beside her was he, than with tears in his voice, he began a sad tale about his fellow exiles driven from their estates in Mexico by the Mexican Republic. He told how even the great lands of the church were no longer free from taxation. What a wonderful chance, he said, there was for some European ruler to establish an Empire there! Yes, echoed Eugenie. And for France! What an opportunity to regain the blessings of his Holiness, the Pope!

When Napoleon III came for the weekend, they presented the dramatic scheme in all its colors. Think, said they, of founding a modern empire on the throne of the ancient Aztecs! There, indeed, was an irresistible thought to Napoleon III. Back in Paris, thumbing over old Mexican histories, the spell of the empire idea grew on him. One must proceed with subtlety; however, difficulties were involved.

The United States, for example, in its Monroe Doctrine positively forbade European powers to interfere with any government existing in the Americas. He must wait for some moment when they would not be able to enforce that doctrine.

In 1861, the proper moment seemed to have arrived. Civil war broke out in the United States, and the collection of debts offered easy entrance into Mexican affairs. So when Spain and England withdrew, French soldiers were dispatched to Mexico. Landing at Vera Cruz, they went marching and fighting their way up the winding mountain road to Mexico City. Juarez had hastily moved his government to a town farther north. So the French marched into the capital, paying people well to cheer and wave flags while they took possession. It was then 1863. Those few Mexicans who expected to benefit from it were then summoned to hold an "election," after which word was sent to France that all was ready for the new Emperor of Mexico!

And who was that new Emperor to be? None other than the fine young Austrian Archduke Maximilian! It was Eugenie who thought of him. Aside from Maximilian's being a most royal person, to offer him that opportunity ought to cancel the ill will that his brother Franz Josef bore Napoleon III because of the Italian War. Franz Josef, though careful not to show too much enthusiasm, raised no objections to it so Mexico's crown was offered to the gentle Archduke.

Maximilian and Carlotta were then living a peaceful, beautiful life in a white marble palace by the seaside at Trieste. While he painted and sketched and played the organ, she wrote poetry and prose. A beautiful life it was, but so unvaryingly peaceful as to be a little boring to Carlotta. She was energetic and ambitious and how she envied Sisi and Eugenie! How she too would love to be an Empress! What joy was hers then, when lo and behold, as out of a fantastic fairy tale, came the glorious, almost unbelievable opportunity.

Maximilian, much less enterprising, did not respond so quickly. What about the Mexican people, he asked. Did they really want him? Indeed they did, he was assured. His sense of honor satisfied by news of the election, Maximilian allowed himself to become enthusiastic. He could see the old Aztec palaces restored. He imagined uniting all the people of Mexico from Indians to archbishops in one peaceful, happy Empire! It all seemed so simple that he gave no heed to those who knew conditions and warned him to beware. And he only half listened to the dull, practical suggestions of his father-in-law, King Leopold, regarding money and military support.

Mexico herself, he was told, would gladly be taxed for his support and the French troops were already there.

"You may count on my everlasting friendship," said Napoleon III.

"You will bring honor to the house of Hapsburg," said Franz Josef in semi-sad farewell, advancing 200,000 gulden.

So, in a solemn ceremony in their chapel at Trieste, Maximilian and Carlota (with her name now changed to Spanish), were acclaimed Emperor and Empress of Mexico. And on a beautiful day in April, 1864, on board an Austrian frigate flying their new imperial flag, they set out on their great adventure, with high hearts, fearless of the future, and with no premonition of the tragedy in store for them. . . .

RUSSIA'S SERFS ARE FREED

THE YEAR that the American Civil War began was also one marked in Russian history, for that year Russia freed the serfs. On Sunday, March 3, 1861, the day before Abraham Lincoln took the oath of office, Alexander II, the Czar of Russia, issued to the serfs the proclamation of their freedom. To the imperial council and the nobles upon whom he had called for support he spoke of the difficulties ahead.

"But I feel sure," he said, "that God will prosper this undertaking most vital for the future welfare of our beloved Fatherland."

The first day of Lent, as the proclamation was read to them from the altar steps of every church, the serfs showed no emotion, until they heard these last few simple words that they could understand.

"Sign thyself with the mark of the holy cross and pray that on thy FREE labor may fall the blessing of God." Then they fell upon their knees with joy. That afternoon, huge crowds gathered in the open square in St. Petersburg to cheer the Emperor as he rode among them. In Moscow later, ten thousand serfs welcomed him with thankful hearts and fell on their knees before their "Little Father."

The next year, 1862, Russia celebrated 1,000 years since the founding of the Empire. But it was not for old Rurik, their first king, that the people cheered, but for Alexander II, the "Czar Liberator!"

Later they would learn that their freedom was little but a name, and that men must earn for themselves that most priceless possession.

1862: THE "MONITOR" AND THE "MERRIMAC"

THAT YEAR 1862, celebrated in Russia, also marked a turning point in the naval history of the world, for it brought the first battle ever fought between metal instead of wooden warships. It was the battle between the *Monitor* and the *Merrimac* fought in that second spring of the American Civil War.

The *Merrimac* was originally a wooden ship, which the Confederates got when they seized the United States navy yards at Norfolk, Virginia. After remodelling it, they covered it with iron, making it look like a "giant crocodile" and then sent it out into Chesapeake Bay to destroy Union warships, which of course were made of wood.

Since their cannon balls bounded from the *Merrimac's* iron sides two of them were soon destroyed by it and sunk. That was Saturday.

On Sunday, March 9, the *Merrimac* steamed confidently out for another day's destruction, to find that something peculiar had arrived from New York that looked like a "cheese box on a raft" and was waiting to do battle. It was the *Monitor*, designed by John Ericsson, a Swede, who had mounted a revolving iron-plated gun turret on the metal deck of a ship, cut off so close to the water as to resemble an old Norwegian timber raft. The funny little *Monitor* put up a stiff three-hour battle against the *Merrimac*, drove the big ship back into its harbor and then chugged off uninjured. Neither ship played any further heroic part in the war. That was their one big day, one on which they made the world say goodbye to wooden warships and turn to making ships of iron.

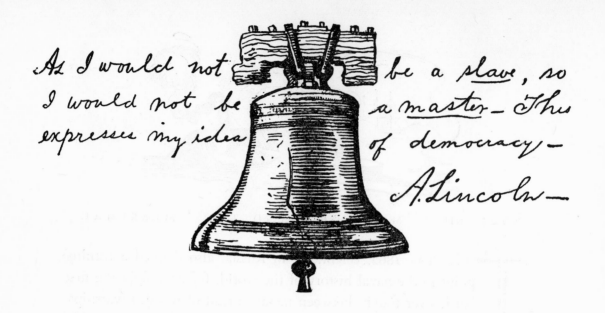

As I would not be a slave, so I would not be a master — This expresses my idea of democracy —

A. Lincoln —

"HENCEFORTH AND FOREVER FREE"

EMANCIPATION OF THE SLAVES was a possibility constantly in Abraham Lincoln's mind in that year 1862, but an act to which he turned only as a means to save the Union, and only after another defeat of the Union forces in Virginia. That year 1862 began for Lincoln with the necessity of making a change in his Cabinet and appointing a new Secretary of War.

One crisp morning in January, Lincoln came out of the White House with his two little boys Willie and Tad, and began a game of throwing pebbles with them along the gravel path that led to the War Department. They had not reached the building when the door burst open and a man with telegrams in his hand, beard and coattails flying, rushed to meet them, apparently in great excitement.

And so he was, for he was Edwin McMasters Stanton, and there was no more excitable man in Washington than the newly appointed Secretary of War. Nor was there ever a more energetic and capable man or one more impatient. He had no patience with crooked contractors, no patience with those who didn't produce results, no time to waste on funny

stories, and no use at all for General-in-Chief Mc-
Clellan, who had let an army sit six months on the
Potomac and DO NOTHING!

"That army has got to get busy and fight!"
exclaimed Stanton, his black eyes snapping as he
faced Lincoln across the desk.

About emancipation of the slaves, Stanton
was equally positive and impatient. Almost a year in office and the President had done nothing about it! He spoke vehemently on the subject,
marching about as if to supply steam, backbone, intelligence, whatever
it was that Lincoln lacked, and push him into it.

Lincoln was no man to be pushed. Not yet, regardless of his own
opinion on slavery, would he interfere with it. According to the Constitution, as it was then, he had no more right to take slaves away from a
citizen of the United States than any other kind of property, and he had
taken an oath to uphold that Constitution.

"But slaves are now property of the enemy," argued Stanton. "They
should be dealt with like any other kind of enemy property."

"Enemy," thought Lincoln. He disliked the word. He preferred to
still think of the Southern states as friends and part of the Union. If the
time should come when that Union could be saved only by freeing the
slaves, and so weakening the rebellious states, he would be willing to do
it, for the Union must be saved. As yet he still hoped to save it by force of
arms alone, by using that army which McClellan must now move. On
that point he agreed with Stanton.

He had waited patiently, he felt, and long enough. So acting as
President, and therefore commander-in-chief, he now set February 22 as
a definite date for an advance towards Richmond.

Before that date arrived, there came to Lincoln a great personal sorrow, the "hardest trial," he said, "of his life to bear." Willie died. He was
only eleven. A child of great promise, he was very close to his father, and
the favorite of his mother, who went almost beside herself with grief.
Gently the President led her away from the child's bedside to the window.

305

"Mother," he said kindly, "try to control your grief, or it will drive you mad." He knew how difficult that was, for he was making the same effort himself. Praying for strength, it came to him.

Two days after the funeral he held a Cabinet meeting, and gradually was back into the routine of work, studying military tactics, receiving delegations, consulting Seward, Stanton, and above all, trying to work out a plan for freeing the slaves that would be just and reasonable. On March 6, in his message to Congress, he proposed one which he hoped would be accepted! It was briefly this:

That the national government should set aside money to purchase the slaves from their owners in any state which would set them free.

Lincoln had great hope that the four slave states along the border, which had remained loyal to the Union would act upon the plan. He was greatly disappointed when they failed to respond. And also disappointed that February 22 had brought no move towards Richmond.

April, however, saw what was called the "Peninsular Campaign" begin, a campaign on that narrow strip of Virginia land between the James River and the York. There McClellan landed his troops with the plan of marching up that "peninsula" to the Confederate capital. The marching turned out to be largely wading, sloshing through the Chickahominy swamp, and floundering about in marshes and bogs.

McClellan, however, managed to drive the Confederates from Yorktown, and Williamsburg, and by the end of May the Union soldiers were within ten miles of Richmond, and actually in sight of the church spires. Then they got no farther, largely because then and there, after the Battle of Fair Oaks, General Robert E. Lee was put in command of the Southern forces. Lee began at once a daring, brilliant game. With less than three-fourths the number of McClellan's troops, Lee made his seem like many more. Confusing, out-maneuvering the Union general and by cutting off his supplies, he forced him back to the mouth of the James River. McClellan retreated in good order. But Lee, leaving Richmond almost unprotected except for some wooden "scare" cannon, followed him closely. Day after day from June 25 to July 1 Lee attacked the Union forces in what were known as the "Seven Days' Battles." They ended after terrific losses on both sides, with Richmond still in the hands of the Confederates, and the "peninsular campaign" a failure.

"Almost any time day or night" during that campaign Lincoln, it was said, might be seen in the telegraph office of the War Department. Day after day he read the dreadful bulletins, his face drawn in agony. At the final failure of the campaign he was almost inconsolable. All those boys dead, and nothing accomplished. Troops, money, supplies poured into the campaign and a failure. What was there to do now but play his last card, as he called it. Nothing. The time had come.

One day he asked the manager of the telegraph office for a piece of paper, saying that he had something special to write. "He sat as he wrote," said the man, "looking out of the window, his left elbow on the table, his hand scratching his temple, his lips moving. Frequently he spoke the sentence in a half whisper. Then satisfied that he had the proper expression he would write it out."

On July 22, three weeks after the peninsular campaign ended, Lincoln called a Cabinet meeting and told the members that he had resolved to issue a proclamation to free the slaves. He would read what he had written and ask for suggestions. His plan was this:

On January 1, 1863, all slaves would be set free in any state still at war with the United States, but not in those slave states that were loyal. Until January 1, 1863, the rebellious states might return to the Union and thus keep the slaves. Otherwise they would "then, henceforth and forever be free."

The sweep of the measure went beyond the expectations of them all —even of Stanton. Secretary Seward had a suggestion to make:

"Mr. President," said he, "while I approve of the measure, I suggest, sir, that you postpone its issue until after a military victory."

307

Lincoln agreed that it would be wiser than following a defeat, and therefore set the proclamation aside to wait for a victory. And night after night he was heard pacing the floor, as August brought not victory, but another defeat—the second Battle of Bull Run!

This time, Lee, being the victorious general, did not fail to follow up his advantage. Heading for Philadelphia, he pushed north, and above Washington, crossed the Potomac River into Maryland. There he was stopped by McClellan. And near Antietam Creek, in one of the bloodiest battles of the war, McClellan defeated Lee, drove him back into Virginia, and gave Lincoln the long-awaited victory.

On September 22, exactly one week after the battle of Antietam, Lincoln called the Cabinet together to hear, as they expected, his finished draft of the Emancipation Proclamation. His face was gray as he took his seat at the table, and opened a small book. He then read a ridiculous squib written by one Artemus Ward. Stanton sniffed. The others smiled politely. They needed a good laugh, thought Lincoln, surveying the solemn circle. So he read another.

"Then," said Secretary Chase, head of the Treasury, "the President took a graver tone and turned to the subject of Emancipation, and read again what he had written."

The next day the proclamation appeared in the papers. Many people who read it were doubtful that it would ever be enforced. One of them was Mrs. Harriet Beecher Stowe, who soon put on her bonnet.

"I am going to Washington," said she, "to satisfy myself that the Emancipation Proclamation is not going to fizzle out." Off she went.

She arrived at Thanksgiving time, visited Lincoln himself, and came to the opinion that "Father Abraham" meant to "stand up" to his proclamation. She saw her son whose regiment was encamped near the city, and was thrilled at the sight of five hundred Negro fugitives having a Thanksgiving dinner. She wrote of the strange rhythmical chant which they sang, that haunting Negro spiritual:

"Oh go down Moses. . . . Way down into E-gypts La-a-nd. . . . Tell King Phar-a-oh. To let my people go! . . .

New Year's Day came, January 1, 1863.

In the morning Lincoln rewrote the Proclamation in its final form, sent it to be copied on parchment, and then went into the East Room to receive guests at the regular New Year's Day reception.

In mid-afternoon Frederick Seward said that he and his father brought the proclamation to the President's office in the White House for his signature. They were there alone.

"Mr. Lincoln," he said, "dipped his pen in the ink, then seemed to hesitate. Looking around he said, 'I never in my life felt more certain that I was doing right than I do in signing this paper. But I have been shaking hands this morning till my arm is stiff and numb. Now, this signature is one that will be closely examined, and if they find my hand trembled, they will say, "he had some compunctions!" But, anyway, it is going to be done!' So saying he slowly and carefully wrote his name to the bottom of the proclamation. This is next to the last sentence and the signature."

And by virtue of the power, and for the purpose aforesaid, I do order and declare that all persons held as slaves within said designated States, and parts of States, are, and henceforward shall be free;

Abraham Lincoln

Thus on January 1, 1863, the slaves in all states then in rebellion against the Union were set free. Two years later, at the end of the war, the slaves in all the remaining states would also be given their freedom, by an amendment added to the Constitution.

That THIRTEENTH amendment declaring that henceforth slavery should exist no longer anywhere in the United States completed one of the great events in American history. It made good by law the words of the Declaration of Independence, that to "Life, Liberty and the Pursuit of Happiness" all men have been given equal right by their Creator. . . .

PRUSSIA MARCHES TO WAR

ISMARCK had now become Prime Minister of Prussia in 1862, and Wilhelm I of the spiked helmet was Prussia's King. With that old soldier as King, and the wily Bismarck at the head of affairs, Europe was now to see how soldiers and swords, "Blood and Iron," could settle the questions of the day! Some years before, on a visit to England, Bismarck had announced exactly what he intended to do when he conducted the government of Prussia. He had to laugh, because he spoke the truth and knew that nobody would believe him, and nobody did—except Disraeli.

"Take care!" said Disraeli. "That man means what he says!"

As of course he did. What Bismarck said was this:

"My first care shall be to reorganize the army. Then I shall seize the first possible excuse to declare war on Austria. I shall then dissolve the German Confederation, and establish a United Germany under the leadership of Prussia."

Bismarck, in control, soon made it possible for Wilhelm I to reorganize the army, increase its size, and raise the required service of every able-bodied man from five years to seven.

That done, Bismarck looked about for an excuse to pick a quarrel with Austria, and decided that by handling it skillfully, he might make use of a situation that existed in Denmark. The situation concerned two provinces, Schleswig and Holstein, and was such a tangled one, that in England it was said flippantly, few but Prince Albert ever could explain it, and now he was dead.

Schleswig and Holstein were part of Denmark in 1862, but whether they should belong permanently to the King of Denmark or to a certain Duke who claimed them, had been argued for the past fifty years.

The King of Denmark was an old man now, and he knew that just as soon as he was dead, the Schleswig-Holstein question would pop up again. Therefore he got England, France, Russia, Austria and Prussia to sign a guarantee that those two provinces should belong to his successor who would become Christian IX.

But Bismarck, also looking ahead, had another idea. Holstein, you see, belonged to the German Confederation. Schleswig did not, but the few German people who lived there wished that it did.

Should it seem sad then for Germans who were and wished to be part of the Confederation not to be rescued from the rule of Denmark?

And if Prussia should go to the rescue, and ask Austria to help, could Austria as head of the Confederation very well refuse?

Then after Schleswig and Holstein had been "rescued" jointly by Austria and Prussia, could not some disagreement over the final settlement probably be arranged? Very probably. What, then, had Bismarck to do but wait for the old King of Denmark to die? Thereupon he would persuade Wilhelm I, who said honestly that he had no claim to those provinces, to dull his conscience for the good of Prussia. Then Prussia joined by Austria would first speak sharply to Denmark, and then invade the country.

To have Prussia carry out those plans against Denmark was to prove most embarrassing for England. And for Queen Victoria, because with her daughter "Vicky" already married to the King of Prussia's son, her son by that time would be married to the King of Denmark's daughter—the Princess ALEXANDRA.

"Sea-kings' daughter from over the sea," Tennyson called the lovely Danish Princess when she came to England in the spring of 1863 to become the bride of the Prince of Wales. She was blond and slim, with an enchanting smile, and a "sort of awe and wonder" in her face, it seemed to Charles Dickens, on her wedding day.

The ceremony took place in the chapel of St. George at Windsor Castle. It was one of "utmost magnificence" attended by the great Lords of England and their Ladies, in colorful uniforms and wide rustling silks. From a small old pew hung high in the wall above the chancel, a little figure all in black looked down upon the scene. Her eyes filled with tears. If only Albert were there with her, to see their son standing in his splendid uniform waiting for his bride, and to watch the lovely bride as she came down the aisle in a cloud of white! Followed by eight bridesmaids also all in white they seemed to Thackeray as they floated past, "like princesses in a fairy tale who had been turned into swans."

Alexandra, too, may have felt that day that she was living in one of those very wonder tales which she had so often heard Hans Andersen himself tell at home in Copenhagen.

For Hans Christian Andersen was still living in Denmark in 1863. He was there when the old King died in late November. . . .

"Then I knew," said he, "that dark days were at hand and a heavy bitter time. The bloody waves of war were to wash over our Fatherland. A kingdom and an Empire stood united against our little country. I knew that from great Germany the railways would hurl soldiers against us, as the sea in a storm casts its waves against the strand. Every day our soldiers left for the seat of war, young men—singing. In the early morning I was awakened by the song and tramp as they came past my dwelling.

"But what avails a little band against well-appointed armies?

"No sunshine fell upon us. Ships brought the wounded and mangled back to Copenhagen. . . . For more than a year I wrote no Wonder Story, my soul was so burdened."

"*mit* BLUT *und* EISEN!"

Bismarck was well pleased with the outcome of the war on Denmark. England, in embarrassment, had looked the other way. France and Russia also became absentminded about the treaty they had made with the old King of Denmark, and so they also stood by and let the little nation be robbed. In October, 1864, Christian IX ceded the two provinces of Schleswig and Holstein to Austria and Prussia, to do with them what they liked. Franz Josef, Wilhelm I and their two advisers then met in Vienna to dine on gold plates and serve up the spoils.

Austria's suggestion that Schleswig-Holstein be made a new state in the German Confederation was skilfully sidetracked by Bismarck. He then put through the arrangement, more useful to him, of having them held jointly for a time by Austria and Prussia.

King Wilhelm still protested that he had no right to them, but he grew used to the idea, and even convinced that as a good Hohenzollern it *was* his duty to God to extend the size of Prussia.

Quite aglow over this first expansion, he conferred upon his Prime Minister the title of COUNT, which was very gratifying to Bismarck, though he found the note which explained the honor most amusing. It had been conferred, wrote King Wilhelm, "as an outcome of my system of government, which you have followed with such great and distin-

313

guished circumspection." . . . Followed, did he say? Yes. . . . Followed! Count Bismarck had to laugh. . . .

And laugh again in 1866. For then, when everything was lined up, when he had persuaded Italy to help in order to get Venetia, when he felt sure that France would not help Austria, Bismarck sprung his trap. He began by having Prussia find fault with the way that Austria was governing in Holstein, and then go to war about it. Starting June 16 and ending August 23, it was the shortest war in history. In less than seven weeks, Prussia dealt the old Empire of Austria a knockout blow from which it never would recover.

"You are a great man, now, Excellency," said an aide to Bismarck very frankly, "but what if the Crown Prince had not arrived with his troops just in time at the battle of Sadowa? The war would have been lost, and you would now be one of the greatest of all rascals!"

No one knew that better than Bismarck. And that was not all he knew. What if the other nations had stood by their treaty with Denmark? Or, inasmuch as they didn't, what if they had united and refused to let Austria be attacked, for no good reason whatsoever? Where would his plans be then? He knew.

But they hadn't interfered!

The first German Blitz-Krieg was successful. Austria was dropped completely out of the Confederation, and Prussia became head of all the united German states north of the Main. The powerful nation planned by Bismarck had now formed itself and from now on, from this fateful year of 1866, when they had stood by and let it happen, the Blood and Iron of Prussia were to make sad history for the nations of Europe.

To the third and fourth generation the children would pay for the sins of their fathers. For there is no changing of the LAW—the future is born in the past.

Only a little over four years and France would be defeated by Prussia, the Empire overthrown, Napoleon III made prisoner, and old soldier Wilhelm crowned the first Emperor of the newly created German Reich in the palace at Versailles!

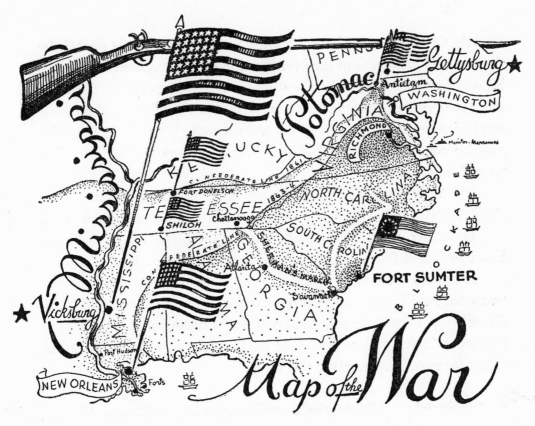

Map of the War

1863: VICKSBURG AND GETTYSBURG

NOVEMBER, 1863, when the King of Denmark died, giving Bismarck the chance to promote his rule of "Blood and Iron," Abraham Lincoln dedicated the battlefield of Gettysburg, where five months before thousands of men had given their lives that a government of and by free people might live on.

JULY 4, 1863, the day after the battle of Gettysburg had taken place, brought another victory for the Union armies. For that day July 4, out on the Mississippi River, U. S. Grant, now a Brigadier-General, had captured Vicksburg. His luck, if you call it luck, had turned at last. And that capture at Vicksburg ended a long, hard struggle to open the Mississippi River, one which Lincoln had followed as anxiously as he had the campaign in Virginia.

Lincoln knew the river. He had poled the length of it on his flat boat from the Ohio to New Orleans. He knew that to get control of the Missis-sippi was as important to the North as the direct attack on Richmond, because it would divide the Confederacy in two, cutting off the three states west of the river from contact with the east. While he had watched one Union general after another fail and retreat in Virginia, he saw with growing confidence the results turned in by Grant, as the river campaign went slowly forward.

The navy started at New Orleans, while the army starting from Cairo, Illinois, began to push south through Tennessee and Mississippi.

FEBRUARY, 1862, the campaign began with the capture of two forts, Fort Henry and Fort Donelson on the northern line of Tennessee.

It was at Fort Donelson that the first great Union victory of the war was won. And it was that victory that first brought the name of U. S. Grant before the people, and gave him the new nickname "Unconditional Surrender." After a three-day battle, the Confederate General had asked Grant for terms, and received this reply:

No terms except an unconditional and immediate Surrender can be accepted.

U. S. Grant

Those words were joyfully caught up, and though the nickname would often be drowned out in curses, those were the terms Grant would stick to as he dragged through mud and blood and agony to the end.

By the capture of Fort Donelson, the Confederate line was pushed back to the southern border of Tennessee. There at Shiloh, in early April, 1862, came the next great Union victory. For that victory, Grant very rightfully took little credit, saying that he owed it to General William Tecumseh Sherman, who had then been transferred west from the Army of the Potomac. So Sherman, with his fighting spirit, and his snappy tongue, was with Grant as they left Shiloh and pushed down through Mississippi to Vicksburg, almost the last fort to be captured, for in

from Currier & Ives print: ～*The Mississippi in Time of Peace* ～

APRIL, 1862, Admiral Farragut and the navy had captured New Orleans. New Orleans, as you can see on the map, was guarded by two forts farther down the delta. Between them heavy chains had been stretched across to block the river channel, while on guard above the forts were fifteen Confederate vessels, two of them ironclads, like the *Merrimac*.

A month before the battle between the *Monitor* and the *Merrimac* which had occurred in March, Admiral Farragut had taken fifty of those Union warships from Chesapeake Bay, and set out for New Orleans. It took six days and nights, after he reached the mouth of the river, before he could break through the chains, run past the forts, and capture the city. The levees for miles were then ablaze with burning ships and cotton bales, but the river was open north to Port Hudson, which would fall soon after Vicksburg. But in that spring of 1862, the fall of Vicksburg was still more than a year away.

Vicksburg was too well protected. It stood on a bluff so high above the river that it could not be fired upon from the boats. And from the northeast by land it was almost unapproachable, because of swamps and bayous and streams full of swirling yellow water.

Grant tried. But months of building bridges, clearing streams of fallen logs, knocking out levees and digging a canal ended only in what the newspapers damned as a "stupid and disgraceful failure." And besides he lost his false teeth in the river!

It was then decided to put the troops on ships, try to run past the batteries, land and come up against Vicksburg from the south. The daring attempt was made one dark night in April, 1863, and was amazingly successful. Though the Confederates burned the houses of Vicksburg to light up the river, so that the gunners could see the transport ships, only two small boats were lost. The army landed.

Then for ten days Lincoln heard nothing from Grant. He was too busy to telegraph. He was striking right and left at two Confederate armies forty miles apart, for another army under General Johnston had then arrived at Jackson, Mississippi. Pemberton came out of Vicksburg. Grant struck left and drove him back. Then struck right at Johnston and drove him out of the state capital, and whirled back for an attack on Vicksburg. Grant and Sherman shelled the town for days and nights continually, but Pemberton did not surrender. So Grant began the siege to starve him out. That was the first of May, 1863.

MAY, 1863, in Virginia saw the Union Army of the Potomac again headed for Richmond, and again defeated by General Lee, this time at the town of Chancellorsville. It was the last Confederate victory, and one in which Lee suffered the tragic loss of his so-called "right arm," General "Stonewall" Jackson, who was accidentally shot by one of his own men. After this victory, Lee tried as before to move north into Pennsylvania with the hope of reaching Philadelphia. This time he got over the border as far as a town called Gettysburg.

JULY 1 the famous battle there at Gettysburg began, the only battle fought on northern soil. Lee was defeated by General George Meade, who later failed, however, to follow up his advantage.

It was a three-day battle, with the armies facing each other from two high ridges separated by a mile of open valley. On the first day the

Union army failed; on the second day the Confederates were driven back.

On the third day General Lee, sitting on his horse Traveller, scanning the valley, decided to charge the center of the Union line. That charge made by fifteen thousand of the bravest soldiers in the southern army was one as desperately fatal as the Charge of the Light Brigade in the Crimea. At the signal to start, the valley was filled with clouds of smoke from the artillery fire which began the day. From where he sat, Lee watched the men in gray start out in wedge formation, and through the rifts of smoke could see them going across the valley. Halfway there the rifle fire of the Union soldiers began to tear holes in their ranks, the holes filled up and on they went, till they were fighting hand to hand. And before the retreat sounded, a boy named Armistead, leading them on, had vaulted a stone wall on the crest of the ridge, and fallen there still holding his cap high on the point of his sword.

Next day in pouring rain, nearly fifty thousand men in gray and blue were left dead on the battlefield, as Lee, blaming no one but himself, led the troops which remained to him, back into Virginia.

NOVEMBER 19, a little more than four months later, a ceremony was held on the battlefield to dedicate a portion of it as the burial ground for the men who had died there. As Lincoln took his place on the platform on that bare November day, he looked out over the faces of one hundred thousand living people, gathered in that valley where so short a time ago half that number were lying dead.

The President of Harvard had been chosen as the orator of the occasion. He spoke for two hours. Then the choir sang. Then Lincoln rose to make "a few appropriate remarks" as he had been asked to do.

Seward knew that the President had been so pressed for time that he had been obliged to finish writing his speech after they left Washington, but he was not prepared to see him stop before he had fairly started, and sit down. The photographers had not been able to adjust their cameras, the crowd had barely stopped rustling and prepared to listen, when he was through.

"I'm sorry for it," whispered Secretary Seward to the President of Harvard. "He has made a failure. The speech wasn't equal to him."

Neither Seward, nor the crowd, nor the President of Harvard—no one then seemed to realize that they had just heard one of the finest things ever written in the English language. But they knew it later, for these are the words that Abraham Lincoln spoke at Gettysburg, that day, words in which the soul of America rose from that brown battlefield:

FOUR SCORE AND SEVEN YEARS AGO OUR FATHERS BROUGHT FORTH ON THIS CONTINENT A NEW NATION, CONCEIVED IN LIBERTY AND DEDI-CATED TO THE PROPOSITION THAT ALL MEN ARE CREATED EQUAL.

NOW WE ARE ENGAGED IN A GREAT CIVIL WAR, TESTING WHETHER THAT NATION OR ANY NATION SO CONCEIVED AND SO DEDICATED CAN LONG ENDURE.

WE ARE MET ON A GREAT BATTLE-FIELD OF THAT WAR. WE HAVE COME TO DEDICATE A PORTION OF THAT FIELD AS A FINAL RESTING PLACE OF THOSE WHO HERE GAVE THEIR LIVES THAT THAT NATION MIGHT LIVE.

IT IS ALTOGETHER FITTING AND PROPER THAT WE SHOULD DO THIS. BUT, IN A LARGER SENSE, WE CANNOT DEDICATE, WE CANNOT CONSE-CRATE, WE CANNOT HALLOW THIS GROUND. THE BRAVE MEN, LIVING AND DEAD, WHO STRUGGLED HERE HAVE CONSECRATED IT FAR ABOVE OUR POOR POWER TO ADD OR DETRACT.

THE WORLD WILL LITTLE NOTE NOR LONG REMEMBER WHAT WE SAY HERE. BUT IT CAN NEVER FORGET WHAT THEY DID HERE.

IT IS FOR US THE LIVING, RATHER, TO BE DEDICATED HERE TO THE UNFINISHED WORK WHICH THEY WHO FOUGHT HERE HAVE THUS FAR SO NOBLY ADVANCED. IT IS RATHER FOR US TO BE HERE DEDICATED TO THE GREAT TASK REMAINING BEFORE US, THAT FROM THESE HONORED DEAD WE TAKE INCREASED DEVOTION TO THAT CAUSE FOR WHICH THEY GAVE THE LAST FULL MEASURE OF DEVOTION; THAT WE HERE HIGHLY RESOLVE THAT THESE DEAD SHALL NOT HAVE DIED IN VAIN; THAT THIS NATION, UNDER GOD, SHALL HAVE A NEW BIRTH OF FREEDOM, AND THAT GOV-ERNMENT OF THE PEOPLE, BY THE PEOPLE, AND FOR THE PEOPLE SHALL NOT PERISH FROM THE EARTH.

RED CROSS

THE AMERICAN Civil War, the worst and bloodiest war that had
ever been fought thus far in the history of the world, had now
completed its third year. Great victories had been won. "Victories, yes! but oh, the cost," said Clara Barton. "Dead everywhere! On every battlefield they lie. In dark ravines . . . tangled forest!
In miry swamps. On lonely picket line! And by the roadside . . . I saw
them fight and die."

Yes, Clara Barton *had* seen them fight and die. She had followed out
onto the battlefield, while the smoke was still in the air, to give first aid
to the wounded, and to help bring them back. She had improvised hospitals, cooked and supplied food, soothed those who were dying, and
helped bury the dead. And when it was all over she was to hunt for the
missing men. Then upon her doctor's orders that she must have "three
years of absolute rest," she went to Switzerland.

There she first heard that in 1864 a great international organization had been formed to care for the wounded in war, and to which twenty-two nations now belonged. When she found that the United States was the only civilized nation missing and had refused two invitations to belong, she said she "grew more and more ashamed." It was interesting to her to learn how the organization had been formed.

"Although the horrors of India," she said, "and of the Crimea and the work of Florence Nightingale had led up to such a movement, it was not until the campaign of Napoleon III in northern Italy that any definite steps were taken."

Monsieur Henry Dunant, a Swiss gentieman, was traveling in Italy in the year 1859, and was in the neighborhood of Solferino the day of the great battle. This led to the publication of the description of what he had observed on the battlefield and in hospitals, as well as a proposition for founding in every country societies for the relief of the wounded.

The work resulted in calling the International Convention of Geneva of 1864, which drew up a treaty and a code. It was necessary to fix upon some common sign to be recognized by all nations.

The design proposed was a RED CROSS upon a white ground.

In the war so soon to come between Prussia and France, Clara Barton was to see the Red Cross put to its first test.

"As I saw the work of these Red Cross societies in the field," she said, "accomplishing in four months under their systematic organization what we failed to accomplish in four years without it—no mistakes, no needless suffering, no starving, no lack of care, no waste, no confusion, but order, cleanliness and comfort wherever that little flag made its way —a whole continent marshalled under the banner of the Red Cross—as I saw all this, and joined and worked on it, you will not wonder that I said to myself 'if I live to return to my country I will try to make my people understand the Red Cross and that treaty.' " And in 1882, through the efforts of Clara Barton, the United States adhered to the treaties governing the Red Cross.

THE LAST YEAR OF WAR

APRIL, 1864. The dandelions were bright on the White House lawn, the leaves were green in Virginia. Spring had come again. The fourth spring to begin a year of war. What would this year bring? What did it hold for the tired man in the White House, now also entering the fourth year of his term? Would the people cast him aside, in November, or would they re-elect him, that he might go on until the war was over and his work was done?

And what of that other President in the Confederate capitol in Richmond, Virginia? How long would he be there?

How long? Just so long as Richmond could be defended. Just so long as the brilliant technique of Robert E. Lee could stand against the well-directed blows of Ulysses Grant. For it had come to that. It would be Lee against Grant in this spring of 1864.

U. S. Grant, summoned to Washington by the War Department to command the Union armies, was planning a new campaign in Virginia. Lee in his army tent on the Rapidan River was preparing to meet it.

Grant's Potomac army numbered 115,000, and behind him were the almost unlimited resources of the North, the efficiency of Stanton, and the wisdom, patience and understanding of Abraham Lincoln.

Robert E. Lee, standing almost alone, had an army of 60,000 men. They had neither clothes enough to wear nor food enough to eat. He was

323

thankful that they had ammunition. Arms and munitions were now being made in the South, many at the foundries in Atlanta, Georgia. And they had spirit, those men of the army of Virginia. The battle of Gettysburg had broken the faith of many Southern soldiers and thousands since then had deserted, but the old guard of Virginia were loyal to Lee, and Lee had their welfare in his heart.

"Keep the Army of Virginia in your thoughts and prayers," he wrote a cousin. "It is preparing for a great struggle."

May 1, the move towards Richmond began. Grant started directly for the Rapidan River. But that was only half of the Union plan. Out in Chattanooga, Tennessee, Sherman waited for the signal to start down through Georgia. Then, by making a wide circle north, he would cut off Richmond and Virginia from the states to the south.

"War is Hell," said Sherman. No use softening the blows, it would only prolong the agony.

May 1, then, Grant started. Lee knew it. The morning of May 4 his staff officers heard it. They were seated with him at a meager breakfast in his tent.

"General Grant," Lee said calmly, "crossed the Rapidan last night." Then as his old Negro servant filled each cup with the unusual treat of coffee, he explained his plan to wait—not to attack Grant in open country, but to let him come on until he had reached the "Wilderness," where Grant would lose advantage of a larger force.

This "Wilderness" of which Lee spoke was a deserted stretch of rough ground about twelve miles square, full of abandoned ore pits, gullies, scrub oaks, scraggy pines, and dense undergrowth.

May 5, Grant was in the Wilderness, hoping to go through the tangled thicket before the attack began. But about noon came the opening guns. In no time the echoing woods were filled with smoke and fire, and the pits and gullies heaped with wounded. The second day, which began at sunrise, saw another day of frantic and confused fighting in the tangled flaming woods filled with choking smoke.

324

Surely now, thought many of the Confederate officers, Grant would retreat. They did not know Grant. He changed his direction, but he did not retreat.

May 11 he sent this telegram to Lincoln from Spottsylvania:

"I PROPOSE TO FIGHT IT OUT ON THIS LINE IF IT TAKES ALL SUMMER."

And fight he did, day after day, sidling to the left, working, fighting, hammering his way mile by mile, almost foot by foot, around the right end of Lee's line constantly sidling towards Richmond until, on June 2, he was only six miles away, just where McClellan had stood two years before. And again, as then, Lee blocked the path. Grant attacked him at Cold Harbor; he lost 7,000 men in twenty minutes. Still he did not retreat. He circled again to the left, and two weeks later he was south of Richmond, twenty miles away near the town of Petersburg. There at Petersburg he settled in for a long siege, determined to hammer and pound and blast away at Lee's army until that town and Richmond, too, were captured. That was to take almost a year, all fall, all winter, until April came again.

During that time Grant's headquarters at City Point grew into a regular town, with people coming and going on all kinds of business. Mrs. Grant and the children came to spend the winter, and old Jesse strutted down to see his now famous son. Newspaper reporters, of course, were everywhere. Soon after the fall of Vicksburg they had begun asking Grant, to his embarrassment, if he would run for President in 1864. The very idea made him quake. Couldn't even make a speech; how could he be President? He was a soldier, not a statesman. He'd stick to his job. And stick to it he did, for that was Grant. . . .

Meanwhile, where was General William Tecumseh Sherman? Well, where would he be, but down in Georgia? Wasn't that the plan? On the dot, as soon as he got a telegram that Grant was in the Wilderness, Sherman set out from Chattanooga, Tennessee, and fought his way down to Atlanta, Georgia, which he captured by September. Thereupon he set fire to the Atlanta factories, destroyed all ammunition foundries, mills and machine shops. Then hearing that the Confederate Army, instead of protecting Georgia, had been sent off by Jefferson Davis on a wild goose chase up into Tennessee, Sherman swept right on down from Atlanta to Savannah. The army left behind them, sad to say, a strip of devastated country sixty miles wide straight through the heart of Georgia "from Atlanta to the Sea."

From the seaport of Savannah he sent back this snappy telegram:

"Savannah, Georgia, Dec. 22, 1864
"To his Excellency, President Lincoln, Washington, D. C.:
"I beg to present you as a Christmas Gift the City of Savannah, with one hundred and fifty guns and plenty of ammunition; also about twenty-five thousand bales of cotton. W. T. Sherman."

The telegram, which had to go by ship to Chesapeake Bay, reached Washington on Christmas Day, and was gratefully acknowledged.

November 4 had also brought Lincoln a message for which he was deeply grateful, the approval of the people. Although he had been called almost every ugly name from baboon to tyrant, they had re-elected him as President. That meant he'd go on to finish his work.

Then had come Thanksgiving, the first one to be celebrated as an annual national holiday, on a date fixed by the President, the last Thursday in November. And so the year 1864 came to a close.

AND SPRING CAME AGAIN. Spring, 1865, the fifth one to begin a year of war, but this time it brought hope of peace.

Only three of the original eleven Confederate States were still left fighting, Sherman was on his way north into the Carolinas and, though Lee still held out against Grant, the Army of Virginia, starved through the winter, was dwindling away.

President Jefferson Davis was still in Richmond, though Mrs. Davis had sold her carriage and gone south, but General Lee warned Davis to be prepared any time to move the government. Unless he could get food

326

for his army, he could not keep it together any longer. Messages bringing no results, in March General Lee went himself to beg Congress for food for his starving troops. Seething with anger and distress he returned to the small house in Richmond, where his invalid wife and family were then living. That evening he paced back and forth before the open fire, and then turned to his son, Custis Lee, who was a Major-General.

"Mr. Custis," he said, "I have been up to see the Congress and they seem unable to do anything except to eat peanuts and chew tobacco while my army is starving. When this war began, I was opposed to it, bitterly opposed, and I told those people that unless every man should do his whole duty, they would repent it . . . and now they will repent."

Robert E. Lee was low that night, but next day his spirit was up, and later at the promise of possible fresh recruits, his black eyes snapped.

"If I had 15,000 fresh troops," he said, "things would look very different." It was only another promise. Lee went back to Petersburg to make the best of what he had, in a last brilliant showing, but it was obvious to the North that he could not hold out indefinitely.

March 4, 1865, therefore, was a very different day in Washington from Lincoln's first inaugural day, when he had had to slip into the city secretly, and every window of the unfinished Capitol had to be guarded by soldiers as he took the oath of office.

Now the Capitol dome was finished, even to the bronze figure of Liberty on top. A great applause swept over the happy crowd gathered on the grounds as they saw Lincoln step forward on the platform. At that moment the sun, which had been under a cloud, came out and shone down on the wet green leaves of spring, the golden dome, the upturned faces and the tall black figure standing before them with the sheet of white paper in his hand. Then he spoke to them of peace and of finishing the war, of bearing no resentment for what was past, and of believing always through whatever was to come that THE JUDGMENTS OF THE LORD ARE TRUE AND RIGHTEOUS ALTOGETHER.

Therefore **"with malice** toward none," he **said,** "with charity for all, with firmness in the right as God gives us to see the right, let us strive on to finish the work we are in; to bind up the nation's wounds; to care for him who shall have borne the battle, and for his widow and his orphan; to do all which may achieve and cherish a just and lasting peace among ourselves and with all nations."

Looking out upon the crowd as he finished, Lincoln saw the face of Frederick Douglass, the Negro leader. He saw him again at the reception which was held that evening in the East Room of the White House. At sight of him, Douglass said, Mr. Lincoln's "countenance had lighted up," and he shook hands cordially.

Walt Whitman, the poet, was also there, but he saw the President looking "rather disconsolate" as the crowd surged by him. He was dressed in black, the poet said, "with white kid gloves and a claw hammer coat, receiving, as in duty bound, shaking hands," but "looking as if he would give anything to be somewhere else."

By midnight the reception was over; the White House lights went out, and it was still at last. But Lincoln was completely exhausted. He could still feel people shaking his hand as he lay down to rest, and closing his eyes he could still hear the voices of the crowd—voices dying into silence and the deep stillness of sleep.

And then into that deep stillness, some nights later, came the sound of sobbing. Or was it sobbing? He listened, then rose from his bed and followed the sound through the empty halls down the stairs, until he stood in the door of the East Room. There before him was a bier upon which rested a corpse, wrapped in funeral vestments. There was a throng of people weeping pitifully. "Who is dead?" he asked one of the guards. "The President," was his answer. "He was killed by an assassin." Then came a loud burst of grief from the crowd, which woke him from the dream.

"I slept no more that night," Lincoln said, telling of it later. "But it was only a dream. So we'll let it go—I think the Lord in His own good time and way will work this out all right. God knows what is best."

In that faith lay Lincoln's courage. He could walk through life, or into "the valley of the shadow of death," without fear of evil.

THE AGE OF BRASS,
or the triumphs of Women's Rights

(from a Currier & Ives print 1869)

LOOKING TO THE FUTURE

I GIVE YOU Upper Canada," said Artemus Ward, for fun, proposing a toast to a convivial group of newspapermen in Virginia City, Nevada, one night in 1863. Ward was the humorous gentleman whose stories gave Abraham Lincoln so much amusement. Listening to him that night in Nevada was a bushy-haired young fellow who had just then taken the pen-name of Mark Twain, borrowed from his old job as river pilot on the Mississippi, and one to which he had no desire to return. He liked writing better, and was then doing a humorous column, somewhat after the fashion of Artemus Ward.

Ward's way was to poke fun in a misspelled dialect on all the topics of the day, from "Wimin's Rites" to the Atlantic Cable and Cyrus Field, whose "Fort" he said was to "lay a sub-machine tellegraf under the boundin' billers of the Oshun and then hev it Bust!" So now it was Upper Canada. "Gentlemen," he said, "I give you Upper Canada."

"And why?" asked one of the companions.

"Because," he responded, "I don't want it myself!"

329

Canada would have been glad to hear such a positive statement made by the United States. And John A. Macdonald, also, who was now Canada's Prime Minister, would have been glad to be assured that the United States did not want Canada. Though sixteen years had passed since the idea to reach the Pacific  Ocean had swept over the neighbor to the south, Canada had not forgotten when and how the great piece of Mexico had been acquired.

Now that the Civil War was drawing to a close, might not the same thing happen to Canada? What would General Grant do with that great army of his when the war was over? The United States might very possibly, they thought, look north now instead of west, with hopes of annexing one or more of the British provinces.

That might not be too difficult either, since only the two provinces, Upper and Lower Canada, were then united. And people in them were still dissatisfied with the system of government.

So now this need to unite for protection, and for better government, led to one of the important events in the history of North America, the founding of the Dominion of Canada.

In Quebec in the autumn of 1864, delegates met from United Canada, New Brunswick, Nova Scotia, Newfoundland, and Prince Edward Island. Under the leadership of John A. Macdonald, they drew up a scheme and resolutions for a Confederation which they hoped would eventually include Hudson Bay territory. Like the United States, they also felt it their manifest destiny to reach the Pacific Ocean.

The sessions were secret, like those held seventy-seven years before in Philadelphia to form the Constitution of the United States. And in planning the government, the founders of Canada looked both to that Constitution and the British system. They made Canada a union of provinces or states similar to the United States, but at the head they placed not a President but a cabinet or committee headed by a Prime Minister like that of England. There was to be a governor general representing the Queen, but having little power.

Then rose the question of what to call the nation.

"I propose we call it the *Kingdom* of Canada," said Macdonald.

Others felt that some other name than Kingdom would be more agreeable to the United States, and so settled upon the name DOMINION.

The plans being completed, they were not adopted by the separate provinces without great agitation, and much weighing of benefits to be gained against possible sacrifices, fear and jealousy taking a hand as usual. In the end, however, New Brunswick, Nova Scotia and United Canada (Quebec and Ontario) decided to coöperate. The plans were then sent to the British Parliament for approval. A committee, headed by John A. Macdonald, went to England to help put through the negotiations. There he was received by Queen Victoria, and kissed her hand.

A week after that audience, Parliament passed and Queen Victoria signed the British North America Act and brought into existence the Dominion of Canada, on July 1, 1867.

John A. Macdonald became the First Prime Minister of the new nation and was to be, for the next quarter of a century, the leading figure in building this Canada which he had helped to found. The founding of the Dominion came just ten years after the Sepoy Rebellion in India, and Sir John regretted that the event had not been given more prominence.

"The declaration," he said, "of all the British North American provinces that they desired as one Dominion to remain a portion of the Empire showed what wise government and generous treatment would do, and should have been marked as an epoch in the history of England."

Today, Canada is free, but still united with England in a Commonwealth of Nations, whose formation marked a step in the history of the world. For the British Commonwealth, formed of self-governing nations, is a union of the largest groups of society ever joined together since families first united into tribes, tribes into states and states into nations. Looking from the past to the future, many people believe that in time all nations will be free to govern themselves, and all united for mutual benefit in a Federation of the World.

Perhaps England lost sight of the importance of what had happened

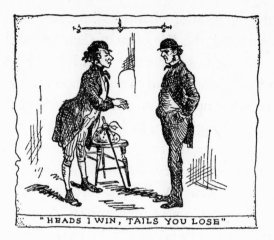
"HEADS I WIN, TAILS YOU LOSE"

in Canada in 1867, because of a great reform which took place that year, by which the vote was given to most of the working class in the industrial cities, and England became, at last, a democracy.

The Reform Bill was put through by the two great leaders in Parliament, and the two greatest rivals, Mr. Gladstone and Mr. Disraeli, caught working together for once in their lives. Gladstone, now leader of the Liberal Party, believed in the Reform. With Disraeli it was a sort of heads I win, tails you lose proposition, as you see in the cartoon from *Punch*.

As the Conservative leader, Disraeli did not want Reform. The year before, when Gladstone had introduced a Reform Bill, he had fought against it, helped defeat it, and so put the Liberal party out.

But "you cannot fight against the future," Gladstone had kept saying. The rule by the people and for the people was bound to come.

Disraeli was shrewd enough to see that, too. Even though he did not want it. But since he knew that it was coming, he thought his party might as well get the credit for it. So when the Conservatives came into power he turned about-face, introduced a Reform Bill, which Gladstone kept adding to until it suited him, and then Disraeli manipulated until he got it passed. So in 1867, the year that the Dominion of Canada was formed, England became a democracy.

Elizabeth
Cady
Stanton

Susan B. Anthony

During the debates in the House of Commons over the Reform Bill, one member, John Stuart Mill, made a strong plea in favor of granting the vote to women. Two years later, in the United States, under the leadership of Elizabeth Cady Stanton and Susan B. Anthony, the first National Woman's Suffrage Association was to be organized. That same year, in the territory of Wyoming, women were actually to be given the vote. But on the whole, the idea of woman suffrage was looked upon as a joke, in those days, both in England and the United States.

Artemus Ward made great sport of the "Wimin's Rite's Associashun," whitch he said as a feroshus female explained "beleeves wimin has rites—whitch beleeves in razin' her to her proper speer—hense 4th & forever." Women's Suffrage was still funny in 1867.

But the Atlantic Cable was no longer a joke. In July, 1866, Cyrus Field had succeeded in "laying his tellegraf beneath the boundin' billers," and it was possible to telegraph between Ireland and Newfoundland the year before the Dominion of Canada was formed.

North America was to see two other changes that year, 1867:

Alaska was to be purchased from Russia by the United States for $7,200,000.

The Republic of Mexico would be restored to its great Indian President, Benito Juarez. First, Napoleon III was to withdraw the French troops. Maximilian, deserted by those who had made him an "Emperor," would calmly face the firing squad on the Hill of Bells. Carlota, having then lost her mind, was to live on insane for sixty years. Though the nations of Europe would have sent urgent appeals to Juarez to be merciful, to Juarez this was a time for justice and not mercy. They had shown no mercy to Mexico. The law must take its course.

Looking ahead to 1867, however, is to go beyond the world that Abraham Lincoln knew. For in 1865, with the end of the American Civil War, would come the end of Lincoln's life. Sitting in a box at the theatre he was to be killed by an assassin. Time and again Stanton had warned the President to be careful, that his life was constantly in danger, but Lincoln paid as little heed to him, as to the eighty-odd notes he had received threatening him with violent death.

"I can die but once," he said, "but to live in constant dread of it, is to die over and over again."

Yet the thought of death was often with him. He was so weary, so incredibly weary. He wanted quiet, a long quiet peaceful sleep, one in which there would not even be dreams to trouble him. Several times one day early in April, 1865, a friend heard Lincoln read these lines from Shakespeare, saying Macbeth was to be pitied, and not Duncan, whom he had killed, for . . . "Duncan is in his grave;

> "After life's fitful fever, he sleeps well;
> Treason has done its worst: nor steel nor poison,
> Malice domestic, foreign levy, nothing,
> Can touch him further!" . . .

Lincoln sat for a few moments with the small book open on his knee, then closed it, and slipped it in his pocket. His face lighted up, he turned to casual conversation, watching with interest the shore line of the Potomac River, as the boat moved upstream towards Washington. For that was where Lincoln was, on the Potomac River.

It was Sunday, April 9, and he was returning from a two-week visit to General Grant's headquarters at City Point. Just the Sunday before, while Lincoln was still in camp, Petersburg had at last been evacuated by Lee, and Richmond, the Confederate capital, had also fallen!

On Sunday morning, April 2, in Richmond, President Jefferson Davis had been in church, listening to the sermon, when someone tiptoed up the aisle and handed him a dispatch. It was a message from General Lee saying that Petersburg had fallen, and that Richmond must be evacuated.

Thinking that Davis would go with the army, Lee made known to him the route he proposed to take, in order to join the other Confederate army, under Johnston, now in North Carolina.

Davis protested at first about having to hurry and leave behind so many valuables, but he finally left. In North Carolina he heard of Lee's surrender on April 9, and so continued on down into Alabama, where he met his family. He hoped to get across Mississippi, and escape from there into Mexico. But leaving their tent one night with his wife's shawl over his head, he was captured, and then taken off to prison to Fortress Monroe. Later he went to England.

The road to Fortress Monroe lay through Augusta, Georgia. There, from the window of the parsonage, a pale nine-year-old boy wearing spectacles saw the President of the Confederacy being led through the streets under Federal guard, the man for whom he had heard his father pray, since the first gun fired at Fort Sumter. That Southern boy, whose name was Tommie Woodrow Wilson, would one day be President of that great Union of States, which his good father, Jefferson Davis, and many other sincere and upright men had honestly believed should be broken up, that an outworn institution might be preserved.

No one would come to realize more keenly than this boy, who was to plan for an even larger Union, that theirs had been a lost cause from the beginning. For slavery belonged to ages in the world's history that were past. And to break down a union instead of trying to preserve it was also looking to the past and not the future. And so in the very cause itself lay its defeat, for whether you wish it or not, "the great cause of the world will go forward." . . .

"YOU CANNOT FIGHT AGAINST THE FUTURE."

335

VICTORY AND DEFEAT

O N SUNDAY, April 9, 1865, as Lincoln was sailing up the
Potomac, General Robert E. Lee surrendered the pitiful
remnant of his army to General Ulysses S. Grant, in the
village of Appomattox Court House, in Virginia. There was
nothing else left for him to do. Early in the morning word had come from
his cavalry leader that the Union army lay straight across their path, that
he had "fought his troops to a frazzle" and could do nothing more.

"Then," said Lee, more to himself than to officers who were with
him, "there is nothing left for me to do but to go and see General Grant,
and I would rather die a thousand deaths."

Sitting by a fire of fence rails, he talked with various officers and
members of his staff, and they agreed that it was the right course to take.
Several notes had then gone, under white flags of truce, between the two
commanders. The first one which Grant had more or less hesitatingly
sent, suggested that General Lee surrender his army to avoid further
useless bloodshed. In a later note he suggested that they might both
appoint officers to confer, in case Lee did not wish to do so himself.
Grant had known too often and too well the pain of humiliation. He
did not wish to inflict it upon anyone else.

General Robert E. Lee had not thought of delegating the disagreeable task of surrender to anyone else. Early that morning, rising before dawn, he had dressed himself in his best gray uniform, fresh linen, and hung his finest sword from a new sash of scarlet silk. He wished to make his best appearance, in case he should have to become Grant's prisoner before the day was over.

Shortly after noon, following the final exchange of notes, General Lee mounted Traveller and, accompanied by three of his staff, rode off beyond the line of battle, across a stream where he stopped long enough for Traveller to drink, and then west on down the road towards the village of Appomattox.

By a strange coincidence, the small brick house chosen for the meeting place belonged to a farmer who had been living near Bull Run Creek when the first battle of the war took place. He had moved south to get away from it, and now the war had followed him, and was going to end on his little round parlor table!

Lee dismounted, and entered the house with his three officers. He laid his gauntlets and hat on the small table and seated himself beside it. After a half hour of heavy silence, he heard horses' hooves.

In a few moments Grant, who had had farther to come, drew rein and dismounted before the small brick house. He was dressed for the field, no coat, dirty trousers tucked into the top of boots, covered with mud, and no sword—no sign of his rank except the shoulder straps on his shirt. He felt embarrassed as he tramped up the front steps of the porch, hoped Lee wouldn't feel that his appearance was meant for disrespect—hoped Lee wouldn't recall the time in Mexico when he had rebuked him for his slovenly appearance—feared— But then the door opened and he was inside.

General Lee rose, surprisingly tall in the low room. The two men shook hands, Lee resumed his seat by the window, Grant took a seat in the center of the room. Twelve of his men entered and ranged themselves behind him. A slight pause, then Grant cleared his throat.

"I met you once before, General Lee, in Mexico."

"Yes, I remember that occasion," answered Lee, and the conversation turned to reminiscences of Mexico. Grant hated to open the subject of the interview, Lee was too nervous to stand the suspense.

"I have come to meet you here, General Grant, to ask upon what terms you would accept the surrender of my army."

Now that the subject was opened, Grant mentioned briefly the terms—generous ones—saying that the officers and men might go home on parole, and that the officers might keep their arms and horses.

Lee suggested that it be put in writing. Grant agreed, and for a few moments the only sound in the room was the scratching of his pencil. Lee wiped his glasses and put them on.

"There is just one thing," he said. "Our privates in the cavalry also own their horses." His face showed the request he did not make.

"In that case," said Grant, "all the men who claim to own a horse or mule may take it home with them, to work their farms."

"That will have a very happy effect," said Lee. After some further mention of details, he signed his name to the terms of surrender, rose, shook hands with Grant, took his hat and gauntlets, and returned the salute of the Federal officers. Outside on the porch he stood for a moment, looking off over the valley, clapped his hands together once or twice, then walked down, mounted Traveller and rode away.

A few minutes later Grant swung himself into the saddle and was off down the dusty road. So the two great soldiers had met, the one as dignified in defeat as the other was generous and considerate in victory. Here in this little Virginia house their ways had crossed and parted. Four years later Ulysses Grant was to be pushed by the foolish people into a position for which he was wholly unfitted when they made him President of the United States. . . . But he had been a great soldier!

Robert E. Lee was to be more fortunate. He was allowed to retain his dignity. Holding no trace of bitterness nor resentment for the past, he was to do all in his power to restore the friendly feeling of Virginia's people towards the government of the United States, and to urge them "To fulfill every duty of peaceful citizens, loyal to the Constitution of their country." His spirit was never defeated.

DAY OF LIGHT AND SHADOW

APRIL 14, 1865, was a great day for the United States and a happy one for Abraham Lincoln. For that day, almost exactly four years after it had been fired upon, the Stars and Stripes were raised again above Fort Sumter! War was over! The Union had been saved. Slavery had been abolished. All, and more, that Lincoln had pledged himself to do had been accomplished.

His work was done. The care that had weighed so heavily upon him for the last four years seemed to have slipped now from his shoulders. His lined face that had grown so drawn and haggard was almost radiant.

The last day he began as usual working at his desk, and then had breakfast at eight. Robert, his oldest son, now twenty-one, was with him. Just returned from camp, he was full of news from the army at City Point. He had a picture of Robert E. Lee to show his father. Lincoln looked at it earnestly. "It is a good face," he said.

After breakfast came several interviews before the Cabinet meeting which was called for eleven o'clock.

"Today," said the President, "General Grant will be with us."

Frederick Seward, acting for his father who was then dangerously ill, was the first to arrive. One by one the others came in, entering into casual conversation over the day's news, and speculating as to where the leaders of the rebel government had now gone.

"I suppose, Mr. President," said the Postmaster General, "you would not be sorry to have them escape out of the country."

"Well, I should be for following them up pretty close to make sure of their going," answered Lincoln in a comical tone.

There was some further speculation as to how soon word could be expected from General Sherman in North Carolina. Then a half cloud passed over Lincoln's face, and he told of a strange dream that he had had the previous night. The dream itself was not so strange, he said, as the fact that he had had it several times before—and each time it had preceded some great victory or disaster. . . .

It was a vague feeling of being on a strange phantom ship, sailing, or floating towards some vast indefinite unknown shore. . . .

Someone ventured the suggestion that the anxiety in his mind each time over what might happen may have led to the dream.

"Perhaps," said Lincoln thoughtfully, "that may be the explanation."

And here Stanton burst in—carrying a large roll of papers, and the group around the table was complete. General Ulysses S. Grant was then cordially introduced. Grant nodded and told in the fewest possible words the incidents of the surrender at Appomattox.

"And what terms did you give the common soldier?" asked Lincoln.

"I told them to go back to their homes and families, and that they would not be molested if they did nothing more," said Grant.

The President's face lighted with approval. That was right. There must be no hate shown or vindictiveness. Now that the war was over, everything must be done to help the bankrupt people of the South back to prosperity. So the talk turned to post-war plans. Stanton spread out his big roll of paper, showing charts for reconstruction. These were discussed until the meeting broke up at two o'clock.

As they were leaving, Lincoln spoke of going to the theatre that evening to see "The American Cousin." Turning to General Grant, he said that he hoped that he and Mrs. Grant would accompany them. But there seemed to be some misunderstanding, because, though it had been advertised in the papers, General Grant said that they were to leave town that evening. Lincoln, himself, was not too eager about going, but since it had been announced, he thought he'd better go. . . .

He made an appointment for the following day, and then went to lunch, from which his next callers saw him return munching an apple.

Then followed a talk with Vice-President Andrew Johnson, the man who was so soon to be faced with an overwhelming task. For now the time was growing short; it was past three o'clock. Lincoln could not stay much longer. There were only a few last things for him to do.

Towards late afternoon, for a short rest he put on his high black hat and went for a drive with Mrs. Lincoln, alone. No, "just ourselves," he had told her when she had suggested guests. It was a fresh spring day, the lilacs were in blossom, the willows along the river were green, the dogwood was opening. Lincoln's face glowed.

"I never felt so happy in my life," he said, drawing a deep breath.

Returning, he walked across the gravel path to the War Department and "was more cheerful and happy," Stanton thought, "than he had ever seen him." But to the guard who walked back to the White House with him in the gathering dusk, he spoke of men who he believed would take his life. And when they reached the steps it was "Good-bye, Crooks," that he said for the first time, and not "Good night."

The strands of happiness and tragedy that made Abraham Lincoln's life were twisting closely now . . . for in the next moment, seeing two friends from Illinois, the governor and a congressman, he called to them in the cheeriest tone. Laughing and chatting, he led them to his office, and there read them one ridiculous story after another. Tad came to call him to supper, and he said he'd be right there. But first he wanted them to hear just one more story, the one perhaps in which the author poked fun at the "Goriller Linkin," whuz rane "he had hoped wood be a short wun."

But now he said, "The Confederacy is ded. It's gathered up its feet, sed its last words, and deceest . . . Linkin will serve his term out—our leaders will die off uv chagrin and inability to live long out uv offis. And so, Farewell, vane world!" And Lincoln left them laughing.

After dinner the Speaker of the House came for a few minutes, to say that if there was to be no special session of Congress during the summer he would take a trip to the West Coast—where, by the way—the transcontinental railroad was now being built.

The clock ticked on; it was just time to go to the theatre, if go they must, when the congressman from Massachusetts was announced. After a few words Lincoln arranged to see him in the morning. Taking a small card he wrote a few words on it, and signed his name—for the last time.

They were now at the door. Outside the carriage was waiting. A breath of fresh cool air came in as the door was opened, and they walked out onto the portico in the moist spring night. Abraham Lincoln stood for a moment, then stepped into the carriage, its door closed behind him, the horses started, the carriage rolled down the driveway, the sound of the wheels on the gravel grew fainter and then died away—and he was gone. Abraham Lincoln was gone.

And only then could the people of Abraham Lincoln's world realize how great he was. He was too tall when he walked beside them.

INDEX OF CHARACTERS

Scott, Winfield, American general: * 137; Mexican War, 197; Civil War, 290

Sequoyah, Indian leader, * 62

Seward, William H., American statesman: * in Senate, 234; and Lincoln, 283; and war, 290; and England, 296; and emancipation, 307; at Gettysburg, 319; ill, 339

Shelley, Percy B., English poet, 113

Sherman, William T., American general: * 286; in Virginia, 294; on Mississippi, 316; Georgia, 324

Smith, Joseph, Mormon leader, 193

Stanton, Edward McM., Secretary of War: about Bull Run, 292; and Lincoln, * 304; 334; 340

Stanton, Elizabeth C., woman suffrage leader, * 333

Stephenson, George, inventor: * 63; 118; son, 264

Stowe, Harriet Beecher, American author: * 62; as a child, 73, 77; to Cincinnati, 152; * 211; and Uncle Tom's Cabin, 235; and Lincoln, 308

Sucré, Jose de, South American general, 90

Sutter, Johann August, early Californian: 195, 200

Tao Kwang, Emperor of China: 147; and opium, 167

Taylor, Zachary, twelfth President of the U. S.: * 137; in Mexican War, 197

Tecumseh, Indian chief: * plans union, 23

Tennyson, Alfred, English poet: * 184; quotation, 219; quotation, 241

Thackeray, William Makepeace, English author: * 184

Thoreau, Henry D., American naturalist, author: * 184

Tolstoy, Leo, Russian author: 238; 241; * 287

Travis, W. B., U. S. soldier, 160

Trevithick, Richard, engine builder, 118

Van Buren, Martin, eighth President of the U. S., 173

Vanderbilt, Cornelius, American businessman: youth, 79; and yacht, 232

Victor Emmanuel, King of Italy: boy, 124; * 211; and Garibaldi, * 248

Victoria, Queen of Eugland: * child, 63; born, 95; * child, 99; * with Albert, 137; * Queen, 169; * married, 180; Peace Festival, 217; entertains Napoleon III, 243; with grandson, 245; and India, 255; * widow, 287, 297; and son, 312; 331

Victoria ("Vicky"), daughter of Victoria: 217; weds Crown Prince of Prussia, 245; and son, 245

Vittoria, President of Mexico, 84, 87

Wagner, Richard, German composer: 207; * 210

Ward, Artemus, American humorist: 329; 333

Washington, Booker T., Negro leader: * boy, 287

Webster, Daniel, American statesman: * 3; War of 1812, 31; on Missouri, 77; tries case, 81; oration Bunker Hill, 93; Hayne debate, 132; treaty with Canada, 191; and 1850 Compromise, 234

Webster, Noah, author of dictionary, * 62

Wellington, Duke of, English general and statesman, * 2; against Napoleon, 45; at Waterloo, 59; Prime Minister, 127; to protect London, 203

Whitman, Marcus, American medical missionary: * 163; trip east, 191

Whitman, Walt, American poet, 328

Whittier, John Greenleaf, American poet, 237

Wilberforce, William, English Abolitionist, 151

Wilhelm I, Emperor of Germany: youth, 48; * 211; Prince of Prussia, 216; * 217; 227; with family, 245; and Bismarck, 313

Wilhelm II, Emperor of Germany: * baby, 211, 245

William IV, King of England: * 99; 127; dies, 169

Wilson, Woodrow, twenty-eighth President of U. S.: * boy, 211; sees Jefferson Davis, 335

Wordsworth, William, English poet: * 184

Young, Brigham, leader of Mormons, * 192

Ypsilanti, Greek patriot, 113

INDEX OF NATIONS, PLACES AND EVENTS

(* indicates map)

Africa, the dark continent, 165

Argentina: free, 34; and San Martín, 88

Atlantic Cable: fails, 262; succeeds, 333

Australia: settlers, 171; gold found, * 201

Austria: and Napoleon, 6; Congress of Vienna, 57; and Italy, 123; revolution of 1848, 204–6; Franz Josef and family tree, 213; loses Italian provinces, 248; defeated by Prussia, 310

Brazil: gains independence from Portugal, 108

Canada: * rebellion, 174, 201; Dominion formed, 330

Chile: freedom from Spain, 35, 88

China: 147; Opium War, 167; * Taiping Rebellion, and foreign treaties, 256–60

Colombia, 88

Denmark, *attacked by Prussia, 310

Ecuador, 88

England: rulers, * 99; growth of democracy in time of George IV, 9; Reform Bill of 1833,